Matador of Murder

Matador of Murder

AN FBI AGENT'S JOURNEY IN
UNDERSTANDING THE CRIMINAL MIND

Patrick J. Mullany

© 2015 Patrick J. Mullany
All rights reserved.

ISBN: 1515077284
ISBN 13: 9781515077282
Library of Congress Control Number: 2015911443
CreateSpace Independent Publishing Platform
North Charleston, South Carolina

Dedication

To those who made the journey:
my wife, Patricia;
our Jeannette, Courtney, Keith, Kim, and Ryan;
and
all those brave men and women
called
Special Agents of the Federal Bureau of Investigation

Disclaimers

Contents of this book contain the author's opinion and are not those of the FBI.

Contents of this book contain graphic photos of crime scenes.
Parental discretion is advised.

Table of Contents

Chapter 1   Monastery to Madness · 1
Chapter 2   RFK and Vietnam · 15
Chapter 3   Creating Profilers · 33
Chapter 4   Susan's Kidnapping · 59
Chapter 5   Mad Greek · 98
Chapter 6   When Washington Stood Still · · · · · · · · · · · · · · · ·112
Chapter 7   To Touch a Saint ·139
Chapter 8   Murdering Nurses ·178
Chapter 9   The Spy Who Couldn't Spy · · · · · · · · · · · · · · · · · 200
Chapter 10 Terrorism and Corporate America · · · · · · · · · · · · 223
Chapter 11 Giving Up the Badge · 245

CHAPTER 1

Monastery to Madness

It was a hot July afternoon in Barrytown, New York, and the warm wind blew from the south, rustling the trees and creating a gentle stir in what was otherwise a silent afternoon. Quietness was part of this beautiful place on the Hudson River; because it was the novitiate home of the Christian Brothers, a world-renowned teaching order dating back to the eighteenth century in France.

Jean Baptiste de la Salle had started the order in Rheims, France, and many of his followers spread out well beyond France, to the United States and beyond. It was a very strict order, and many members were not only well educated but also famous for their educational achievements. The order was originally founded to teach the poor, and that was its mission for many years. It excelled in bringing poor, uneducated children into a world where education was valued.

What made me journey to Barrytown this July 1965 was a desire to be alone. I wanted to spend a week or more reflecting on my life and considering whether my future should include continuing as a Christian Brother. After I expressed my doubts, I was encouraged to take whatever time I needed to determine my life's direction.

There was a need for me to look deeply into myself in an effort to avoid making the mistake of continuing in a life not meant for me. The leader of our province had just appointed me director of vocations for the New York province, yet I struggled with whether this life was meant for me.

In 1953, having just finished high school, I joined the Christian Brothers, beginning a very positive experience. The early years of training were full of discipline and hard work. In many ways, we were literally cut off from the world, living a contemplative life of prayer, silence, and self-discipline. Looking back, it felt as though we were put in a bottle, cast out to sea, floating for five years. Landing back on shore, we had to learn what was happening in the world all over again. Modern-day songs meant very little, and world events seemed insignificant. What was significant in those years was discipline and learning to be a teacher of youth. It was our whole life, and being good at it meant success.

Standing with the warm wind hitting me in the face and causing my long, black robe to blow freely, my mind rushed back to the first classroom of seventy-one young boys assigned to me in the fifth grade. Teaching was an art. If one lost discipline on the first day, it would be impossible to regain respect. Seventy-one young, energetic boys presented not only a teaching nightmare but also a management dilemma.

Early on, I realized I was responsible for teaching them everything from penmanship to spelling to arithmetic and history. The only subjects I did not have to teach were music and art. After the regular day of teaching, I ran home to change and then met the class on the ball field to play the sport of the season.

What was clear in those days was that seventy-one boys were all very unique, with distinctive needs. The neediest would often either avoid or cling to the teacher, while the brightest usually fended for themselves, even helping others on occasion. Many days a young student named Brian Flanagan would join me as I walked home from school.

Looking back, Brian was a fascinating study in human behavior. He was brilliant, sullen, quiet, resentful, and very much in need of acceptance. In fifth grade, he joined choir. By eighth grade, he found himself still in choir, unable to quit because doing so would create other members wanting to leave. Brian would stand behind the altar with jaw locked while all his choir mates made the angels in heaven pay attention. For Brian it was a drag, an inescapable disaster with no relief in sight. Yet when the service was over and Brian tore off his choir outfit, he always waited outside for the long walk home. He was great company, friendly when alone but in need of something.

Brian's grandmother raised Brian after his mother and father divorced. I might never know what was going on in his mind, but this was the time Brian was forming the foundations of his life.

Brian graduated from grammar school and won a scholarship to Regis High School, the most prestigious Catholic high school in New York City. Later on, he vanished for a time in the labyrinth of college life at Columbia University, only to reappear at another time and place.

Sometimes teachers lose sight of the huge influence they have on their students and of the fact that their influence can live on for years and become critical to the development of some individuals. It is easy to remember teachers we loved—and even easier to remember teachers we grew to detest. As in every profession, there are good ones and bad ones. Even the bad ones influence lives. As a member of the Christian Brother order, the pressure to avoid having a negative influence was powerful. It would have been difficult to exist in the close confines of other teaching Christian Brothers and not be a good teacher.

The warm, July afternoon was conducive to a period of reflection as the clouds billowed in the sky, gathering as though there could be a late afternoon storm. Sitting on a bench, next to a tall pine tree, I remembered the many summer assignments in the orphanage and reformatory. I had such powerful memories of those times, with incidents that seemed to introduce a conflict between the role of a "man of the cloth" with that of man and survival.

The reformatory, Lincoln Hall, was located in Lincolndale, New York, and the courts of New York would refer students to Lincoln Hall—sentencing them to Lincoln Hall. When the students turned eighteen years of age, those who hadn't completed their sentence would be transferred to a state prison. The mission of teaching the poor was carried out in Lincoln Hall, and a person could consider himself fortunate to be assigned there for the summer months. Those assigned on a permanent basis developed unique skills and dedication necessary to be effective long term.

One could not help but reflect on all the years of training and education that went into the development of a Christian Brother, with an emphasis on prayer and self-control, who was assigned to a position similar to that of a warden.

Such a person had exposure to the early development of the criminal personality. No matter how much attention and direction you gave some kids, you knew in your gut that they would likely lead a life of crime that might well end in violence. Then there were the others, in need of structure, looking for direction, and responsive to guidance, who would live long lives as good citizens, looking back on the good done by a nameless person in a black robe.

The orphanage in Albany, New York, was different but in many ways the same. Being sent to the La Salle Orphanage generally meant that your parents gave you up because you were a severe discipline problem. In a few cases, young students were referred to La Salle because they had no parents or missing parents, or because of court removal. As a person pursuing my master's degree in counseling psychology, I was most impressed with the numerous cases of students who were severe bed wetter's.

La Salle School had more than a handful of students who fit the triad of the homicidal personality—namely bed wetters, animal killers, and fire setters. The prognosis on many of these cases was poor. A common denominator was always that the family was in near total disarray.

Reflecting on these two institutions caused great faculty concern and frustration—concern because the numbers always seemed to increase in both places, and frustration because little other than containment was being accomplished. The closer you worked with students assigned to these institutions, the more you realized that by their teens, they had for the most part developed their life habits and choices.

What was impressive was the simple example set by the men who worked full time in both Lincoln Hall and La Salle. The outside world probably viewed them as holy men in black robes, spending most of their lives in prayer. That was only one aspect of who they were; they were tough men, masculine, disciplined, willing to face danger, people of principle, athletic, and determined to instill a semblance of order in lives that had been dissipated by lack of love.

The late July afternoon sky was getting heavy, and the evening bell disturbed the wind-blown tree sounds. Walking back to the chapel, I vividly recalled the years I spent teaching in Manhattan Prep. Manhattan Prep was a prestigious high school in New York that accepted a select few. The classes were smaller and the students were bright, some even brilliant. What was most exciting was the challenge to be a great teacher to excellent students.

Manhattan Prep was housed on the campus of Manhattan College, which enjoyed an excellent reputation not only as an engineering school but also as a school of excellent athletic achievements in track and basketball. The school had long since abandoned the hope of a football team. The New York Giants used the facilities at Manhattan College for overall fitness and treatment of aches and pains. During the season, not a day went by that old Doc Sweeney wasn't seen escorting some big giant, such as Alex Webster. Although we worked harder in many ways while there, life became a whole lot more normal among the Brothers. Hand Doc Sweeney a good brand of Scotch, and you could prepare for a full night of inside stories about the New York Giants. Everyone's favorite story was his explanation of why Y. A. Tittle ran out of bounds during a championship game. Tittle, according to Sweeney, was petrified of being hit. After a difficult game with a lot of physical punishment, it would take Tittle hours to come back down off his hype.

Most evenings, the chapel was dimly lit and filled with the noise of the young novices filing into their pews toward the front and of the old and infirmed slowly moving into place at the rear of the chapel. I had great admiration for the older Brothers, some who came in using a cane or in a wheelchair, and some assisted by others. Many of them had labored in the New York schools for years, and now toward the end of their lives, the only reward held out to them was eternal life. They had lived good lives, simple lives, lives of poverty, and lives of prayer. One such brother, Brother Raymond, had been a missionary in the Philippines during World War II and was left for dead behind an altar after the Japanese Army killed and wounded many others. In my eyes, he was a hero, but in his eyes, God had intended that he be there at that time, and what happened to him was the will of God. Each one of the older Brothers carried a story of a different life, but now as the evening fell upon their lives, they shared much in common—a life of near solitude, void of blood family because they had been accepted into a religious family.

The young novices toward the front of the chapel, although quiet and reserved in demeanor, were full of life, energy, and eagerness to see if this life was for them.

As I looked at the younger ones, I realized that a great percentage of them would not last for very long. It was not a reflection on them as individuals but rather an objective realization of how difficult it was to give up all in life to achieve a single goal. Many of these individuals had chosen the path they started on because they had very strong role models in the schools they came from, but it would take more than a role model to carry them through a lifetime.

Between the novices and the retired Brothers was an appropriate place for me to be. It was a place between one group thinking this was the life for them and the other knowing they had no time to doubt; this was what they had done with their lives.

Although it was not an easy decision, I ultimately made the choice to leave the life I was in and pursue a different road. I had no bitterness or disgrace in my decision, but I believed that if I continued in the role of attempting to convince others to join a life that I myself had severe doubts about, no one would be well served.

Leaving a religious order presents some immediate problems. Most of your clothes are black, and unless you intend to become a waiter, it is pretty difficult to show up properly dressed to an interview. The order knew the difficulty you would have and gave you what was referred to as separation money. It was enough to get started.

Not many days after I left the order, when word got out, the phone started ringing at my brother's home where I was temporarily living. Efforts were in place to recruit me to a teaching position on Long Island. Many who left the order immediately positioned themselves in Levittown, Long Island, as schoolteachers, continuing to live much as they had before. I knew this was not for me.

It was late January 1966 when the snow began to cover the eastern coast of the United States. In my pocket was an appointment letter directing me to report to Washington, DC, on Monday, January 31, 1966, where I would be sworn in as a special agent of the Federal Bureau of Investigation (FBI).

The snow started to fall on Friday evening and continued all day Saturday and most of Sunday. The weather forecast was for a heavy storm, but the radio reports had much heavier accumulation than expected. By the time the storm was over, in excess of two feet of snow covered the east coast, from Virginia to Massachusetts.

My letter of appointment, while very brief, was precise in directing me to be present at the Old Post Office Building on Pennsylvania Avenue no later than 9:00 a.m. A huge hurdle had to be overcome because my white Mercury Comet was buried in snow, roads were closed, and trains were not running, not to mention I was in New York. However, with a great deal of imagination and with the helpful persistence of the Greyhound bus company, edging its way down the New Jersey Turnpike in the one lane opened to traffic, arriving in Washington, DC, at approximately 2:00 p.m.

Once situated in the Harrington Hotel, I called the FBI, notifying them that I was in town. A very friendly secretary answered and anxiously stated that if I hurried and came right over, I would be sworn in and given credit for the entire day due to the emergency snow conditions. In less than fifteen minutes, I was escorted into the office of the deputy assistant director of the training division, where I found waiting another candidate in my same predicament, James Garcia.

Within minutes of my arrival, the door opened and a very large man, conservatively dressed, appeared. He had a blustery voice and was very businesslike, introducing himself as Mr. Thomas Jenkins. After very brief congratulations on my having arrived in town under such conditions, he gave a short speech concerning the solemnity of being sworn in as a special agent of the FBI. The one part that stuck with me for most of my career was that I was taking on a very special and different way of life.

We were asked to stand and raise our right hand as we were sworn in as special agents of the FBI. The words that most impressed me during the ceremony were these: "You will uphold the Constitution of the United States."

Going back that evening to the Harrington Hotel, I felt pride at having been selected. I had little insight what the future would bring, but I knew it would include excitement and new adventure. That day, I had no idea that it would continue my journey to understand people as a teacher, a journey that would lead to the mysterious world of understanding the criminal mind as a special agent of the FBI.

The transition from teacher in a religious order to FBI agent was dramatic, to say the least. In many ways, it was a journey from the monastery to madness.

While much was different, there was a strong sense of sameness. The common tread was that once again, as an individual, I reached out to join an organization in which all of the members had a common purpose. Another similar aspect was the high degree of selectivity used in choosing the men to serve. From the first day in training as an FBI agent, we had a common bond. Men from all walks of life were drawn together from all parts of this country to learn what it meant to be an FBI agent. There was a sense, however unspoken, that one day you could be called upon to put your life second to that of your partner. It was this realization, perhaps, that made the training to become a special agent very serious business.

On the second day in Washington, we boarded what looked like a school bus and were taken some forty-five miles south to the Marine Corps base in Quantico, Virginia. This, too, turned out to be a long journey; the snow was still on the roads. We learned quickly that no matter what the weather, the schedule for training had to move forward. For the next four months, the training was intense. Every aspect of law enforcement was covered with a heavy dose of Constitutional law. Each statute that the FBI was responsible for investigating was studied to the point of memorization. Proficiency in the use of a firearm was a must.

Firearm training, in many ways, was a relief from the long classroom hours. In this aspect of the training, more than in any other area, there was a seriousness and sense of urgency. If you failed to become proficient in the use of a firearm, you could not qualify as agent. Firearms gave you the sense that the job you were about to undertake was different from all other jobs. While no one lectured about danger, it was understood that kicking in a door to arrest someone who could face the rest of his/her life in prison was confrontational, to say the least. What was instilled in everyone was the need for safety, especially when using a weapon.

There was so much firearm training in the curriculum that carrying a weapon and being able to use it became instinctual. "Ready on right, ready on left, all ready on the firing line," were words that would ring in your head because of repetition. The need for safety was instilled into every agent through methods such as having a firing line shoot all six rounds of ammunition and wait for the order to "holster an empty weapon."

Once the weapon was holstered empty, the next command was, "With an empty weapon, at the sound of the whistle, draw your weapon and fire six rounds." There were those occasions when the clicking of empty weapons would be disturbed by the loud sound of a live round going off. At the end of every firearm session, weapons were physically checked and all empty rounds kicked out. The order was then given to "holster an empty weapon." To all, this meant that we were neutralized and no longer capable of inflicting harm on ourselves or others.

The cold snow of January turned into the brilliant dogwoods of April. As your knowledge and confidence grew, you anticipated your assignment to one of the field offices throughout the country. No matter how hard you tried to figure out the geographical reasoning for assignment location, you were surprised when it was announced.

Jacksonville, Florida!

Graduation day came. You were handed your credentials and given your Smith & Wesson 38-caliber revolver with six live rounds and told to holster a loaded weapon for the rest of your career as an FBI agent. This was the real thing. Jacksonville was a one-and-a-half-day drive from Washington, DC. I would be expected to report in a day and a half. We graduated on Monday, which allowed me to arrive at Jacksonville in the early afternoon of Wednesday, just in time for lunch. I was assigned to a seasoned agent, Carl Beason. He showed me to my desk and introduced me to the squad supervisor. Carl was edgy and anxious to leave the office. Near the office, we stopped for a quick lunch. After lunch, as soon as we went 10-8 (in-service) in the FBI car, Carl was asked to call the office ASAP.

Carl covered the Mayport Naval Base just outside the city limits of Jacksonville, and the ASAP call informed him that one of his fugitives was in a hotel off Beach Boulevard. With training school dust still on me and lunch on the way down, we took off at high speed to make an apprehension. Within three hours of my reporting to the division, we were putting handcuffs on a fugitive and placing him in custody, only to go back out and pick up the second subject.

Needless to say, the pace did not keep up with that of day one. It was impressive how quickly the learning atmosphere of training disappeared in the reality of dealing with fugitives of justice. The experience I gained within the first year was incredible. Jacksonville in 1966 was a small Florida border town well known for being home to a major naval base in Mayport—a place that increased the activity of an otherwise quiet town. Deserters from the military and selective service violators became routine investigations. Jacksonville, being a border town, was very active in terms of attracting fugitives for crimes committed in other states. Florida seemed to act as a lure for fugitives from the north and Midwest, in particular. A week would not go by without a pretty serious bank robbery. The special agent in charge, D. K. Brown, regarded himself as an expert in bank robbery investigations. He loved the hunt.

A late Friday afternoon bank robbery was reason for all troops to leave other duties to actively join in on the bank robbery investigation. Assignments to search all hotels and motels were common. A bank robbery in Stark, Florida, could be enough to initiate a search of all hotels and motels north to St. Augustine and south to Daytona Beach. Somewhere in the history of the FBI, a bank robber must have been caught in a motel during a similar search, but that never happened on my watch.

Simple events could change just because you were an FBI agent. It was like you would stumble into a series of occurrences that had meaning, forcing you into action. One such event happened while I was driving at the Mayport naval base out near the aircraft carriers. A car was stopped, and a young sailor was standing with another. The trunk to the car was open, and I suddenly observed the second sailor climb into the trunk of the car. I continued around past the aircraft carriers and noted the car's license number. Proceeding to the main gate, I parked outside. Within about two minutes, along came the car in question, exiting the gate. Putting on the red light and siren, I had the car pull over. Approaching the driver, I identified myself as FBI and directed him to make a U-turn and park at the military police office just inside the gate. The driver did so without incident, and I took him inside, where he fully explained what he was up to. When the MPs came out to open the trunk, the occupant was shocked; he held the record for the least amount of time as a deserter from the military.

Being an FBI agent could also bring unwelcome attention to your family. Living in a garden apartment complex just outside of Jacksonville were people from many different walks of life. One such individual was a male approximately forty-five years of age who had a great tendency to brag. One thing he bragged about was that when he was a marine, he trained FBI agents to shoot in Quantico, Virginia. This was totally unheard of, as were many of his outlandish comments. My wife had just given birth to a beautiful baby girl about three months earlier when one day he commented to me at the poolside, "I'll bet you would kill somebody if they kidnapped your baby." The answer to his statement was affirmative. Instead of just ignoring his statement, I became concerned and started checking out just who he was. It did not take much checking to discover he was a con man responsible for passing numerous bad checks up and down the east coast and was wanted by GMAC for repossession of his car. That was an easy one; GMAC came out that night and snatched the car. The next morning, Mystery Man was spotted in front of his apartment making a stolen vehicle report to the Jacksonville Police Department. After the report was finished, he talked the officer into driving him across town, where he went into a new car store to initiate the purchase of another car. Later that day, the Jacksonville police were able to arrest him for writing bad checks.

While I was temporarily assigned to the Lake City, Florida, area for a short time, a strange series of events took place. The FBI was well known in Lake City, and the agents often stayed at one motel that seemed to welcome our business. Having checked in earlier in the day, I went by the reception desk to check for any messages. When the owner of the motel saw me, she let me know that a New York City police officer was in the room next to mine, and she had mentioned to him that I was here in case we wanted to take in dinner together. She added that he had asked her to hold his gun in the office safe and that he was driving a black Cadillac. My antenna went up immediately; what police officer would give up his gun, and why was he here in Florida? The following day, the owner of the motel called and told me that something suspicious had happened. The would-be police officer abandoned his room, leaving all of his clothes there, and never went by to pick up his weapon at the front desk. That immediately told me we had someone on the run. After verifying his quick exit from the motel and obtaining his car license number, I headed to the Greyhound bus station, where I found his car parked in the parking lot of the bus depot. With the name and description of the car, I sent an immediate teletype to New York, where he was picked up the following day for an outstanding warrant for check passing and Sullivan law violations (gun possession).

As an FBI agent, you soon realized that good fortune had to be on your side. Special Agent Phil Cook was assigned a case involving a young black man who had shot and killed a police officer in Detroit, Michigan. Late one summer day, Phil received a call from an informant saying that his fugitive was located in a certain house in the black section of Jacksonville. Phil rounded up about ten agents to assist him on this arrest. Tom Fitzpatrick, Bruce Gordon, and I went in the front door of the residence, and the remaining agents surrounded the house. Bruce and Tom went upstairs while I did a sweep of the main floor, which consisted of a living room and kitchen. Once inside the kitchen, I came upon a young boy about twelve years of age. I asked him, "Where did he go?" The boy responded, "Out the back door." I reached for the door and it was locked, which immediately told me the boy was lying. As I glanced away from the door, my left eye caught movement in a small pantry area. The top of the fugitive's head disappeared behind the couch that was crowded into that room. I loudly yelled, "FBI, come up fingers first!" My yell was to the fugitive but was particularly intended to get Gordon's and Fitzpatrick's attention. Within seconds, the fugitive was up against the wall, searched, and handcuffed. Good fortune was with me. The fugitive was not armed. Had he been armed, there was a good chance he would have had the drop on me when I reached for the door. Law enforcement in many ways is a game of risk. You take the risk and hope that good fortune is with you.

Occurrences such as these were endless, but they were an opportunity to gain experience in many areas in preparation for a much larger office. It was routine to be transferred from your first office of assignment after one year, normally to an office that was larger in scope and responsibility. The bonds of friendship formed during your first office would last a lifetime. Not only did you work together, but also you played together. Everyone was from somewhere else, and no one had family to rely on for the backbone of their social activity.

I never fully realized, at the time, that the experiences I had in those early years would be the foundation for my understanding of the criminal mind. I'd spent several years pursuing a master's degree in psychology, but little did I know that becoming an FBI agent would give me the opportunity to be in a living laboratory of criminal behavior.

During that first year, the most dominant personality I observed was the psychopath (sociopath) personality. This personality very often can result in a person living a life of crime. Simple schizophrenia disorder occurs infrequently. However, one case of schizophrenia left a lasting impression on me while I was temporarily assigned to Lake City, Florida. The sheriff's department asked if I would assist in identifying a prisoner who was in their lockup. I asked a few simple questions, such as, "What has he told you?" Their answer was that he had told them nothing, "He does not talk. He only stares into space." The prisoner was about six-foot-four and weighed about 220 pounds. Approaching his cell, I found him standing and staring into space. He would respond to no questions. There was no doubt in my mind that what we were dealing with was a severe schizophrenic suffering from catatonia. I knew that people coming out of catatonic trances could have the physical strength of ten people. Three days later, when the prison guards were getting ready to move this prisoner, it took five deputies to control him. They wished they had five more to assist.

I experienced very real and practical applications of understanding abnormal behavior and how it relates to law enforcement. The years following would see its application to criminology, criminal psychology, criminal profiling, hostage negotiations, and the interviewing of witnesses with the use of hypnosis. Very little structured study of psychology as it relates to law enforcement was done before 1970. The basic instincts of good police officers became the everyday guide in handling the criminal. There were countless great detectives who used street knowledge to solve difficult cases. At the same time, however, there were many missed opportunities for better handling of the criminal mind, with too little anticipation of the criminals' next moves.

Many forms of crime exist, the worst of which is murder. Law enforcers always felt that murder was a grizzly topic. Every murder was different; every murder told a different story. These stories were compounded when they became a series of murders. In a strange way, the series of murders, however horrifying, would assist the investigators in solving the crime, leading to the apprehension of the murdering mind.

Early on, it was clear that no profiler would ever solve a case by himself or herself. An understanding of the motivation behind committing a crime is an invaluable tool in the hands of a shrewd investigator. The criminal profiler creates the map the investigator follows. The map is only as good as the experience, sensitivities, instincts, and understanding that an open, clear mind can bring to a case—a mind not burdened by politics or prejudice.

My journey was just beginning, and there was much to learn.

CHAPTER 2

RFK and Vietnam

AMERICAN HISTORY FROM THE 1960s through most of the 1970s was marked by extreme social change. Many tragic events took place, including the assassinations of John F. Kennedy, Martin Luther King, and Robert F. Kennedy. Many near-tragic events also occurred, such as the assassination attempts on Gerald Ford and George Wallace. In the early 1980s, John Hinkley almost succeeded in assassinating President Ronald Reagan.

JOHN HINKLEY

Society itself was undergoing a major shift, with every institution under the assault of change: family, neighborhood, education, government, church, and the work environment. The events of World War II had long since passed, leaving a nation very much intact after a war that tested its innermost fiber. The period after World War II was marked by stability in most institutions of society, with relatively little upheaval.

In the 1960s, a new generation of youth appeared on the scene. This generation seemed less connected to family, much more questioning of organized religion, undisciplined in education, and very distrustful of government. Family and neighborhoods were in the middle of a radical change from earlier years. The migration to the suburbs was in full gallop, and many inner cities were being left to decay. Long commutes became the way of life, and while it appeared that people had more to do, they had less to do with each other.

The nightmare of World War II had been replaced by the uneasy period of the Cold War, which from time to time was tested on both sides. The Cuban blockade brought us within moments of a major confrontation with the feared Soviet Union. The American psyche was not prepared for the sacrifice of war, and many youths resisted the notion of serving their nation. A centerpiece to the antiwar mentality of this period was an absolute fear of being killed in war for a cause that was ill defined.

It was a period in society when leadership took a holiday. Education had been designed for the mass population, but teachers were exiting classrooms to take on high-paying administrative positions. Churches were looking at empty seats and wondering where the congregations were going, a situation particularly marked by the absence of young people. Families continued the trend of becoming more fractured. Divorce, once relatively rare, became more commonplace. Children growing up with one parent or even none became an ever-increasing problem. Alternative lifestyles began to appear.

In this newfound liberation, society suffered a hemorrhage in the use of drugs. College campuses were no longer serious places of intellectual pursuit but the center for experimenting with altered states of consciousness. Dress codes were toppled; long hair was a mark of distinction for the nonconforming. A new class was created: the hippie. Rebellion was in, and conforming was out. Unrest of all kinds was the attraction; political, social, familial, religious, neighborhood, race, and governmental. Dropping out was in, and many individuals lost their place in society, never to be found again. Suicide and homicide tripled in this period, leaving us with staggering figures of more than twenty-five thousand people being murdered on our streets in the span of one year. The psychiatric community was estimating suicides to be more than twice that number.

This period in America saw an alarming increase in the violence that turned outward toward murder as well as the form of violence that turns inward to suicide. It became the period in which more people were receiving doctorates in psychology but less and less was actually understood about behavior, much less treatment.

In 1968, an event took place that made most Americans wonder where we were going as a society: the assassination of Robert F. Kennedy. Sitting in the living room on Sunday evening, June 2, 1968, my wife and I had the television on but were not paying much attention to it because we were entertaining another FBI agent, Lou Wilson, and his wife, Karen. Lou and Karen were from Louisiana and had that delightful Southern accent, which we loved to listen to. We had a great deal in common: age, occupation, interests, and location near the office. After dinner, they played with our oldest daughter, Jeannette, and our big Irish setter, Brandy. The baby had already been put down to sleep, and our social evening was coming to an end. The television caught our attention with the following announcement: "Stay tuned for a special report." The special report was sketchy with information but clear as to what happened. Robert Kennedy had been shot at the Ambassador Hotel where he was attending a reception, which started at 8:00 p.m. It was already shortly after midnight.

Robert Kennedy had been seeking the presidential nomination for the Democratic Party and had just won the primary in California. There was little doubt that he would be the nominee. He clearly was the front-runner and for all practical purposes had it locked up. This event would forever change the course of history. People will always ask, "Had he not been assassinated, would he have been elected?" If so, how would that have changed the direction America took? We will never know.

Moments after the news announcement, the phone rang. Because we were close to the office, we were immediately available. It took mere minutes to throw a suit on and strap on the gun and head to the office for a car. By the time we arrived at the Ambassador Hotel, the panic and commotion had subsided, and Robert Kennedy was taken to the Central Receiving Hospital on West 7th Street in downtown Los Angeles. The Cocoanut Grove Room had been cleared of the crowds heard cheering just hours earlier, and the kitchen area was being maintained as a crime scene.

Word came early the following day, June 3, 1968, that in fact Robert Kennedy died of his wounds that morning.

Another Kennedy! The next morning, the FBI office bustled with activity. We had been requested to assist the Los Angeles police department in the investigation, and the word was that no stone would be left unturned. The spirit of the investigation was vigorous. Lurking in the background was the criticism of the investigation in the aftermath of the John F. Kennedy assassination. This investigation had to be twice as thorough and leave no room for conspiracy theories similar to those surrounding his brother's assassination.

At first, the information was sketchy. The shooter was a lone Palestinian Arab named Sirhan. He had used a small 22-caliber handgun, and when subdued and searched, he had on him the announcement of the reception for Robert Kennedy along with four brand new hundred-dollar bills.

Information surrounding the shooting revealed that Roosevelt Grier, Rafed Johnson, and George Plimpton played a major role in subduing Sirhan Sirhan, along with Maître d' Karl Uecker, who was escorting Robert Kennedy through the kitchen. Robert Kennedy's last handshake was with busboy Juan Romero. Wounded also in the incident were Elizabeth Evans, Erwin Stroll, Ira Goldstein, William Weisel, and Paul Schrade. They were hit by stray bullets and received nonlethal wounds.

Robert Kennedy had been shot three times. He was shot twice in the area of the right armpit and once behind the right ear. Kennedy lost a significant amount of blood from his head wound. It was this wound that cost Robert Kennedy his life.

Prior to the shooting, Sirhan Sirhan was in the crowded ballroom while Robert Kennedy was making his remarks after winning the primary. Unable to get near him, Sirhan exited the ballroom and walked down a small corridor where the restrooms were located and entered the serving kitchen area of the Ambassador Hotel. Sirhan was within a few feet of the long serving table when he encountered Robert Kennedy and started shooting.

Sirhan had a 22-caliber weapon with eight rounds and fired all eight of them.

Within hours after the shooting, my responsibility was to interview Maître d' Karl Uecker, Juan Romero, and a young college student whose name escapes me. Additionally, two separate neighborhood investigations were conducted in places where Sirhan had recently lived.

The three individuals gave very consistent accounts as to what happened that early morning in the kitchen of the Ambassador Hotel. Sirhan approached Kennedy as close as he possibly could and without warning opened fire. Uecker was holding Kennedy by the arm as he was leading him through the kitchen. Had he gotten beyond the kitchen, he would have used the same corridor that Sirhan had used to come into the kitchen. It was Karl Uecker who initially grabbed Sirhan, forcing him face down on the serving table. Within split seconds, George Plimpton, Roosevelt Grier, and Rafer Johnson assisted in subduing Sirhan. While Sirhan's body and arm were being pressed to the table, his shooting hand was still mobile, enabling him to get off additional shots.

Robert Kennedy fell to the floor of the kitchen between the serving table and the large ice machine. Kneeling over him and holding Kennedy's head was the young college student, and next to Kennedy was Juan Romero. Shortly after Kennedy was shot, he uttered his last words: "How is Bill?" Robert Kennedy was concerned for his personal aide and security man, Bill Barry, who was behind him when the shooting started. Bill Barry was a former special agent for the FBI. Robert Kennedy lost consciousness before he was placed on a gurney and rushed to the central receiving hospital, where he was pronounced dead a few hours later.

As occurred after the investigation of the death of John F. Kennedy, the theories started to circulate around the investigation of Robert Kennedy. The first question was whether Sirhan acted alone. This was a legitimate question and a concern in the investigation. No information was ever substantiated to indicate that Sirhan was part of a conspiracy. Years later, the serious question of whether Sirhan actually did the shooting in the kitchen that morning gained momentum. This theory gained strength from the post investigation of how many shots were actually fired in the kitchen that night and whether there was more than one gun. I remained satisfied that Sirhan got off eight rounds, three of which entered Robert Kennedy's body and one of which one proved lethal. The interviews of several eyewitnesses confirmed those findings.

This case presented the classic psychological profile of the mentally driven assassin as opposed to the hired gun. Sirhan's background, as determined by the investigation, was totally consistent with the individual who assassinates because of some deep-seated psychological reasons. In reconstructing Sirhan's life after the event, it was consistent with a person who was regarded as being very sincere, a loner, a churchgoer, seldom causing any disturbances, not married and with few very close friends, intelligent, well spoken, not well accomplished in a particular career, and rigid in his beliefs. It also reflected one who seldom drinks or uses drugs, prefers being alone, has feeling of superiority, has impaired logic, is distrustful of people, is mission oriented, and has delusions of persecution coupled with periods of delusional grandeur. He was and continues to be an individual afflicted with a paranoid personality. The age of onset to the time he acted out his bizarre thought pattern fits the paranoid personality. It is unfortunate, but this type of individual seldom regards him- or herself as mentally impaired but almost always regards others as being less than normal.

The mentally driven assassin almost always kills his victim from a close distance. The act of killing is the ultimate. Seldom is an escape from the crime planned. When apprehended, the person gives the appearance of someone relaxed, waiting to be congratulated for his actions. In his mind, he totally justifies what he has just done and is, more often than not, willing to discuss the reasons for his actions. For the normal person listening, this is often incomprehensible. For this type of personality to act in concert with someone else is unheard of.

Sirhan was truly the paranoid person who had conjured up in his mind that it was incumbent upon him to better the Arab world he had come from. Robert Kennedy, in Sirhan's mind, was an enemy of the Palestinian state. If Sirhan destroyed Robert Kennedy, he would be forever viewed as a hero in his country. This type of personality disorder seldom improves to the point of normal mental health. This condition does not respond well to treatment because the individual never accepts that his behavior and mentality are subnormal. The condition worsens with age, and when one fixation is removed, another soon develops.

The most common question after a heinous crime such as an assassination is why? The reasons for paranoia are very complex. The study of them is in no way intended to excuse a crime committed but rather should be a tool to prevent similar crimes. Paranoia is one of the deepest-seated forms of psychosis known to medicine. Because of its very nature, it often goes untreated. The roots of paranoia are embedded deep in the psyche of these individuals. Many of their personality characteristics can be traced to the earliest periods of their socialization processes, including infancy. There is an emotional coldness to them; perhaps they never learned the process of being loved. As they mature in life, they become isolated and lacking in trust for other people. These characteristics do not always manifest themselves in youth but more frequently have their onset around age thirty. Truly paranoid people have unrealistic feelings of grandeur, making them feel almost godlike. They are very rigid individuals with a frequent tendency to fixate on a series of beliefs that could have very well originated in true events in their lives. These are people not normally well liked by others. In a work environment, they are often very unpopular and well known for complaining. The vast majority of individuals classified as paranoid personality types do not turn to crime or violent behavior. They normally lead lives marked by loneliness, agitation, and misery. Seldom do they excel to lead their peers in work endeavors. A very small percentage turns to crime, but the magnitude of the crimes such individuals choose to commit can be extraordinary. The mentally fixated assassin is the classic paranoid personality.

The paranoid assassin is the US Secret Service's nightmare, because such an individual appears normal and has the intelligence to gain close access to his target. The paranoid assassin can plan an assassination with great detail and is able to execute the plan with great precision. In advanced cases of paranoia, the assassin can give himself away, having an obsession with writing letters that set forth his delusions. Letters received from people with the paranoid personality should be closely read and not disregarded. Often these letters contain the elements of their potential destructive behavior.

Anyone with a good understanding of the paranoid personality would readily conclude that it would be inconceivable for this individual to be part of a plot to kill with others involved.

Matador of Murder

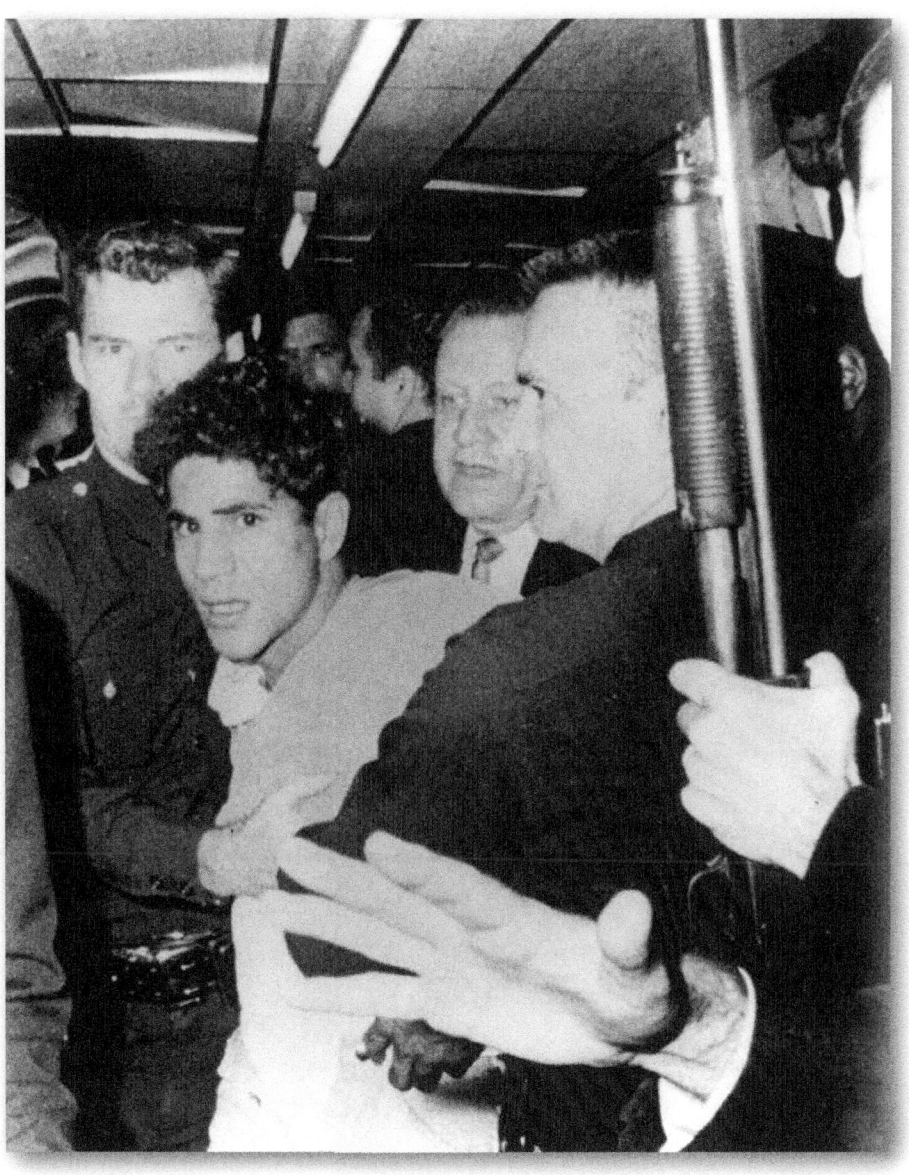

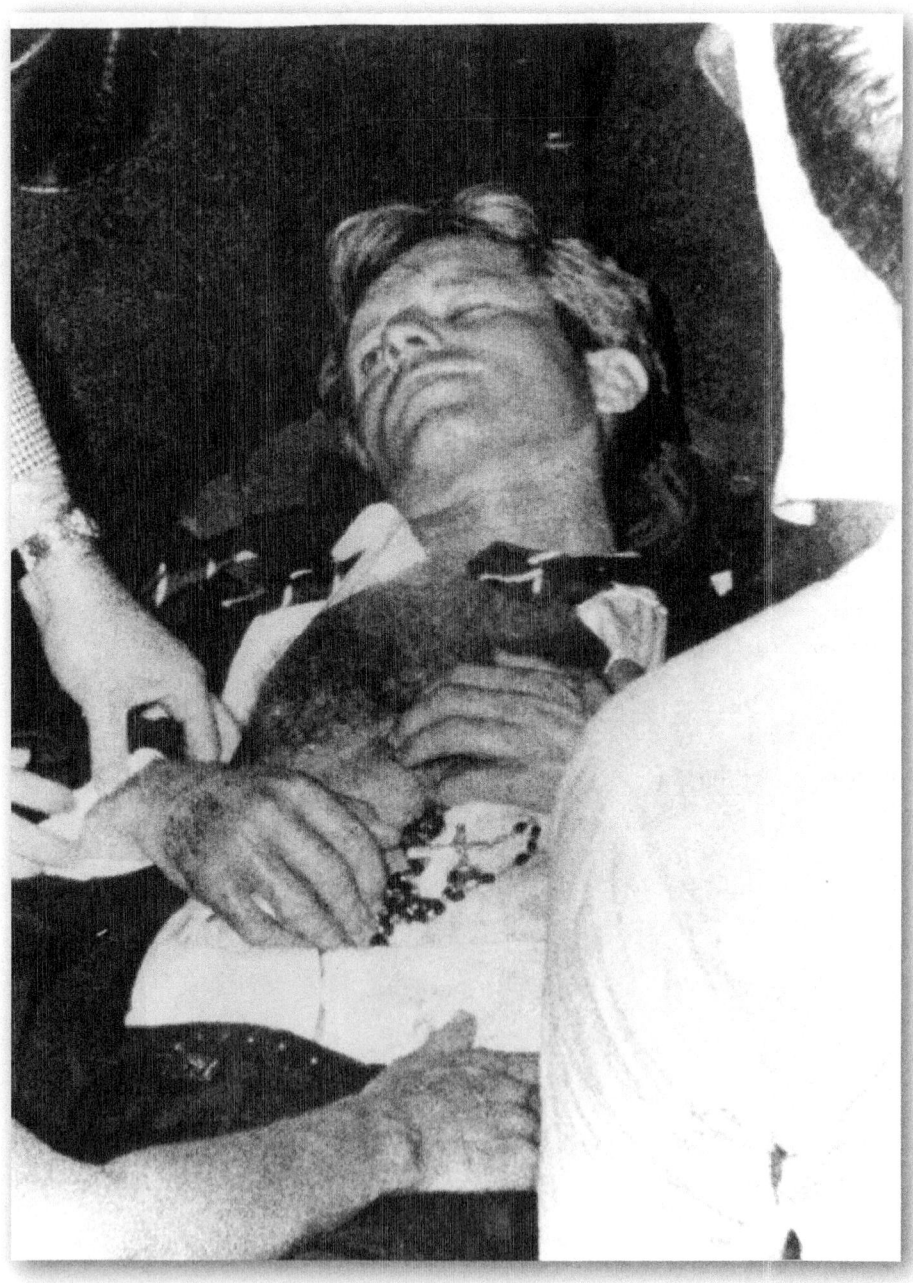

We become victims of this type of personality because the plot to murder exists in the mind of the killer, and he is incapable of sharing these thoughts with others. Sirhan Sirhan's actions accomplished one thing; they changed the course of history in this country. The history of Robert Kennedy ended with that bullet behind the right ear. As he lay dying in his own pool of blood, history redirected itself to what those of us who remained behind had to live with.

The killing of Robert Kennedy came at a period when unrest was being expressed throughout the country about our involvement in Vietnam. Robert Kennedy was against the war in Vietnam, but he did not abandon our soldiers who were fighting the war.

The college campuses on the west coast, such as, Berkeley, USC, UCLA, and University of California at Santa Barbara, were only some of the campuses filled with endless demonstrations and repeated oratory against the war. The demonstrations could give one the impression that these were gatherings of countless mindless individuals allowing themselves to be led by the big-name pacifist of the time. Seldom were the spoken words original; seldom were the targets of these demonstrations well thought out. There was sameness to dialogue and stage. The performers rarely had new faces, and the crowds were generally the same—young college students who could not find Vietnam on a map. What they did achieve and were successful at was manipulating the media. The media planned their day for the anti-Vietnam demonstrations, and most demonstrations were conducted in a timely manner to make the six o'clock news broadcast.

The Democratic Party held its national convention in Chicago in 1968. It was referred to as the Days of Rage. With a backdrop of campus demonstrations and demonstrations moving into the governmental and business areas of major cities, the nationally televised demonstrations surrounding the Democratic National Convention sent a shock wave through America. The word "anarchy" was heard more than once. The top levels of government knew that this behavior would greatly undermine our efforts to win an unpopular war. At all costs, this activity had to be brought under control. The demonstrations grew larger, and control was more difficult.

Arrested during the Days of Rage in Chicago and charged with attempted murder was an individual by the name of Brian Flanagan. Brian was no longer singing in the choir but had joined the more radical element of the period called the Weatherman. Brian was later acquitted of the murder charge placed against him when it turned out that the victim, a news reporter, had indeed thrown a tackle at Brian but missed and hit a hydrant, crippling himself for life. Brian Flanagan was let go free to continue his antigovernment activity. Some three years later, I found myself on surveillance at his residence. Brian had become a suspect in the bombing of the US Capitol. Brian had changed in the decade since we'd interacted with each other, and so had I. There had been no way of predicting the path Brian would take. In my view, his path was narrow and filled with broken promises. His ideals went from peaceful to violent. I never knew what ultimately became of him, but I felt that I had somehow failed him while trying to aid in his efforts to grow up with a positive outlook on society.

There were two major movements of unrest on the American scene: the antiwar movement and the preexisting movement for racial equality. In many ways, those involved in the movement for racial equality felt cheated by the media attention given to the antiwar movement. Much attention had been given to the racial equality movement in the aftermath of the assassination of Martin Luther King, which was perpetrated with totally different motivations from those of the assassination of Robert Kennedy. James Earl Ray was not the mentally motivated killer consumed by an inescapable obsession. Psychologically, he fit more neatly into the pattern of the psychopathic hired gun. In both movements, there were numerous incidents in which extreme violent behavior set aside the lofty rhetoric of some ideal principle.

After three exciting years in Los Angeles, our duty station was changed to New York City. Arriving in New York the Monday after the West 11th Street town house bombing, I was tapped to serve as liaison with the New York City police during the investigation of this bombing. The bombing took place in the early part of March when New York was experiencing bitterly cold weather. Temperatures were below zero during the night and reaching the single digits during the day. What I remember most was that I had not made the transition from west coast clothes to wintertime east coast clothes and did not have even an overcoat.

Chief Seidman, NYPD was heading up the investigation. From day one, it was evident that the relationship between the FBI and the NYPD was friendly but strained. There was a great resistance to sharing information on a timely basis. As the bulldozers were clearing the hole left where the town house once stood, there was a sense of concern because live sticks of dynamite were being discovered. The bulldozer operator was not thrilled, in the least, at the prospects of setting one of them off. On the third morning, we got word that the NYPD dug up the finger of who later discovered was Diane Dungie. From day one, it was noted that immediately after the explosion at least two individuals were seen running from the townhouse. The NYPD had a good idea who these individual might be but needed to be certain. What became clear to me during the time I spent as liaison with the NYPD was that I had a better chance of reading what was discovered from the town house clearing in the *New York Daily News* than I had getting it from Chief Seidman.

Relations were not the very best between the FBI and the NYPD. Each organization felt both pride and overwhelming competition at the idea of solving a case as large as this one. The hostility between agencies was not at the detective-agent level but was felt in the command ranks. There was a great deal of mutual respect, but as far as I was concerned, there was too much competition for press headlines on the part of both organizations.

Dustin Hoffman lived right next door to where the bomb factory was destroyed. It was fortunate he was not injured in the explosion. The explosion not only rocked West 11th Street but also sent a message that the antiwar movement was in the process of increasing violence in the effort to minimize the US role in Vietnam. The antiwar movement started to gain a following among the upper middle class individuals who supported their activities and made every effort to cover for them.

Shortly thereafter, the tragic event on campus at Kent State University took place. The agonizing picture of a college girl bending down over a student shot by the National Guard was seen all over this nation. The war we were experiencing on our streets and campuses was similar to the dark events thousands of miles away in Vietnam.

In honor of the death on campus at Kent State, Mayor Lindsay in New York decided to fly the city flags at half-mast. The flag on city hall was lowered to half-mast at the applause of the peace demonstrators, mostly from Pace College. In the open, park-like area around city hall, thousands of demonstrators were carrying banners of protest in a rather unorganized manner. There was a sense of restlessness because the rumor prevailed that the hard hats were going to march on city hall to raise the flag. The demonstrators pledged to hold their ground and deny them this effort.

Shortly before noon, just south of city hall, a ragtag group, reminiscent of the Civil War period, came marching north behind an American flag. The hard hats were solemn in their march, walking in ranks of four. They were determined that no one would stop them. Looking on, I knew there was little chance that the students would get in their way, but I was concerned with the police ranks that surrounded city hall. As the hard hats reached the city hall square amid cheers and name calling, a degree of panic struck the demonstrators. They started running in all directions. I witnessed more than a handful of individuals run through the plate glass windows of Pace College. The hard hats approached the steps of City Hall and spoke briefly to the police. They seemed to reach an agreement, and a small contingent of hard hats was allowed into city hall, where they proceeded to the roof to raise the flag over City Hall. A very large number of business people had taken the place of the thousands of demonstrating students, and cheers sounded out at the raising of the flag. The next day, the papers all carried the story as though it were a victory in war. The flag was not lowered again that day or in the days to come. Hard hats became heroes, and they flew flags on their work sites and equipment. The division was clearly marked; we were a divided country fighting a very unpopular war.

One of the cases assigned to me when I arrived in New York was titled Prisoners of War in Vietnam. It was an intelligence case for gathering information relating to the prisoners of war (POW) in Vietnam. When I first looked at the case, I wondered what could be done here in New York that would affect the situation of the prisoners of war so many miles away. I very quickly found out.

The peace activists who journeyed to Hanoi during this period became part of an insidious effort against our prisoners. It was hard to determine who the instigator of this propaganda machine actually was. If the peace activists designed the plan, they should receive the due criticism. If they allowed themselves to be used to carry out the plan at the design of the North Vietnamese, they should be held responsible for the duplicity. The concerted effort was to maximize the suffering of our soldiers who were being held prisoners in North Vietnam and Cambodia. The US Military knew which soldiers were missing in action, but they had no confirmation of which ones actually were POWs.

North Vietnam decided to take advantage of the unrest being experienced on the streets across America by putting a huge wedge between the families of the POWs and the government. A list of POWs was provided to the peace activists, which included the National Council of Churches and the likes of Jane Fonda and Rev. Richard Fernandez. Fernandez and Fonda who were well-known Vietnam War dissenters. They, with others, traveled to North Vietnam, giving comfort to the enemy and using their efforts to further their credentials as peace activists in the United States.

As with most subversive organizations, the FBI successfully penetrated the anti-Vietnam War movement. With a well-placed informant, we were able to obtain a full listing of all the American POWs in the hands of the North Vietnamese, facts previously unknown to the US Military. Having obtained this information, the military had a concrete idea of who the POWs were. The peace activists had a different use for the list. The intent was to torture the American families by giving them the knowledge that their son or daughter was being held prisoner and influencing them to speak out against the United States to get out of Vietnam. During December 1971, Rev. Richard Fernandez returned from North Vietnam with 1001 letters from the POWs. This was not a humanitarian effort but a brutal effort to manipulate American popular opinion. It perhaps was reasonable to question whether we should have been in Vietnam and when we should disengage ourselves, but this was dealing in concert with the enemy in using our soldiers, who were most unfortunately captured, as a propaganda tool.

Years later on a trip to Mexico City, I was flying first class and had the opportunity to sit next to Jane Fonda. She was involved in shooting a movie in Mexico and was traveling with a number of colleagues. When assigned in Los Angeles in the late '60s, I frequently ran into Henry Fonda while shopping in the Westward Village area of LA. Henry Fonda was a very decent man, easy to approach and happy to greet people who might recognize him. Sitting next to Jane Fonda was not a thrill. I recognized her immediately but never had any conversation with her. The strong feelings I had regarding her activities during the Vietnam War did not make me one of her fans. I said a silent prayer that the plane would have no difficulty because if we crashed, I would go down on the plane Jane Fonda did. I must admit I did do a quick psychological profile on her when the stewardess presented her with the meal. Jane Fonda angrily looked up at the stewardess over her paperwork and muttered in an ugly tone, "Can't you see I am working? I do not want that now." I felt sorry for the stewardess, who was doing her job. As for Jane Fonda, her behavior was uncalled for, and she appeared most arrogant. I felt fortunate that from the beginning, I did not waste time greeting her. Her efforts in the Vietnam War period were unjustified, and her behavior on the day I witnessed it was uncalled for.

The unrest of the 1960s and 1970s had a profound effect on crime in America. Civility was greatly diminished. People seemed to lack respect for others. There was a tremendous amount of hostility between races. The music of those years delivered a strong message; it had a life of its own and lived for many years beyond. Peter, Paul, and Mary; Willie Nelson; Joan Baez; and countless others left society with something to think about. The Vietnam War left us with veterans who had a great deal of difficulty finding their way back into our society. This was only worsened by the deadly effect that drugs were having on a significant segment of our population. As was stated earlier, homicide and suicide seemed to spike during this period. One of the predominant reasons for crime increasing during this period was drugs. It was bad enough that drugs were resulting in crime to support addictions; worse yet, crimes committed by people under the influence of drugs were more bizarre in nature. There was little doubt that many who came back from Vietnam had been brutalized by a war that made them face death. Many were never able to turn off the energy they had expended in surviving such an emotional experience, and a level of brutality not previously seen marked crimes committed during this period. In chapter 4, we will discuss one such crime. A particular concern surfaced: did the homicidal personality emerge in Vietnam, and was it impossible for them to turn it off when they returned home? Some fifty-eight thousand Americans lost their lives in Vietnam. Those who survived never forgot or forgave what they experienced. Between the victims to drug addiction and the loss of direction among so many who returned from Vietnam, we had a very significant population with a much higher probability of turning to crime. Much of that crime was violent crime.

Almost a decade after this period, while working at FBI Headquarters, I walked into Larry Wilson's office and found him going through a two-foot pile of computer printouts of our soldiers killed in Vietnam. He was very quiet, almost with tears in his eyes, when I asked what he was doing. He and I were assigned to the false identity unit of the criminal division. We had come to understand that it was common to obtain false identity, for whatever purpose, but we now knew that the prime source for names to assume was those killed in Vietnam. Larry told me that he was looking up the names of members of his platoon. I would later learn that those names were many. Larry had reached the rank of captain in the Marine Corps and was deeply involved in Vietnam. He led a platoon as lieutenant colonel that was overrun by Vietcong, and many of his men were massacred. The battle would be called The Battle at Finger Lake. So devastating was this battle that an American air strike had to be called in to give them any chance of survival. Years later, Larry would find out one of the jockey pilots flying a Phantom jet that day would live to be a fellow FBI agent, Tom Gates.

On Larry Wilson's face that day, I could read many thoughts running through his mind. Could he have done more to save his men? How were the survivors doing? For what purpose did we fight so hard and so long? Was it necessary to have so many men die and go so unappreciated? Later that week, I pulled his personnel file to refresh my memory of his role in Vietnam. It read like the journal of a true hero, though Larry would be the last guy to ever call himself hero.

Toward the end of the 1990s, Larry, after much planning, brought together his platoon, or what was left of them. Larry was kind enough to invite me. As we stood out over a bluff looking at the Pacific Ocean, cooking barbecue, I caught myself studying Larry's command in Vietnam. Many of them looked as though the road of life had treated them pretty harshly. Some looked better than others. Some looked as though they were still trying to catch on to society and follow it wherever it would lead them. They all looked with pride to the guy who had yelled orders, enabling them to survive and see another day, but they all slept with the memory of the death they had witnessed.

All war leaves many victims. World War II left major cities with Bowery-type neighborhoods, home to the hopeless. The Korean War left us wondering if our soldiers had lost the spirit to fight and escape if captured. Every war leaves scars, but Vietnam became the war for which no songs were sung, no parades went down Main Street, no academy award–winning movies were made, no real heroes emerged. It was a war for which, twenty-five years later, we learned of the misdeeds of our political leaders. What Vietnam did leave us with was a cycle of violence, both individually and collectively, from which we are still recovering. In many ways, this war brought together all the things that were collectively going wrong in our society. It drove us from churches; broke up families at a more rapid rate; made us critical of government; steered us into being self-centered and unwilling to give ourselves to organizations, especially the military; tore down barriers of self-control; made us less respectful; and led us to increasingly experiment with altered states of consciousness. We killed each other at an increased rate, killed ourselves in record numbers, and gave birth to more bizarre serial killers than anyone would have ever imagined. Understanding the criminal mind was more necessary than ever before in our history.

CHAPTER 3

Creating Profilers

IN THE EARLY 1970s, THE FBI embarked upon building what was later referred to as the West Point of Law Enforcement, the new FBI academy in Quantico, Virginia. The main purpose for this institution was to train local law enforcement officers from all over the world. Its secondary purpose was to train FBI agents. From a small building at the center of the Marine Corps base in Quantico, no one could imagine, in those days, how this institution would grow to become the magnificent academy it is today. It became closely affiliated with the University of Virginia to gain academic credit for its students.

In the late 1960s, a small contingent of special agents bonded together to form the new faculty for the upcoming academy. The idea was to create a meaningful curriculum that would be useful to law enforcement while being applicable to FBI agents. This was no small task. One of the early innovators was Jack Kirsch. Jack reminded me more of an outdoors person interested in hunting and running dogs than one interested in studying the behavior of humans in society. His talent was a combination of his study in sociology and an excellent understanding of organizational behavior. He knew the politics of the FBI. He knew what would work and what would not. Perhaps his best asset was his genuineness and affability wrapped up in optimism. Many of the individuals he surrounded himself with brought very different backgrounds to the table. John Pfaff was his immediate sidekick, experienced in policing major cities. Dick Kohler was a computer systems person, ten years ahead of his time. Jerry Shannahan and Paul Watson were his management experts, along with Gene Crickenberger. Perhaps Jack's favorite was Marty McInerney, who, like Kirsch, was a firearms instructor.

This was the original core of what would later become the faculty of the new FBI academy. When I look back over thirty years and evaluate what these individuals started, I have complete admiration for it.

When I was back at an in-service training class, Jack Kirsch took me aside and spoke about the possibility of me being on the academy staff when it opened in 1972. Jack had apparently conducted a file review to find individuals with advanced degrees in behavioral science, and my name turned up. Needless to say, I was honored. I remember Kirsch telling me, "You are too far away in Los Angeles, and we've got to get you closer." His purpose in getting me closer was to use me as an instructor before the academy opened. He suggested that I change my office of preference to New York and, once there, that I enroll for my doctorate at Columbia University.

Half of the plan worked. I was transferred to New York, and before I knew it, I went before the first session of the FBI national academy teaching Psychology for Law Enforcement. My plans to obtain a doctorate at Columbia, however, were short-lived. Besides being assigned sixty-one cases the first day I reported to the office, I spent the next two years tracking every demonstration against the Vietnam War. I did manage to take four postgraduate courses in psychology at Manhattan College, where I had obtained my master's degree some years earlier.

At Manhattan College, a nun, Sister Elizabeth, who was aligned with the Berrigan brothers, Daniel and Philip, was in one of my classes. She and the Berrigan's were protesting the Vietnam War and the government's involvement. Midway through the course, on a field trip to a mental hospital, Sister Elizabeth confronted me. "How can anyone profess to be a Catholic and be an FBI agent at the same time?" I replied that I found it incomprehensible that one could profess to be religious and at the same time live a scandalous public life breaking laws. We did not become close friends, and I was convinced she felt I was attending this class just to keep an eye on her activities.

Rev. Philip Berrigan, like Daniel, had become a fugitive and was wanted by the FBI. I took great pleasure in telling Sister Elizabeth of my experience arresting Father Berrigan at a Catholic rectory on New York's upper west side. The Agent in charge of the criminal division in New York, Joe Gamble, and I went into the back of the church looking for Berrigan. I remember Joe Gamble genuflecting on one knee while uttering, "I hope the son of a bitch is here."

Father Berrigan wasn't in the church, so we asked to search the house. The pastor assured us he wasn't there. The last room we searched was the pastor's bedroom. When we first opened the door, we couldn't see anyone. But in the back of the pastor's closet, we found another door. Once we opened that door, we found Fr. Berrigan standing quietly. It was indeed a new experience, putting handcuffs on a Catholic priest.

In March 1972 I was transferred from the New York office to the FBI academy shortly before it officially opened. Our first days at the new academy were anything but academic. We spent a great deal of time transferring everything from furniture and weapons from the gun vault out to the new academy. Before the first class arrived in early spring, we made beds and cleaned bathrooms. While it was unusual work for FBI agents, it gave us a sense of pride and ownership to prepare an institution that would, for many years, serve in making law enforcement more professional.

As the early months went by, Howard Teten and I shared an office and many thoughts together. Howard came up with the idea that we team teach. Team teaching meant having two instructors in the classroom at the same time, giving a combined course. He also suggested that we merge criminology and psychology—a very popular form of teaching. I would give the psychological disorder lecture regarding symptoms, prognosis, causation, and potential treatment. Howard would follow with the types of crimes that individuals with particular disorders would commit. It required a great deal of discipline from both of us to not cross over into the other person's territory. I always felt I had the greater burden because it was more exciting to give the criminal application than the more medical factual material.

Howard had been well versed in criminology and would lecture about Cesare Lombrosos, who put a great deal of emphasis on body type and its relationship to criminal behavior. On the other hand, I was more Freudian, pointing out that much abnormal behavior had its roots in unresolved sexual development. The more we lectured together, the more we came to a strong mutual belief that people kill the way they live and live the way they kill. What we started to notice was that particular patterns of behavior seemed to be related to certain categories of crime.

Howard had been a police officer in San Leandro, California, before he became an FBI agent. Neither one of us had a strong background in investigating homicides. We both had a keen interest in human behavior and how it related to crime. The more we lectured to various police officers from all over the world, the greater respect we had for each other and the more respect we got from the classes. Criminal psychology quickly became the most popular course at the FBI academy, and we came close to killing a good thing through overuse. No sooner would a class at the academy end than they would send us out to teach "road" schools one after the other.

Howard was far more scientific than I and paid more attention to detail than I did. I was always more interested in seeing the big picture, however, and had much greater capacity for sensitively seeking a person's motivation. What started to take place initially happened quite by accident. Police officers began to bring unsolved cases into Howard for review, and he would spend hours going over the file, autopsy reports, and crime scene pictures. He was always interested in the early interviews conducted by the police. Very quickly, Howard brought me into the review process. This was the beginning of criminal psychological profiling.

Profiling started, literally, out of a shoebox in a small office in Quantico, Virginia, at the FBI academy. We did not discover the original concept; many individuals did it before we came on the scene. Most of these earlier profilers could be classified as forensic psychiatrists with an acute interest in crime and its causes. Many of the psychiatrists had regular practices and gained notoriety when they participated in difficult police cases. What we did accomplish was to set the stage for criminal profiling to be recognized within a major law enforcement organization— the FBI. Howard and I had both police backgrounds and backgrounds in criminology and psychology. We had what the psychiatrist was missing: street knowledge.

Neither Howard nor I had any idea where these early efforts would lead us. With each success, the word spread, and more cases would come in. Howard had a slide collection of the early detectives who were known as experts in reading crime scenes. The old saying, "A criminal will leave his calling card at the crime scene," made an awful lot of sense to us, just as it had to the more renowned investigators of the past. We were aware of the works of Dr. James Brussel and of his success with George Metesky. We were also aware of the failures of Dr. Brussel. We had studied the "Jack the Ripper" series of murders in England and read Dr. George Phillips's findings on determining a killer's personality by the manner in which he treated the victim.

Howard and I started this work as an outgrowth of our teaching responsibility. We did a very informal review of the unsolved homicide cases and handled them on an ad hoc basis. There was no FBI recognition of the work in progress, and as a matter of fact, we were concerned that the FBI management would consider our findings speculative and not worth official sanction. We were aware that Dr. Brussel made mistakes, and so could we. What made our task easier was that many of the cases we reviewed were almost given up on and viewed as a last-ditch effort to seek a possible solution.

The structure used in establishing psychological case profiling was very similar to the methods we used for the class. In teaching criminology for law enforcement, we created a framework of the classes of mental disorders found in the American Psychological Association's treatment of mental disorders. The three main categories of mental illness we stressed were (1) neurosis, (2) psychosis, and (3) that large category known as personality disorders. We clearly understood that a very small number of murder cases would require psychological profiling.

It is easy to understand a murder case when the motive is rage or the result of armed robbery. The more pronounced the motivation, the less likely the need for a psychological profile. A psychological profile becomes necessary, however, when the motive is less apparent. It is useful when there is an aurora of mystery surrounding a case. When the killer has little or no relationship to the victim and there is no apparent motivation for the killing, the chances of solving the murder are greatly reduced. These are the cases in which a psychological profile of the killer can be most useful.

Psychological profiling is an attempt to get into the mind of the killer. The doorway to a killer's mind is the crime scene that he left behind. Being at the crime scene gives the investigator a three-dimensional view of what has transpired, the opportunity to sense what has taken place, and the ability to measure the violence created. It gives the trained investigator a chance to evaluate the struggle and examine the body for signs of torture or postmortem abuse. Being at the crime scene can also create the risk of overlooking some details, however, because emotions take control of the investigator. Psychological profiling, in most cases, occurs long after the victim has been removed from the scene but before the investigators identify a suspect. It involves the tedious review of every piece of documentation connected to a crime. A group of trained investigators often conduct the review independently and then, upon completion, meet to reach final conclusions.

Following the time-honored belief that the killer leaves part of himself at the crime scene, the profiler meticulously examines how the killer treated the victim. There are very few neurotic murders. Other than those driven by obsessive-compulsive behavior—exhibitionists and voyeurs—most neurotics would never come to the attention of law enforcement. The obscene phone caller might very well fit into this category, but in profiling homicides we seldom dwell on neurotic behavior.

Two categories of mental illness of great concern to us when profiling a homicide were the psychotic and those classified with personality disorders. We found distinct correlations between the crimes committed by persons representing these categories and their personality disorders. Well over 90 percent of the individuals who kill other human beings without an obvious motive fit into these categories. They are commonly called psychopaths or sociopaths. It became clear from the homicide cases we reviewed that the psychopath leaves many clues regarding his identity when he kills. Psychopaths are capable of committing any conceivable animalistic act during their killing spree. The crime scene frequently indicates severe torture before the victim(s) died. The common indicators to a profiler that psychopathology is involved are rape, sodomy, cannibalism, necrophilia, and other abnormal behavior. Psychopaths are vicious killers unconcerned about guilt and fearless of being apprehended. The crime scenes are distinctive in what they leave behind. The intelligent psychopath leaves few clues, while the less intelligent leaves much behind.

The psychotic killer, on the other hand, can be confusing for the profiler to unravel. There are many forms of psychosis, and for each form, there is a totally different crime scene. The psychotic killer, unlike the psychopathic killer, is a controlled killer. The controlling factor for the psychotic killer is measured by his derangement. With many psychotic killers, it is their inner set of beliefs, which can have little to do with reality that motivates them to kill and commit crime. The psychotic killer is in the world where mentally driven assassins live. It is the world where mad bombers play out their dreams, where self-appointed crusaders prey upon prostitutes, killing them for the good of mankind. It is the world where people kill because inner voices commanded them to do so, the world where a mother, driven by mental illness, can murder her children and place them in bed dressed in their newest outfits. It is a world where the mentally isolated psychotic can prey upon a child and, upon murdering them, take them apart like a doll.

Psychological profiling of a homicide requires the study of every piece of evidence, every blood drop, body marking, contusion, burn mark, lab result and everything that is missing, in light of what has gone on. Profiling is stepping back to look at the whole picture and taking the risk of entering the mind of the killer. Having entered the killer's mind at the time of the killings, a good profiler draws up a profile of the criminal. A good profile will shed much light on a confusing crime scene. Things take on different meanings; strangulation should not necessarily be judged as sadistic. A severely shattered head might not necessarily indicate a masochistic rapist. Missing body parts might become the road marker to the psychotic killer or the psychopathic thrill seeker.

One of the early cases we profiled was the killing of an eight-year-old girl as she waited at a bus stop in Enrico County, Virginia. The examination of this case brought together many of the theories of Dr. Brussels and Dr. Phillips and the theories we had been developing—that people murder the way they live. The killer grabbed the young girl who was on her way to school, pulled her into the underbrush, and strangled her to death. At first, Enrico Sheriff's Office perceived this case to be a sexually motivated crime. There was no semen on the body, and the killer had pulled the little girl's clothing toward her head and placed a soda bottle in her vaginal area. The autopsy reported that the cause of death was, in fact, strangulation and that someone had placed the bottle gently in the vagina after the little girl's death. Her clothing was not torn, and there were no other abrasions to the face or body. The findings clarified that while the case had sexual overtones, it was the work of a psychotic killer who lived in a world of his own. The motive for the killing was more curiosity than sexual gratification. You would not find this killer in local bars, and he would not have a previous arrest record for this type of crime. According to our findings, we strongly believed him to be psychotic and suffering from simple schizophrenia. This type of killer often lives in the same neighborhood as the crime; he is known to be a loner and somewhat odd but is regarded as harmless.

Howard and I had been working on the various ways simple schizophrenia manifests itself in crime. Simple schizophrenia is a very serious form of psychosis, which normally has its onset during the teen years. It is marked by asocial behavior, aloofness, a tendency to be alone, the lack of interpersonal skills, and inadequate heterosexual development. Many times these people can be very skilled in activities that require no interaction with other people, such as a music or art. They seldom turn to violence. We had noticed a pattern of killings that were more motivated by curiosity, especially curiosity about the female body. Having killed the victim, the killer would cautiously examine the body. There were cases when the perpetrator would have a sexual release, but not always. From the autopsy and crime scene pictures of this young girl on her way to school in Enrico County, Virginia, it was apparent that the killer spent a lot of time examining the body after the murder. This was most unusual and would be unheard of for a psychopathic killer. We felt strongly that we should not be looking at past sex offenders but rather at loners who were aloof, quiet, and overly reserved. We also suggested that the killer might not be previously known to law enforcement. In the early hours of this investigation, the police had questioned a young man who fit our profile exactly. Within weeks, however, this individual was placed in a mental institution where the police could not interview him. This case has remained unresolved to this day.

Psychological profiling will never solve a case on its own. Good police work—and in particular, good detective work—solves cases. Psychological profiling is only as good as the person or persons doing the review. It is not an exact science, and there will be times when the conclusions a profiler reaches will be dead wrong. We shouldn't abandon the technique because of this face, but we should take care not to blindly follow a profile or ignore obvious leads in a particular case.

We became good at profiling murder cases because of the volume of cases we reviewed and because of the background we took to the review. Autopsy reports and crime scene pictures can reveal a wealth of information about a case. What is missing in many police departments is someone who can sit down in a peaceful environment to digest the full investigation and determine what is missing or what is important. The case investigator seldom gets this opportunity and rarely has a chance to discuss the case fully with someone else.

In the early 1970s, some of the more spectacular cases from around the country came to us for review. There was no shortage of bizarre cases that could teach us some valuable lessons. It did not take long to understand the magnitude of brutal, violent behavior going on in America. When compared with other countries, we outdid them both in number and in brutality.

One such case occurred in Santa Cruz, California. The killer was Edmund Emil Kemper. Kemper was a white, male, and about six-feet-eight-inches tall. He was always fascinated with law enforcement, and had it not been for the fact that he killed his grandparents at a young age, he might have become a police officer. He loved to hang around with the police, picking up whatever information became available. The courts gave him a short prison sentence for the killings of his grandparents and placed him on probation.

He got to every probation meeting on time and did everything his probation officer told him. He impressed his probation officer and court-appointed psychiatrist so much that the psychiatrist wrote in one report. "The motorcycle that Edmund rode to the psychiatrist's office was far more dangerous to society than Edmund Emil Kemper was." The psychiatrist was unaware that on that particular day, Kemper arrived at the office with the head of a young coed by the name of Aiko Koo in the trunk of his car.

Santa Cruz, California, is home to a very popular California State University campus well known for its free spirit and rather free-loving people. While it was not as politically active a campus as Berkeley was, it was still radical.

Living in this area, Kemper had become a full-blown killer. He was very meticulous in planning his crimes and vicious in carrying out his fantasy. Kemper carried a lot of law enforcement equipment in his car: handcuffs, red light, large antenna, rope, and material that could be used for body bags. He stalked his prey intently. Most of his victims were young females attending the university. Occasionally he would pick up two coeds and overpower and kill both of them.

Kemper did not look like a killer, despite his large size, nor did he act like one. He could be very engaging and cunning in speech. He was the true con man who took great pleasure in controlling people. He ended up killing six coeds and brutally dismembering them. Each time, he took the bodies back to his house, and on numerous occasions, he kept the body beside his bed for days. Kemper lived with his mother, who had no clue as to his activities.

Matador of Murder

The community of Santa Cruz was in a state of panic over the killings. The campus felt like it was under siege. Kemper's crime spree likely would have gone on much longer than it actually did except for the fact that he lost control of himself and killed his mother and his mother's best friend.

Shortly after this happened, the Santa Cruz Sheriff's Office got a phone call from Kemper requesting that they come pick him up, promising he would wait at the phone booth he was calling from. His confession to all of these crimes took hours. The police were exhausted at the length of the confession and the minute detail it contained. In explaining his actions during the course of his lengthy confession, at one point he said, "I woke up the next morning and looked down at the body of the girl I had killed the night before and wondered what it would be like to have sex with her, so I proceeded to have sexual intercourse."

Kemper cooperated fully, taking the police to crime scenes they didn't know about. Kemper, throughout his confession, showed no emotion or shame for what he had done no matter how depraved these acts would appear to a normal person. Kemper was not normal. He seemed affable, polite, proud, and contented with his newfound notoriety. He came across as a braggart and suggested they wouldn't have caught him if he hadn't turned himself in.

We weren't sure whether his mother had discovered what he was doing or not. If she did, that could have been the reason he killed her. From a psychological standpoint, it was easy to see why he killed his mother. Kemper had a habit of burying the heads of his victims in his mother's backyard, with the faces pointing in the direction of his mother's bedroom window. Kemper's infatuation with keeping the heads of his victims indicated severe pathology. He freely expressed in his confession that he would use the heads for oral copulation.

In examining this case, we found the deepest, most depraved form of psychopathology that one could imagine. He confessed, "After killing my mother, I cut her head off and placed it up on the kitchen sink. I noticed that her trachea was moving, and that got me very upset, so I cut it out and threw it down the garbage disposal. When I turned on the garbage disposal, it tossed the trachea back out. I remember saying to myself, 'She bitched at me all my life, and now even in death she continues to bitch at me.'" All the evidence pointed to the fact that Kemper mentally tortured his victims before he killed them. He used the handcuffs and rope to tie them up. Controlling and dominating his victims was a major part of his killings. His smooth talk would have his victims believing that he was a police officer. The victims were usually hitch hikers who fell for his story. The depth of Kemper's obsessive-compulsive sexual depravity is somewhat incomprehensible.

Years after the killings, Robert Ressler, an FBI agent who worked with us, interviewed Kemper in prison. Ressler had been assigned to the behavioral science unit in Quantico and became an exceptional profiler who brought many new initiatives. He started the program to interview individuals who killed more than one person. Bob Ressler is responsible for the concept of the serial killer, one of whom was Edmund Kemper.

When Ressler and another agent interviewed Kemper, the imprisoned man attempted to dominate and command the situation. Kemper knew that his height, six feet eight inches, intimidated people. Knowing that these two interviewers were FBI agents did not deter him from trying to dominate them as he did his victims.

This case, when properly studied, gave us more complete insight into the psychopath. Psychopaths truly wear a mask of sanity. Everything about them defies classifying them as mentally ill. They do not hallucinate. They are not necessarily delusional. The acts that they commit when they turn to violent crime are mind numbing. These individuals always play a game of one-upmanship. They are without measurable guilt and never show remorse. They are emotionally cold, outgoing, manipulative, and cunning. They place no value on life and seldom learn from past experiences. This is the mentality that clogs our criminal justice system, and this profile fit Kemper almost perfectly. Most sadomasochistic behavior has its roots in psychopathology. Unfortunately, individuals with this disorder are beyond rehabilitation.

When the psychopath kills, he almost always also tortures his victim. This torture is compounded if the killings become a series of killings. The killer will pick up new methods of killing and new patterns with each killing. Often these patterns can be studied, and the perpetrator can be linked from one crime to the next. What makes this emotionally difficult for the profiler is that the study of the process reveals a clear understanding of what the victim had to endure prior to death. Can you imagine what went on in a victim's mind before he or she was killed? Our studies showed that when a psychopath turns to killing, he inflicts bodily damage before murdering the victim. This bodily torture can go on for days until the killer is bored and finally commits murder.

He sometimes starts to dismember his victims before actually killing them. When the victims panic, the killer, in maniac form, often becomes very methodical and calm. The more horrified the victim, the more the predator feels in control. There is no doubt that killers within this category experience a perverted sexual pleasure from their behavior.

The case of Edmund Emil Kemper gave us a benchmark in the early days of profiling. It showed us how far a person could go in setting up his victims with a con scheme: Kemper posed as a policeman to gain the trust of his victims. It also established the variety of activities the psychopathic killer can become involved in, such as necrophilia, cannibalism, and masturbation. It gave us reason to conclude that no behavior was off-limits for the psychopath. Kemper's history of killing was on the upper end of the bell-shaped curve of murderers. It did not take long after that to fill up that end of the curve with names such as John Wayne Dacy, Ted Bundy, Richard Rameriz, David Berkowitz, Jeffrey Dahmer, and Richard Speck. Each case became more grotesque than its predecessor. After that, the United States quickly gained first place when compiling the most bizarre killers known to mankind. They were ours.

When we first began our profiling, the chief of police in Santa Barbara, Al Trimbly, brought in a case to Howard Teten for review. I mention this case because it confirmed our belief that people kill the way they live. It was a homicide that took place in the late evening hours along Ocean Boulevard in Santa Barbara. Today, the Fess Parker Doubletree Hilton Hotel stands on the site where it happened. During the time of the crime, it was a lonely stretch of road that was bordered by a rather deep, overgrown area of brush. The victim had been a waitress at a nearby restaurant and was walking from her place of business to join her boyfriend at a popular lounge. She never made it to the lounge. The crime scene pictures showed massive trauma to the head; she was nearly unrecognizable. The nipple portions of both breasts were missing. She had been wearing a white blouse that was buttoned down the front with a short skirt. Her shoes were off but near the body. In the crime scene pictures, it was clear that a branch had been placed in her vagina. The investigators didn't find semen on the body, but there was semen found on a nearby jacket belonging to the victim. The autopsy report cited the cause of death as severe trauma to the head, with multiple skull fractures. The report also noted the nipples of both the right and left breasts were missing. The vaginal tracings showed little or no injury to the vaginal track even though a branch had been placed in the orifice. Other than the severe beating to the head, the coroner couldn't find any injury to other parts of the body. Insomuch as he could determine, the nipples had been cut off after she died.

When Howard Teten and I reviewed the case, the autopsy and crime scene pictures became of paramount importance. The Santa Barbara Police Department had taken excellent crime scene pictures. This case was about six months old by the time the chief brought it in for review. We felt that it was an aggravated sex crime. We went over the crime scene pictures very closely, using a magnifying glass to examine every portion of it. What we spotted amazed us. At first sight, this crime appeared to have an excess of passion to it—severe beating, objects injected into the body, and breast nipples removed. Upon close examination, however, we noticed that her blouse had been meticulously opened before it was raised over the victim's head. There was not one button missing or any buttonhole torn. The bra was lifted but not torn. From the autopsy report, we determined that the killer had very carefully placed the branch into the vagina. The nipples were not torn or bitten off but rather cut by a sharp instrument, probably a pocketknife. The murder instrument was a boulder found near the body.

Howard and I reached the same conclusion fairly rapidly. This was not the crime of the typical psychopathic rape. This was a crime during which the perpetrator spent a great deal of time exploring the body. It was somewhat akin to what a toddler child might do to a doll, taking it apart to see what was inside. When we examined the profile, we came to believe that the killer was sexually inadequate, perhaps psychologically unable to have a normal relationship with a person of the opposite sex but nevertheless full of sexual curiosity. The killing was most unsophisticated; he used brute force, with little if any prior planning.

Our profile, which we handed over to the chief, indicated that he did not have an active sex killer on his hands. It was clear in our findings that this murder was the work of someone who fit the psychological category of the simple schizophrenic. There was evidence that the perpetrator was deeply psychotic, and we told the chief that we didn't think an informer would have any information that would lead to an arrest.

Our profile had the perpetrator as a white male, twenty-five to forty years of age, a loner, possibly a drifter, single, and sexually inadequate; he likely had a past criminal record involving indecency or public nuisance–type violations.

He was physically strong, was a product of broken marriage with a maladjusted family background, and lived near the scene of the crime. We were concerned because a large population of homeless individuals lived nearby. This case has remained unsolved since the mid-1970s and was still unsolved as recently as August 2000.

Most homicides that take place in the United States are solved without much difficulty because we can easily find a motivation for the killing. Homicides that have little or no motivation, committed by strangers, are very difficult to solve. The case in Santa Barbara bears that out. It is always possible that the perpetrator jumped the next freight train out never to be heard of again or that he was taken off the streets and placed in a mental institution. The serial killer is particularly hard to catch because the motivation for killing can be almost anything. The Green River killings in the Northwest are a good example. There are countless missing persons, mostly female prostitutes, attributed to this killer, though the motivation for killing is unclear. The case remained unsolved for decades. It was not until recently that an individual was arrested, based on DNA evidence, and charged with four of these hideous crimes. The total killings, estimated at forty-nine, had great similarities, and the individual arrested fit many of the characteristics of the early profiles. Seldom is a crime scene so obvious that we can determine the motivation for this type of killing. Motivation can be accurately determined only by understanding the individual who committed the crime.

One such case that we studied involved the killing of Sharon Tate by the Manson gang. The murders this gang committed were extremely brutal, yet the motivation for the killings was extremely difficult to determine. The Manson gang killed Mr. and Mrs. Labianca while they were sleeping. Mr. Labianca had been wearing a pair of blue pajamas, Mrs. Labianca a nightgown. Someone carved the word "WAR" in large letters on Mr. Labianca's stomach. Mrs. Labianca had put up a fierce struggle for her life. The gang brutally stabbed her numerous times in many parts of the body, but the most severe wounds were to her torso. Both of these cases, when we reviewed them together, indicated to us that the killers had been heavily influenced by the use of drugs.

Murdering with a knife brings an intenseness not experienced with any other weapon and often indicates an excessive closeness between the killer and the victims. Both crime scenes were marked by an overabundant use of force and multiple stabs. Sharon Tate, some eight months pregnant, was stabbed three times below the left breast in the heart area. It appeared that she did not give much resistance to her assailants. The hairdresser in the house that night was also severely beaten and stabbed to death. The crime scene was laden with blood. A heavy rope was tied around the head of the hairdresser, loped over a ceiling beam, and tied to Sharon Tate.

Both of these crime scenes involved senseless criminality. What was the motivation? Who would have ever been able to interpret "helter-skelter" before we heard the psychotic ramblings of Charlie Manson?

The Manson Cult killings opened a new door on homicide cases. On the one hand were psychologically weak people allowing themselves to be led by a deeply disturbed leader. Charlie Manson has been classified as a paranoid schizophrenic all his adult life. His world is one of voices and clashing visions of violence. This mixture of human group dynamics, on the other hand, is set in an unpredictable pattern of behavior under the influence of drugs. Drugs act as a lubricant in removing inhibitions that might control otherwise uncontrollable people. Under the influence of drugs, a group's actions become spontaneous and heinous. The crime scene is often very puzzling and disturbing. The normal reasons for killing are missing, such as revenge, hate, anger, and the need to escape a crime. What is left behind is a crime scene that is psychotic in itself, depicting madness.

Matador of Murder

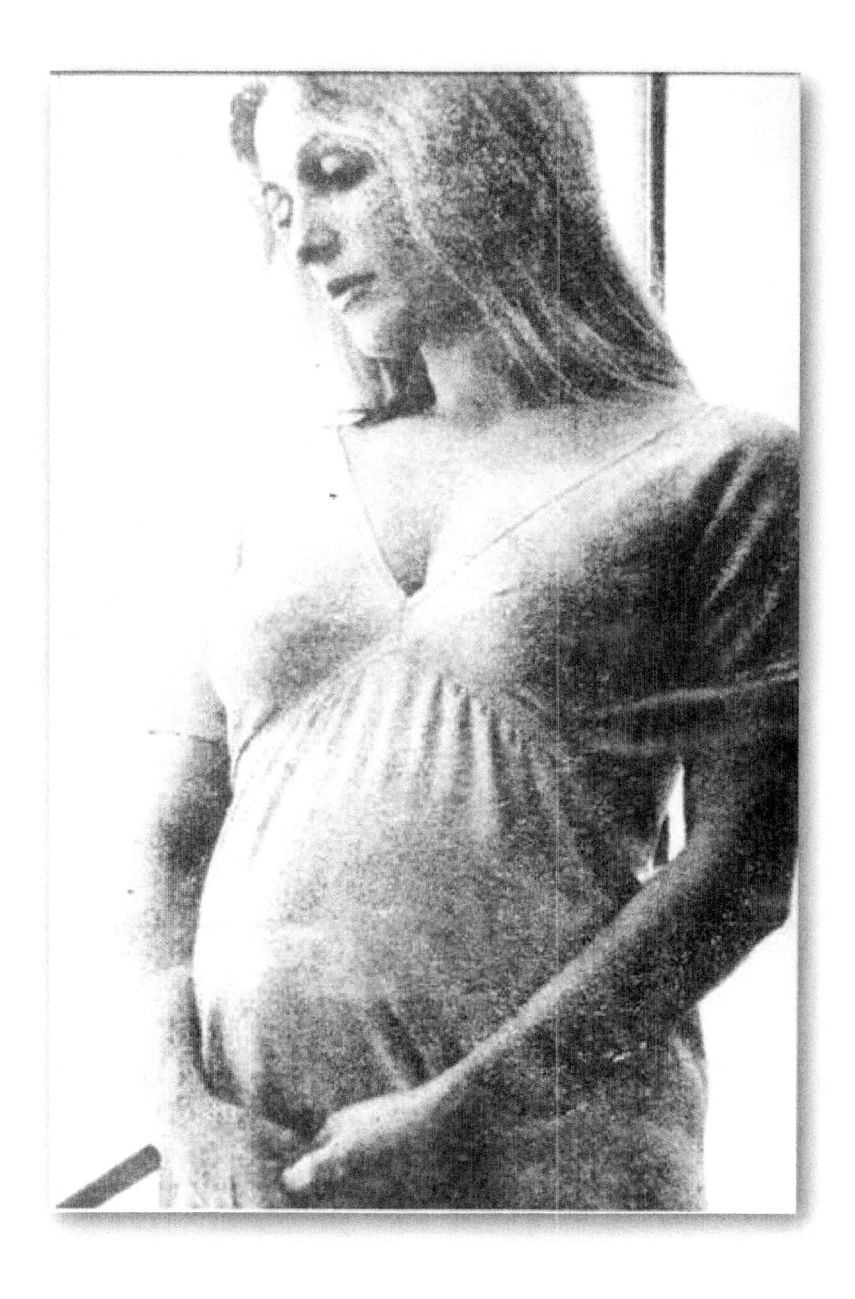

Patrick J. Mullany

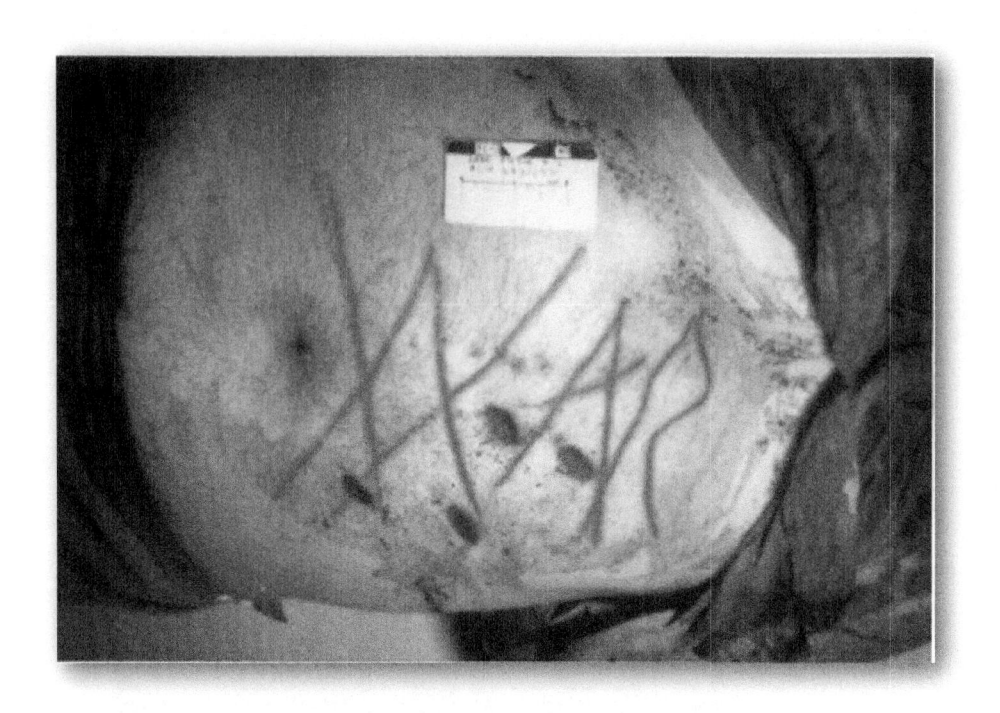

After we reviewed hundreds of cases, including some of the most publicized in the country, we realized that our early perception was right. *People kill the way they live and live the way they kill.*

The early work that Howard Teten and I had undertaken as an unproven concept became a reality. In 1976, I was invited to attend the American Psychological Association's (APA) meeting in Toronto, Canada, to present a paper on the work we had been doing. It was clear to me that the psychiatrist/psychologist would press for the empirical evidence to prove our assumptions.

We had no empirical evidence to draw irrefutable conclusions; that was not our purpose. My paper and presentation pointed to the strong correlation between certain crimes and specific mental disorders. I was honored to be on the same stage with Dr. Carl Menniger, who acted as our moderator. He was intrigued by our research and, more importantly, by our early successes. We closely followed the APA's menu of mental disorders. Here were some of the findings I presented:

* The psychopath was capable of any and all crimes, accompanied by an endless appetite for violence.

- The paranoid usually acted independently. This was often the mind-set of an assassin.
- Manic-depressed psychotics were well known for suicides and murders. This disorder was displayed in cases of mothers killing their young children and committing suicide, often leaving a note behind begging forgiveness.
- The simple schizophrenic sometimes had a tendency to linger with and explore the body. (The attendees were intensely interested in this.)

The conference members expressed a belief and frustration that we were experiencing an increase in all types of crime, both violent and nonviolent. They sensed that murder was becoming more brutal and animalistic, pointing out the increased drug involvement and a general breakdown of what holds people together in society: family, school, and church.

Perhaps the most difficult case for us to review came out of Texas. It involved the death of a seven-year-old girl—the daughter of a young couple whom the police arrested for murder. The parents had kept the baby for her entire life in a dark room with a solitary crib placed in the center. Alongside the crib was a rabbit cage. Inside the rabbit cage was a well-cared-for rabbit. From all evidence, however, the parents never held or cradled the child but kept her confined to the crib. The investigators found a diaper on the body that appeared to be weeks old. The baby never learned how to talk but, according to the parents, squealed much like an animal, perhaps like the rabbit. The body showed great deformity and excessive hair growth along the back and shoulders. Her hands revealed a pattern of partially healed deep cuts on the fingers. There were also recent cuts.

In the interview, the parents stated that the only way they could shut up her squealing was to "cut her fingers with a paring knife." The body showed signs of severe malnutrition. You could see that the crib mattress covering had not been changed in months and that they had allowed the child to sit in its feces matter. The physical development of the child, for all practical purposes, ceased at sixteen months of age, and the child appeared to be a baby rather than a seven-year-old girl. This case represented the most extreme case of child abuse and neglect that we ever witnessed.

Matador of Murder

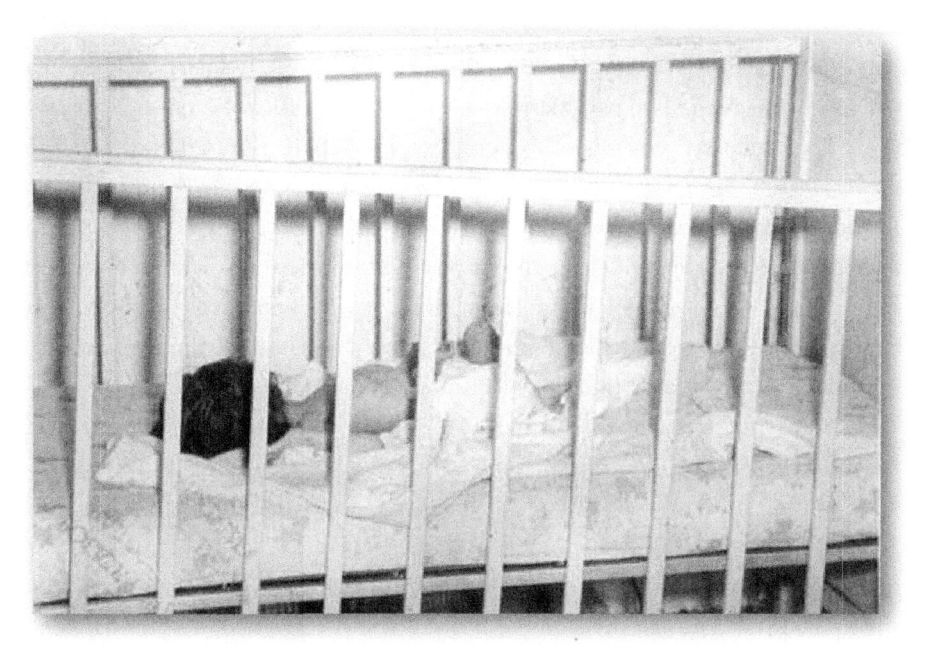

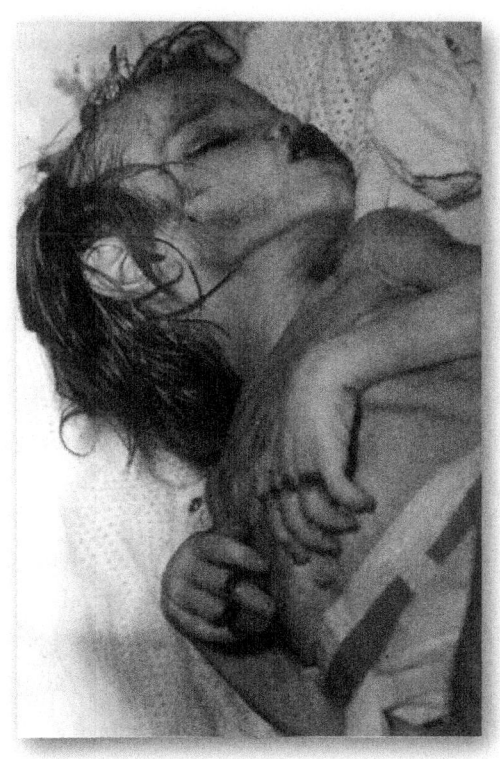

The police officers investigating this case were greatly upset by it and had to have counseling. The psychiatrist counseling the officers cautioned them to remember that for every one of these cases they were forced to investigate, *there are hundreds of Sunday school picnics—good people leading productive lives. There are Dr. Cooley's and Dr. DeBackey's out there creating cures for people who would otherwise not make it.* This is a point that can escape a police officer involved in investigating some of the most violent and repulsive crimes. Being asked to investigate the work of monstrous killers can take an enormous toll. In many ways, the investigator can become the silent victim of crimes of this nature.

The behavioral science unit began to take form in the early 1970s. Inside this unit the FBI had such components as sociology and police community relations as well as criminal psychology. Howard Teten and I started teaching in 1971, and the new FBI academy opened in 1972. In 1973, we began to review numerous unsolved cases, doing this unofficially until 1975 or 1976—the time when the criminal division began to officially recognize it. This happened because they were referring so many cases to us by then and using us in many of their criminal investigations. Psychological profiling remained in the behavioral science unit until 1977, when it broke away and became the National Center for the Analysis of Violent Crimes (VICAP).

From those early years in the 1970s, new people joined the behavioral science unit and started psychologically profiling homicide cases. Howard Teten and I were the first generation of profilers, and Thomas Strentz and Conrad Hassel closely followed us. These two individuals did not stay with profiling long but went into operational matters. The second generation of profilers, Robert Ressler and Richard Ault, proved to be an excellent addition to the effort. Robert Ressler took profiling to a new level. He was a risk taker and innovator. It was he who started the interview program of the most notorious killers in America: Charlie Manson, Edmund Emil Kemper, John Dacy, and Jeffrey Dahmer. Many minor players also made limited contributions, such as Bob Fitzpatrick, Bill Peters, John Mindermann, Jim Siano, and John Douglas. Roy Hazelwood arrived before I left the unit. Hazelwood was extensively involved in sex crimes, and Douglas traveled and worked with Bob Ressler.

One of Douglas's achievements was to work with Hollywood in making the film *Silence of the Lambs*. Clearly, these agents were part of the third generation of profilers. The person responsible for keeping the unit together and seeing that it developed from the shoe box phase to VICAP was Roger DePue, a former marine and sociologist.

Criminal profiling has experienced remarkable growth and acceptance from its beginning in the 1970s until now. Once the FBI institutionalized criminal profiling, most major police departments followed closely behind. Many local law enforcement agencies currently participate in sharing information, enabling the national center to become a clearinghouse of difficult cases to solve. It has been a tremendous tool for solving multiple homicides that cross state boundaries.

Though it is a tremendous tool, we knew from the early inception of psychological profiling that there is an inherent danger, a danger manifested itself in a series of sniper killings in the Washington, DC, area. Many newly recognized and recently retired profilers allowed themselves to become involved in the media frenzy that surrounded the sniper incidents. After each shooting, the pressure was building within the media to cover the story. Unfortunately, what took place was not psychological profiling but gross speculation that served to fuel the imagination of the two killers. The profilers appearing on television served the purpose of scripting the assassins, feeding off each analysis they listened to. They fell into the trap of selecting the statistically acceptable suspect—the lone, white male. This allowed the actual killers more time to avoid arrest.

Psychological profiling is the systematic review of every element of a crime. It is best served when all of the material is present for review and sufficient time has elapsed to allow investigators to gather all the evidence possible. Psychological profiling is not the discipline of speculating in public while killers are actively selecting targets and eluding capture.

Anyone close to profiling knows that the process never replaces the hardworking detective. But we firmly believed that it provides an invaluable tool in the arsenal for apprehending vicious killers.

Perhaps what motivated us the most was the belief that our efforts could possibly save that next victim thumbing a ride on a road in "Somewhere, USA." Capturing a notorious killer gives police and profilers a rush beyond belief. Most homicide detectives live with a sense of the horror a victim lives through in the final moments of his or her life. To be able to stop a rapist, murderer, sex pervert, and animalistic killer is a major contribution to society. To bring them to justice is a service beyond reward. To understand them in order to stop them is a challenge. Unfortunately, the challenge to understand, stop, and apprehend occurs too frequently in our society.

Yes, murder is a grizzly business. As with any disease, it must be studied and understood to make any inroad against its occurrence. We continue to be the most advanced and civilized country in the world and are now regarded as the most powerful nation. Yet we are the most violent. We kill more than any other society. With all of our study and advancement in understanding crime, what we understand the most is how far we have to go to make a difference in our appetite for killing each other.

CHAPTER 4

Susan's Kidnapping

ABOUT THIRTY MILES EAST OF Butte, Montana, is the Missouri Headwaters, next to a small town named Three Forks. Three Forks sits nestled in the Rocky Mountains, not too far from Bozeman, Montana. This is a beautiful, picturesque part of the world famous for fishing, hiking, horseback riding, rafting, backpacking, and hunting. In the wintertime, temperatures can dip down very low, and the region is good for skiing. It is a place far from the hustle and bustle of the big cities, a place where families can enjoy good outdoor fun and relaxation. It is ideal for a vacation.

Bill and Marietta Jaeger left their Detroit suburb town of Farmington, Michigan, after school had ended for the summer in June 1973 for the vacation of a lifetime. With them were their five children, three boys and two girls. The girls' names were Heidi, age thirteen, and the youngest of the children, Suzy, age seven. Behind their trailer, they pulled a camper. Marietta Jaeger remembers the trip as the best time they had as a family, and it was Suzy's first real vacation.

After seeing such places as Mt. Rushmore, they settled into the camp area along the river at Three Forks. The plans were to stay three nights. The Jaeger family had no way of knowing that almost five years earlier, a terrible tragedy happened at the same campsite. A young Boy Scout, Michael Raney, age twelve, was brutally stabbed in the back as he lay sleeping in his tent.

During the day, the sky was a deep blue, and at night it was filled with stars. The tall pine trees and rolling mountains were home to a rustling Missouri River. The peacefulness was disturbed only by the distant sound of a freight train making its way slowly through the countryside. It was truly the place that movies were made about; it was peaceful and in many ways enveloped the visitors with a sense of serenity and trust.

When the Jaegers made camp, the mother and father slept in the trailer, and the five children slept side by side in the tent that was set up for them. Each had his or her own separate sleeping bag because it could get cold at night.

On the third night, after three days of great fun and outdoor play, Marietta and Bill tucked the five children into the sleeping bags and buttoned down the tent for the night. Little Suzy gave her mother the usual big hug before she drifted off to sleep. During the night, Heidi got up and exited the tent to go to the bathroom. She would later confess to having an inner sense of fear that someone was watching her, present in the darkness. Not giving it much thought, she went to the bathroom and made it back into the tent without harm. About two hours later, Heidi woke up again, feeling a draft and chill coming into the tent. It was then that she noticed a large slit was made in the tent where Susan's sleeping bag was. There was no Susan. Left behind were Susan's two stuffed lambs, one resting on the ground just outside the tent.

Heidi immediately knew that tragedy had struck that night in the campsite at the Missouri Headwaters. She immediately woke her parents, and the search that would last a lifetime began. The first deputy to the scene was Deputy Ron Brown of the Three Forks Sheriff's Department. Deputy Brown carried with him to the campsite the vivid memory of the young Boy Scout who had been viciously stabbed in the back, and he wondered if these two crimes could be connected.

Within a matter of hours, Deputy Brown was joined by Pete Dunbar, who was the FBI special agent assigned to the area. With other law enforcement assistance, they spent endless hours searching every piece of terrain they could imagine, including flying low over the river with a helicopter for any possible clues. They even went as far as dragging the river for evidence. Nothing could be found. Susan had disappeared.

The local residents around Three Forks and Bozeman rallied around the Jaeger family. Bill and Marietta had four other children to care for, and the time grew longer and longer without any news. The local papers carried the story daily, and very few promising suspects were turning up. After about five long weeks, the Jaeger family decided to try to put their lives back together with the one major piece, Susan, missing. They made the difficult decision to return to Farmington,

Michigan. It was getting close to that time of year when the four children needed to be back in school, and despite the harsh reality, life had to continue.

Bill Jaeger never was able to find peace with himself over what had happened. Perhaps he blamed himself for failing as a protector. The loss of his baby, Susan, was overwhelming. According to his wife, it was this tragedy that, years later, took a second life—her husband, at fifty-six years of age, died of a massive heart attack. No one will ever know the life that Bill Jaeger lived after his child was senselessly murdered. One can imagine that the void was a chasm never to be filled. He never forgave himself and certainly never forgave Susan's murderer.

Marietta Jaeger chose a very different path. While she was still very much a victim to what had taken place, she refused to allow it to control her. When she was interviewed for an ABC *20/20* special called "Vanished," she shared her feelings. As the investigation dragged on, she felt ravaged with hatred for the person who kidnapped Susan. Marietta initially wanted to seek revenge and was willing to kill the person who committed such a crime. She gradually reasoned that if she continued on this path, the anger built up inside of her would eventually destroy her. She vowed to herself that she would not let that happen.

Looking at her husband and the four remaining children, she realized the importance she was to each of them and that if she remained in anger and kept the strong feeling of revenge, she could not be of help to her family, much less to herself.

Marietta revealed that one week after the kidnapping she had a terrible nightmare. She dreamed that Susan was in an abandoned building, disrobed, and screaming in terror. According to Marietta, there was a chilling aspect of reality to her dream. In her innermost self, Marietta felt that she let go of Susan after that dream, knowing she was no longer alive. There was a powerful sense that God had sent her this dream and that the message He was sending was that Susan was suffering no more because she had entered the peaceful embrace of death.

Weeks and months went by without a clue where Susan was. There was no ransom demand for her return. There was absolutely no word at all. It was not because the case went ignored. The FBI, the Gallatin County Sheriff's Office, and the Three Forks Police Department followed up on many clues and tips, but none led to the proper solution.

In early spring 1974, Pete Dunbar came to the FBI academy in Quantico, Virginia, to take a course on criminal psychology. As Pete sat there listening to the course, his mind could not help but race back to the Susan Jaeger case. Howard and I got very heavily involved in describing the blending of simple schizophrenia and psychopathology. We were discussing the disorder that had all the characteristics of the psychopath, capable of any crime, who was without compassion and ruthless. We noted that in rare instances, these characteristics appeared in the simple schizophrenic and led him to be very aloof and capable of living in a world of his own. We mentioned that it was not unheard of for a person with this disorder to fly through a lie detector test and even perform well with sodium amytol or sodium penethol. We felt that all of these truth tests relied greatly on a person having normal physical reactions to the questions asked. It was our belief that when the disorder traits were combined, the individual often lived self-contained in a world of his own. Knowing this, we believed that these test would be at least inconclusive or could possibly show no involvement to the case in question.

This concept intrigued Pete Dunbar so much that he came to Howard and asked if we could review his entire kidnapping case and see if we had any insight that perhaps he had overlooked. Pete did not have all the information with him, but as soon as he arrived back to Bozeman, he packaged it up and sent it to us in Quantico.

Howard and I gave this case top priority. It was the first active FBI case for which psychological profiling was used. We did not have very much to go on. No autopsy reports, no really good crime scene reports, and—most importantly—no body. We asked Pete if there had been any similar cases in that general area in the recent past. We were looking for the traits of a killer picking on victims of the same age and using the same modus operandi (MO).

No such luck. Pete came back and gave us a menu of crimes that had taken place in the past five years around Bozeman. He included Three Forks, Manhattan, and Bozeman but did not include Butte. The profile of cases was quite odd. Two girls disappeared on bicycles; the bicycles were found abandoned. A young boy was shot while climbing on a nearby bridge. A teenage girl was missing from Manhattan. A Boy Scout was stabbed to death at the same Three Forks campsite. In Missoula, a woman was tied in her home, bound, sexually attacked, and killed. In Billings, a husband and wife were killed in their home. A young lady was killed near Forsyth, Montana. The body of a young lady was left in Idaho Falls after she was killed outside of Bozeman.

We were not shocked that this peaceful area had so many unsolved homicides. We were very curious about the many female victims, but we gave this no special attention. What we did say to ourselves was that this was no typical kidnapping. Whoever took this seven-year-old child took her to keep her for his own sordid purposes. By the time we received the case, it was at least 10 months old, so we were by no means on a hot trail. We had a sense that in many cases, the actual perpetrator is very often contacted and interviewed as a suspect but is let go because of a lack of evidence. We asked Pete for a complete list of his interviews along with his reactions.

Howard and I had in mind a profile before we started the interview review. We felt that the suspect was a white male in his mid to late twenties, was unmarried and a loner, lived in the area, was well known in the area and regarded as odd, had military experience, was a repeat offender, had a dominant mother and no father or an absent father figure, was asocial, and had an impaired history of heterosexual relationships. We also felt that his work history would reflect a solitary position, not requiring interpersonal relationships. Perhaps most shocking to Dunbar was our certainty that if the suspect was apprehended and his house searched, body parts would very likely be found. We felt that the suspect had killed more than once.

We spent hours reviewing the material that Pete Dunbar sent. As usual, we would always independently review and then get back together to share insights. Robert Ressler helped us a great deal on this case, and we had limited input from others as well. The burden of the review was with Teten, Ressler, and me. When the review was over, we unanimously selected a person who was interviewed early in the investigation but was dropped as a possible suspect. His name was David Gail Meirhofer.

When we called Dunbar, he was very skeptical. Dunbar went on to tell us that while Meirhofer was regarded as a possible suspect, he was given sodium amytol and sodium penethol truth serum tests, and he passed both. Dunbar stated that in Manhattan and around Bozeman, Meirhofer had a following of individuals who accused the authorities of picking on him. One such ardent supporter of Meirhofer was the doctor who administered the truth serum tests. Dunbar was uncertain, but he did tell us that David fit most of our profile. He was a white male, twenty-four years of age, single, a loner, a carpenter, raised by his mother, had past difficulty in school when he had tried to stab a boy, intelligent, Vietnam veteran, lived in the area, seldom dated, was asocial, and was regarded as strange.

Meanwhile, back in Quantico, we were not moved by Pete's argument. We recommended that he have David Meirhofer polygraphed by an FBI examiner. What was amazing was that Meirhofer's attorney made him available for all such testing and Meirhofer was willing to submit to it. A polygraph examiner came up from the Denver division and polygraphed Meirhofer. According to the FBI examiner, Meirhofer had no guilty knowledge of the crime. Years later the charts of this polygraph examiner would be disputed regarding the conclusions he reached.

Bearing in mind that the truth serum test did not reveal Meirhofer as guilty, we cautioned Pete Dunbar that the polygraph might be unsuccessful as well. The support for Meirhofer grew in the Bozeman area. All the while, the conviction that we had put our sights on the right man was being reconfirmed in Quantico. We did sense a little uncertainty in Pete Dunbar regarding our findings. It was perfectly logical for him to conclude that we were a bunch of nice guys who didn't know what the hell we were talking about.

We did leave Pete with something he could act on, and his fellow law enforcement colleagues in Bozeman went along with it. We had a strong sense that this was a very emotional crime committed. We felt the subject had a connection to the crime, much like an individual to a wedding anniversary. We felt there was a very high degree of probability that the subject would make an anniversary contact with Susan's parents. We convinced them that we had nothing to lose and everything to gain by having a tape recorder placed on the Jaeger residence phone in Farmington, Michigan. We also recommended that the phone call, if made, be traced. Both suggestions were met with little hostility and were implemented.

In the early morning hours of June 25, 1974, the silence-piercing ring of the telephone disturbed the Jaeger family's sleep. Marietta Jaeger answered the phone.

MJ: Hello.
Caller: Is this Suzy's Mom?
MJ: Yes, it is.
C: Can't hear you.
MJ: Yes, this is. I am Suzy's mother.
C: Well, I'm the guy who took her from you exactly a year ago to the minute today.
MJ: You did?
C: Yeah.
MJ: Where is she now?
C: I can't hardly tell you that.
MJ: Is she alive?

C: Yes, she is, ma'am.
MJ: Can we have her back?
Can we have her back?
C: I can't hear you.
MJ: Can we have her back?
C: Well, I am in a kinda awkward position to do that. Actually I have gotten kinda used to her.
MJ: I can't believe you that she is still alive. How can you take care of a little girl?
C: Well, how would you take care of a little girl?
MJ: I have a home, and I am here all day long.
C: I do also, and I probably have more money than you have.
MJ: How can you support her, and how can you take care of her and go to work?
C: I don't have to work, ma'am. We have been awkward; well, we covered the West pretty well, just sightseeing. Me, I've gotten used to her.
MJ: Ahh [crying in low voice].
Click: phone disconnected.
MJ: Hello.
C: Hello, ma'am, we musta got cuten off.
MJ: Oh, I thought you hung up on us.
C: No.
MJ: Ah. Why can't we have Suzy back? She is our child, she belongs to us, and we will pay any amount of money. Ugh, you know.
C: I realize that, ma'am, but I am in kinda an awkward position.
MJ: Why is that?
C: Well, once I have turned her over to you, she can identify me.
MJ: Not in a court; she is too young. They won't put a child in a court to identify someone.
C: I know better than that; it don't need to be in a court anyway. Right now, as it is, I am pretty safe because they have no suspicion of me at all; haven't even been contacted. 'Cause I am pretty smart for them.
MJ: I don't believe that you really still have her. You are trying to play games with us, like so many other people.

C: No, I am not playing games.
MJ: Can you tell me a particular piece of identification about Suzy?
C: I can tell you lots of things.
MJ: All right, tell me.
C: Well...
MJ: Prove to me that you do have her.
C: All right, first of all, it was I who called the Denver FBI on Saturday, June 30, late in the afternoon. It is also I who called you, who called Mrs. Brown on July 2, sometime after 10:30 at night. It is also I who called you on September 24, early in the afternoon and you weren't home; later on a relative of yours who spoke with me, and finally I talked to your oldest son, and if that is not enough—you are waiting, aren't you?
MJ: Yes.
C: The nails of her first fingers are hooked.
MJ: All right, what else can you tell me? Now, with that piece of information, you are a little late with your call because it has been leaked; there are some people who know about that and who are able to tell us about that. But you are trying to play games with us.
C: As far as I know, it has not been leaked.
MJ: What, ah, tell me something else about her. If you have been with her and traveling around with her, if she is still really alive and with you, then you must know a lot of things about her. Has she talked to you about us? What has she told you about us? Surely you must talk?
C: Well, the thing is, I have been kinda working on her mind. Almost got most of the memory of you, your home, and your other children wiped out of her mind through psychotherapy.
MJ: How are you qualified to do something like that? I don't believe that is possible. She had a good home here, she was loved very much, and she was treated well. I can't believe that you can erase those kinda memories.
C: (long pause) You better believe it.
MJ: Did she mention what pets we have? Did she say the things we used to do?

C: [pause] Look, if you don't believe me, you just as well hang up, and you will never hear from me again.

MJ: Well, I want to believe that she is alive. I have gone the whole year hoping that she was still alive, just to know positively that she still is, but all you can tell me—

C: That is precisely why I called you. To tell you that she is.

MJ: But, you can't prove it to me; all you can tell me are the things you have done. Is that all—you called just to tell us she is alive?

C: I expect to get her back to you one of these days; like I said, I have been working on her mind, and I want to get her to wipe me out of her mind, just like she has wiped you out of her mind.

MJ: What's the point?

C: Just takes time.

MJ: What is the point of doing all of this?

C: She can't come back to you knowing who I am.

MJ: Have you been good to her?

C: Yes I have.

MJ: Why did you take her?

C: Well, it is kinda a long story. I always wanted a little girl myself [crying]…always wanted a little girl of my own.

MJ: Did you ever have a little girl of your own, your very own?

C: No.

MJ: Are you married?

C: Not now.

MJ: Has she been abused; have you hurt her?

C: No, just that first night—I had to choke her some.

MJ: When you took her out of the tent?

C: Yeah.

MJ: Did she wake up?

C: Not right away. I grabbed her around the throat.

MJ: How did you get away? No one could figure out how you possibly got away.

C: Are you recording this?

MJ: No.
C: Are you sure?
MJ: How could I record it?
C: With a microphone on the phone.
MJ: No.
C: You're lying to me.
MJ: In the middle of the night, I should put a recorder on the telephone? No, I am not, but I am concerned about Suzy. If you could tell me something to prove that she still really is alive and what you want us to do...because we will do anything you want us to do on our own without notifying the FBI, the sheriff, or anybody.
C: I realize that, but what comes after that is bothering me.

The phone call went on in a rambling manner for over an hour. Marietta Jaeger asked penetrating questions in an effort to get some signs that Susan was still alive. The caller became more depressed the longer the phone call went on. At the end of the phone call, the caller was unable to hang up and pled with Marietta Jaeger to hang up the phone. Marietta even confronted the caller with the fact that he did not have the courage to tell them that Susan was no longer alive.

The strength and courage that Marietta displayed in her telephone conversation was incredible. A mother of five children, never trained in law enforcement or in interrogating individuals, she was keen with her insightful questions. The major theme that she tried to get out of the caller was whether her daughter was still alive. Her ability to keep the caller on the line was magnificent. Toward the end of the phone call, the caller heard tapping sounds that upset him, but Marietta was able to convince him that she was not recording the conversation. Years later, she expressed concern that she had lied to the caller.

Marietta ended the phone conversation by telling the caller that she felt sorry for him and would pray for him. The caller was speechless and sobbing, pleading with Marietta to hang up.

Whatever hope Marietta had that Susan was still alive was extinguished by the phone call. The FBI had never given up hope that Susan might possibly be alive, but from the beginning we knew that, statistically, it was very unlikely. The phone call convinced us that she had been killed because there was no evidence in the long call that she had lived for any great length of time after the kidnapping.

The investigation that languished for so long now had the hopes of a fresh start. The caller had no way of knowing that, because of this call, he would be eventually caught. It was not so easy to actually catch him, however. The FBI had set up a trace on this long, extended phone conversation. The length of the call might indicate a very good probability for a successful trace, but phone companies' technology in the mid-1970s was not what it is today. Many long distance calls would pass through two or three relay stations. For every pass through, the risk of the trace being redirected was increased. Unfortunately, this trace was redirected, and it went southeast into the state of Florida. Several weeks went by with intense investigation in Florida, all to no avail. Such a long phone call and a bad trace left Pete Dunbar and the authorities in Bozeman at a loss to explain their bad fortune.

Fortune was about to change and in a big way. What was most interesting to the profilers was that no one in the Bozeman area was able to identify the voice on the recorded phone conversation. Even the direct request to match it to the selected suspect, David Meirhofer, brought indecision and uncertainty about the caller's identity.

A few years earlier, David Meirhofer had worked on a large ranch just outside of Manhattan, Montana. The owner of the ranch was paying his telephone bill when he noticed a call on the bill that he did not recall making. He asked the phone company to assist him in identifying to whom this call was made. The phone company came back in a very short time with the identity of the party called: Mr.and Mrs. William Jaeger, Farmington, Michigan. It was a name well known to the ranch owner. He immediately contacted the sheriff's office and the FBI.

The authorities were all over the ranch looking for clues as to how the phone call originated from the ranch. The phone line came into the ranch through a series of phone poles along the property. They came upon one phone pole with what appeared to be the tire tracks of a pickup truck beside it. A careful examination revealed that the phone line had been tapped into. There was little doubt that the hour-plus phone call was made from this location. Deputy Sheriff Ron Brown and FBI Agent Pete Dunbar looked at each other and remembered David Meirhofer was trained in the military as a phone technician. Without a doubt, he was capable of doing this. Still no one was certain that the voice from the recording was that of David Meirhofer.

The days did not get easier for Brown and Dunbar. Eight months after the kidnapping of Susan, a nineteen-year-old girl by the name of Sandra Marie Dyckman Smallegan disappeared from her apartment in Manhattan. There was no trace of her whereabouts and no reason she would mysteriously disappear. David Meirhofer once again reappeared as a suspect. David had once tried to date Sandra, but Sandra showed no interest in having any relationship with Meirhofer.

Looking for logical places where a body could be stored, the sheriff's department went out to an abandoned ranch known as the Lockhart ranch. At the Lockhart ranch, they noticed a number of strange things. Inside the ranch, they found a closet that had been nailed shut recently. Although it was now open, it appeared that it had been nailed shut on numerous occasions and renailed. There were blood tracings inside the closet. They also noticed a large oil drum on the side of the house that had charred bone remains. Immediately, they isolated the area. In the early days, when the police were investigating the Lockhart ranch, a male in his early twenties showed up at the fence line and inquired of one of the deputies if they found anything. After he left, the deputy asked who he was. It turned out that it was David Meirhofer.

An intense search of the Lockhart ranch turned up human bone fragments scattered around the property. The Smithsonian Institute was called to analyze the bone fragments in the oil drum. The institute came back with a report that there were both human bone fragments and bones of animal, most probably chicken bones. This ranch was yet to reveal its innermost secrets.

There was a general consensus that David Meirhofer was the most likely suspect in both of these crimes. Most of the information surrounding Meirhofer was strictly circumstantial, however. There was no physical evidence linking him to either crime or to any crime for that matter. Meirhofer was in total denial and came across as believable. It was very difficult to get him crossed in a story or alibi.

Howard Teten, Bob Ressler, and I were back in Quantico tasked with coming up with a suggestion that could crack Meirhofer. We knew the mentality we were dealing with and the difficulty we would have penetrating such a personality. So far, our profile was working, but it too, had reached a standstill. Based on his profile, I recommended something that I knew would never fly with approval from on high in the FBI. I felt that if Meirhofer were confronted with a strong female personality about the crime, it would get him off-center and he could make a mistake. Aware that he followed the Susan kidnapping very closely, the idea of having a female FBI agent pose as Marietta Jaeger to confront him seemed to have little merit. What did have merit was to have Marietta Jaeger herself confront David. If this were placed in the form of a memo to an assistant director in the FBI, it would have been immediately turned down for fear of what could happen to Marietta. I told Pete Dunbar to have the sheriff's office make the request. Marietta Jaeger knew the request came from the FBI, and she did not hesitate to go along with the plan.

Marietta traveled west one more time, and the confrontation was put in motion. When she met Meirhofer on the street, he was polite but vehemently denied any knowledge of the missing child, Susan. After the confrontation, Marietta was convinced that David had kidnapped her Susan.

Marietta, disappointed and saddened, returned to Michigan, wondering if the kidnapping would ever be solved. The confrontation was to pay off. Once back in Michigan, the phone rang again in the Jaeger residence. Marietta answered. The voice was the same, but this time he had a name: Mr. Travis. He accused Marietta of telling the police and FBI and said that because she had done that, she would never see her daughter again. Marietta called the caller David, and this sent him into a rage. This time the phone trace worked, and it went to a hotel in Salt Lake City.

The FBI and sheriff's office had what they needed. They waited for David Meirhofer to drive back into Manhattan. When he arrived, he was arrested for the kidnapping of Susan Jaeger. In Meirhofer's pocket was the hotel receipt, and written on it was the Jaeger phone number in Michigan. Now there was no doubt in anyone's mind.

In the original profile, we cautioned against two things. First was that they were likely to find body parts when they searched his home. Second was that he had to be watched very closely once apprehended, because he was an extremely high suicide risk.

The Gallatin County Sheriff's Department and FBI had a search warrant issued to search David's home. What they were to find would make anyone question whether there were any limits humanity could stoop to in violent behavior. Meirhofer's attorney, Douglas Dasinger, was advised, and he rushed to the house to witness the search. In opening the top freezer portion to the refrigerator, the Police encountered numerous packages of wrapped meat. One such wrapping was marked "Deerburger." On the wrapping were printed the initials "SMDS" (Sandra Marie Dyckman Smallegan). The lab would determine the packages contained human body parts.

Two weeks before David Meirhofer's arrest, he attended a church picnic. He brought a meat casserole to that picnic.

Douglas Dasinger defended David Meirhofer to the very end, believing that law enforcement was selectively targeting David for everything that happened in the greater Bozeman area. When he walked into David's home, one of the deputies handed him a wrapped package from the freezer. It contained one of Sandra Smallegan's fingernail-polished hands. Dasinger went outside and regurgitated in the dark.

Dasinger was angered that David had never been truthful with him. He insisted that they go immediately to the sheriff's lockup and interview Meirhofer. Shortly after he came out of David's cell, Dasinger asked Ron Brown if they could make a deal. Brown asked what he could offer, and Dasinger said, "Four homicides."

On September 29, 1974, David Meirhofer took off his mask of sanity and gave the following confession:

CONFESSION OF DAVID GAIL MEIRHOFER, GIVEN SEPTEMBER 29, 1974

    PD: I am with the FBI. You know Mr. Olson?
    DM: Yes.
    PD: County Attorney of Gallatin County. Your defense attorney,
          Douglas Dasinger is here, right?

DM: Yes.

PD: It's now 3:20 a.m., OK? Now, David I have told you this before, right? And I'm going to repeat it just so that there's no doubt. Before we ask you any questions, you do know you have the right to remain silent, that anything you say can be used against you in court. You have the right to talk to a lawyer who is here now for advice and to have him present, which he is during this questioning. If you decide to answer our questions now with your lawyer present, you will and can do so, but you also will have the right to stop and not answer any questions. You also have the right to not answer questions until you do confer with your attorney, Mr. Dasinger. Now, do you understand this?

DM: Yes.

PD: The next thing, David, I am going to ask is if you know that this is in accordance with the Fifth Amendment, and if you do answer questions, you are waiving a right, so I would like you to consult with your attorney and know that you understand this and knowingly waive this right and go ahead and we can talk about things. Ok?

DM: Yes.

PD: And if Mr. Dasinger will read this, explain it to you, and I would like him to have you sign it, with his, with his having read it.

DD: Pete, Mr. Dunbar, has handed me what is called a waiver of rights. You and I have discussed this matter, and under my advice, I have advised you that I feel it is in your best interests, under all the circumstances, to waive your rights under the Fifth Amendment and to make the statements and answer questions that are about to be asked, and I am advising you at this time to sign the waiver of rights, which means that you are in effect, you are waiving your right to refuse to testify against yourself, and that's what I'm handing you now.

DM: Do you have to have a written guarantee?

DD: It will be on a tape recorder.

PD: Yeah. Everything, David that we are talking about is being recorded, OK?

DM: I mean guarantee for what…

DD: For what we talked about?

DM: Yeah.

DD: That will be there, and this will be transcribed if necessary.

PD: Would you put the time in too, David? It's 3:23.

DM: Bozeman?

DD and PD: Yes

PD: Now, I'll ask, can I go ahead, Mr. Olson and Mr. Dasinger, and state all the things we've talked about, or do you want to do this?

DD: Let me make a brief statement…

PD: Please do, yes.

DD: As to my understanding as to this, and then I'd like to have Mr. Olson, unless you'd rather state first.

DD: I have conferred with David. We've discussed some matters. We have also discussed, I have also discussed with the county attorney, Mr. Olson, and with you, Mr. Dunbar…

PD: Yes.

DD: The fact that in return for a guarantee from the county attorney that he will strongly recommend against the death penalty in any of the charges, that David would be—I would advise David and he would be—willing to make a statement, uh, regarding the two crimes of which he is charged and other events. Uh, that he would be willing to answer questions—and again, this would be based on the guarantee of the county attorney that he would recommend against any death penalty and that, uh, I have also advised David that in my opinion, the death penalty is applicable only in the case of State of Montana v. David Meirhofer, re: Sandra Smallegan, that in any other instance we are discussing, it is my opinion that the death penalty is unconstitutional and could not be applied to him. I have further advised him that I feel that under the circumstances of the case of the evidence of which I am aware and all of the factors, that he, uh, is in grave danger of being, uh, convicted, and in my opinion it is almost a certainty that he would be convicted and that under our law, the death penalty is mandatory unless there are mitigating circumstances. That is my understanding.

TO: This is Tom Olson, the Gallatin County Attorney, speaking. I concur with Mr. Dasinger and Mr. Meirhofer's understanding. I will strongly recommend to the district judge that the death penalty not be imposed on the condition that the defendant, David Meirhofer, make a full and complete statement concerning the Sandra Smallegan case, concerning the Susan Jaeger case, and concerning any other case that will be brought up at this proceeding. In addition, the defendant will waive any plea of not guilty by reason of insanity and would enter a plea of guilty to the two cases I have mentioned that have been filed in court and any other cases that would be filed as a result of this conference.

DD: Turn off the tape.

TO: Uh, the tape will now be shut off at the request of the defendant's counsel.

PD: OK, now both the county attorney and the defense attorney have made their statements. Now I am talking to you, David, as the investigating agent, Pete Dunbar, with the FBI. You know me as such, right?

DM: Yes.

PD: Are you now willing, David, and will you answer questions that I pose to you?

DM: Yes.

PD: OK, do you realize, David that this is on record?

DM: Yes.

PD: Being very blunt, very truthful, cutting this to the bare essentials, did you on June 25 take Susie from a tent? Susie Jaeger, in the Headwaters State Park at Three Forks.

DM: Yes.

PD: Did you cause Susan to be hurt, and if so, how?

DM: Yes, I had to choke her.

PD: Was she killed when you choked her?

DM: No.

PD: When was she killed?

DM: Uh, a little later.

PD: All right, let's start, David. I know this is difficult, but it's the only way I know to do it. When you took her from the tent and choked her, where did you take her?

DM: Uh, it was about one hundred yards north and then over to the highway and back down the highway fifty yards back across the highway up on top of the hill where the monument is, down the road on top of this hill about half a mile to my pickup, which was waiting alongside the river.

PD: Did you put her in the pickup?

DM: Yes.

PD: And then where did you take her?

DM: Went out to the ranch owned by Bill Bryant.

PD: The Lockhart ranch, right? Did you then nail her in the closet—I mean put her in the closet and nail the door shut?

DM: No.

PD: Well, what happened then?

DM: Well, I undressed her, and then, uh, well, uh, I proceeded to feel her body, and she got pretty wild, I guess, and I choked her. She died.

PD: She what?

DM: She died.

PD: OK, and then did you conceal her body?

DM: Yes.

PD: Where?

DM: Uh, I cut her up.

PD: And where is the body located?

DM: Well, not much left of it.

PD: What's left? Where, where did you put the pieces?

DM: I put her head in that outhouse behind the ranch, and all the rest of it was burned.

PD: And what did you burn it with, David?

DM: Just wood.

PD: Pardon?

DM: Just wood.
PD: With wood, and...
DM: It was done in different places on the ranch.
PD: And where did you spread these pieces?
DM: Well, the, uh, the main part of the torso, upper torso, was burned alongside a culvert on the road between the Lockhart ranch and Menard.
PD: And Menard.
DM: Uh, huh.
PD: And was it spread along, or was it in one area?
DM: No. It was all, it was right there; it—I had wrapped it in a bunch of blankets and stuff and then.
PD: Where, where could it be found, for, for, burial purposes?
DM: Well, it was burned completely.
PD: Just with wood. Is that correct, just with wood?
DM: Yeah.
PD: OK, uh, what did you use, David, as an instrument to cut the body up?
DM: My hunting knife.
PD: Just the knife?
DM: Yes.
PD: No saw or anything else?
DM: Yes.
PD: OK, now, David, did uh, did you or will you tell us what happened to Sandra Smallegan?
DM: Yes.
PO: And in your own words, just the same way you did with Susie, go ahead.
DM: Well, I went up to her apartment about two o'clock in the morning of the tenth.
PD: Of February; is this correct?
DM: Yes.
PD: OK, pardon.
OO: Year.

PD: 1974, OK?

DM: And, uh, I, she was sleeping, and I jumped on her and choked her and then tied her up and put a piece of tape around her mouth, and then I was gonna, while I was putting some of her clothes and stuff in the car, she evidently died. She couldn't get any air through the tape.

PD: She was dead, then, before you left Manhattan.

DM: Yes.

PD: OK. And then what happened?

DM: Then I put her in the car, too, and went out to the Lockhart ranch.

PD: OK, and then what?

DM: And I proceeded to cut her up, too.

PD: With what?

DM: My hunting knife.

PD: Nothing else?

DM: I think I did use a saw.

PD: What kind of a saw, David?

DM: A handsaw.

PD: OK, and uh, what did you do with her pieces?

DM: Well, I burned them right there at the ranch.

PD: With what?

DM: With wood shingles and stuff that was piled alongside the buildings.

PD: Nothing else?

DM: No.

PD: Where, where would Sandra's remains be?

DM: Right in that campfire, in that fire beside the house.

PD: Nowhere else? OK. Did you, David, have occasion to hurt in any way a Boy Scout at the camp in Three Forks where Susie was?

DM: Yes.

PD: And do you know his name?

DM: Michael Raney.

PD: Did you know him before this happened?

DM: No.

PD: OK, then what happened with Michael Raney?

DM: Well, I went to the park where the Boy Scouts were camped, and I was going to get somebody, and I opened this tent and saw this little boy, and I couldn't force myself to take him, so I stabbed him in the back.

PD: And then did you hit him with anything on the head or anything?

DM: No, I did not.

PD: This was just a stabbing; is that correct?

DM: Yes.

PD: You did not hit him with a club or your fist or anything?

DM: I did not.

PD: Just stabbed him? And what happened then?

DM: Well, I ran back to my truck.

PD: Did you know whether Michael Raney died or not until you read it in the paper?

DM: I did not until I read it.

PD: David, do you know or do you recall having caused injury to a boy on the bridge directly behind Manhattan, or north of Manhattan across the Gallatin River—the Nixon, is it the Noxon or Nixon Bridge?

DM: Nixon Bridge.

PD: Nixon Bridge.

DM: Yes.

PD: And did you know this boy by name?

DM: Yes.

PD: Before, what happened then? Just in your own words.

DM: Well, I had been up in the hills and came down past the bridge and two boys were, I seen them playing there, and I went down the road and parked about 100 yards, 150 yards, and walked out around with my rifle, .22 caliber, into the bushes on the other side of the river, I guess on the south side of the river. And then I saw Bernie Poelman playing on the, climbing up on the pillar of the bridge, and then I shot him.

PD: Did you see him fall into the river?

DM: Yes.

PD: Did you know he was dead?

DM: I didn't know for sure.

PD: In other words, you shot him and saw him fall into the river, and what happened then? Did you leave the area?

DM: Yes, the other kid took off running, and I went back to my truck and went back up through the hills and come out at Logan.

PD: But you did know this boy by name before you shot him? Is that correct? In other words, you knew who you shot, then; is that correct?

DM: Yes.

PD: All right, now I am going to ask you a couple of other questions, David, that your attorney perhaps does not know, and I think it will resolve something, just, uh, which you, too, would want to resolve. Did you go over to Silver Cloud Camp and attack a young girl and be startled during the attack and leave, recently in August?

DM: Silver Cloud Camp?

PD: Yeah, over by Anaconda.

DM: No.

PD: Now, if you did this, David, it would, you have admitted many things, and everything would indicate that you probably were the person who went into the Girl Scout camp and were in the process of bending over a girl and tying a rope around her neck and choking her when the light came on and then you left. With what we have said, there would be no reason that I can see, and I hope your attorney would agree, if you did do it, uh we should know it. It's the same camp that you had the map drawn of, in the same area, in August of this year.

DD: This would be the same day that we went over to Warm Springs to take the sodium amytol test.

PD: The same day that you took the sodium amytol test.

DM: No, I wasn't over there.

PD: You were not? OK, we, we, we'll drop it. I just felt if you did, this would be the time to say so. OK?

DM: Yeah.

PD: If, David, you are responsible for any of the other persons who have been attacked around Montana, we should know about it now. Do you agree?

DM: Yes.

PD: Are you responsible?

DM: No, I am not.

PD: And I am specifically asking now, and I will go point by point, OK? Two girls missing in Marion, Montana, on July 31, three days after you delivered your combine to Kalispell.

DM: No.

PD: OK, Sharon McGinnes, a little girl who was attacked in Missoula, taken from Missoula to a culvert west of town and put in the culvert.

DM: No.

PD: OK, Dawn Collins, a woman who was tied in her home at Missoula, bound, sexually attacked, and killed.

DM: No.

PD: Mr. and Mrs. Barnhart, killed in their home in Missoula, Montana—or, I'm sorry, David, Billings, Montana.

DM: No.

PD: Donna Harding, killed July 4, 1974, uh, near Forsyth, Montana.

DM: No.

PD: OK, Donna Lemon, killed somewhere between July 4 and July 8, between Bozeman and Idaho Falls, Montana, or her body was left in Idaho Falls.

DM: No.

PD: Do you know her?

DM: No.

PD: OK. Now, if we can go back—again, this is not for publication; this is for our own purposes—just to fill in details. We'll go back to Susie, OK? When you took Susie from her tent, uh, if I am correct, death occurred actually at the time when you were, uh, you took her from the tent, choked her a little, and then when you were starting, as you said, to feel her, this is when she became wild, and you killed her. Is this correct?

DM: Yes.

PD: What caused death?

DM: Strangulation.
PD: OK, was she sexually attacked?
DM: No.
PD: There was no sexual intercourse?
DM: No.
PD: Was this at the Lockhart ranch?
DM: Yes.
PD: OK, was it in the house at the Lockhart ranch?
DM: Yes.
PD: When you strangled her and she died, she had not yet been cut up; is this correct?
DM: Yes.
PD: And, in other words, after death you cut her; is this correct?
DM: Yes.
PD: Am I correct, David, that you spread her legs apart and cut from the top side down, or in other words, the front rather than the back?
DM: Yes.
PD: How many cuts did you make?
DM: Well, I cut her legs off and arms off and her head.
PD: The head is in the outhouse now; is this correct?
DM: Yes.
PD: Is it in one piece?
DM: As far as I know.
PD: Her legs, where are they?
DM: They were burned.
PD: Did they completely dissolve with burning?
DM: Yes.
PD: Were there any bones left?
DM: No.
PD: Uh, you did know that Susie had a unique fingernail. Is this correct, on the index fingers?
DM: Yes.
PD: Where are those fingernails?

DM: They were on her hands.
PD: Where are the hands now?
DM: They were burned too.
PD: In the same place that the legs were burned?
DM: Yes.
PD: Did they dissolve completely?
DM: Yes.
PD: The torso, now, if I am correct, is between the Lockhart ranch and Menard. Is this correct? On the regular road?
DM: Yes.
PD: Could you take us to where the torso is?
DM: Yes.
DM: This is just the upper?
PD: Yeah.
PD: And it is burned too?
DM: Yes.
PD: Is there anything left of it?
DM: No.
PD: Completely dissolved?
DM: Yes.
PD: Only the head exists. Is this correct?
DM: Yes.
PD: Then, now, we know and you know that the lower tailbone, in other words, the sacrum—or, I may not be pronouncing it right—exists. How does that exist? It was in the outhouse too.
DM: I don't remember, quite; when I cut the legs off, it was hanging down there.
PD: Did you put it in with the head?
DM: Yes.
PD: Nothing but the head and that bone?
DM: Right.
PD: You're sure?
DM: Yes.

PD: Is there anything we can find other than the head?
DM: No.
PD: And the head is not in the outhouse that's in the house. It's in the outhouse separate from the house. Is that correct?
DM: It was in the outhouse outside.
PD: OK, how deep?
DM: It should be in the same place as the other bone.
PD: No lime, no burning, no nothing.
DM: No.
PD: OK. In the case of Sandra Smallegan, you went to her house at 2:00 a.m. Did she see you?
DM: No.
PD: You, you choked her and covered her mouth without her knowing it?
DM: Well, yes.
PD: How did you get her into the car?
DM: I had her tied up.
PD: And carried her?
DM: I carried her, yes.
PD: To her car? Did you drive her car?
DM: Yes.
PD: To the Lockhart ranch?
DM: Yes.
PD: Did you take the route from Manhattan to the Lockhart ranch, or did you go by the way of Logan?
DM: I went through Logan.
PD: To the ranch?
DM: On the interstate. Not through Logan but on the other side of Logan.
PD: In other words, you didn't go straight north of Manhattan on that road.
DM: No.
PD: But you do know that road.
DM: Yes.

PD: OK, you took her directly to the Lockhart ranch. Is that correct?
DM: Yes.
PD: She was dead?
DM: Yes.
PD: Where did you actually cut her up?
DM: On the floor of the house.
PD: In the Lockhart ranch?
DM: Yes.
PD: How did you cut her—by this, was she lying on her back?
DM: No.
PD: On her stomach.
DM: Yeah—on her back, excuse me.
PD: OK, how many cuts were made there?
DM: The same. I cut off the arms, the legs.
PD: Head?
DM: And the head.
PD: Where is the head?
DM: It was burned.
PD: Did it dissolve?
DM: Yes.
PD: Where was the burning?
DM: Right alongside the house.
PD: Of everything?
DM: Yes.
PD: You only burned in the one spot. Is that correct?
DM: Well, it wasn't all put on at once.
PD: How, how long did this take?
DM: Well, I had to go back there the next night and burn the rest.
PD: OK, now, you took her on Saturday night or early Sunday morning, really. You came back and changed oil for your neighbor in his car.
DM: Yes, I was back in town by eight o'clock.
PD: Uh, had any of the burning taken place then?
DM: Yes.

PD: How much?
DM: The head and upper torso.
PD: And then you went back to finish.
DM: Yes.
PD: Is there any of Sandra located anywhere except on the Lockhart ranch?
DM: Yes.
PD: Where?
DM: I don't know where they're at now.
DD: Tell him what he's indirectly talking about.
PD: Pardon?
DM: I had one of her hands and a couple fingers in my freezer.
PD: This, this is correct. Is there anything of Susie located anywhere that we could locate and identify for the family other than the head and that bone?
DM: No.
PD: In other words, you have nothing of her in your home, right?
DM: No.
PD: What I am getting at, David—and I am sure you know this—when we searched your house, remember, and your warehouse, the sheets, remember, that we picked up and the bedspread all have human blood on them in great quantity. What were they used for? Sandra or Susie?
DM: I don't know. I didn't use them.
PD: There is a great deal of human blood on them.
DM: I did not use them. They were in that building when I bought it, and they had been...
PD: In other words, what you told me before was completely correct. Is this right?
DM: Yes. They was in that cooler in there when I got it. I did not use them.
PD: There is nothing that we can find of Sandra, then, except what we have already found. Is that correct?
DM: That's right.
PD: You probably know about as well as we do what has been found. There is nothing else; is that right?

DM: Right.
PD: Except the hand that was located today.
DM: Right.
PD: OK, now is there anything of Susie that we can find?
DM: No.
PD: Other than what you have told us. We can find the head, right?
DM: Yeah.
PD: You can take us to the head and show us where it was.
DM: Yes.
PD: It isn't put in lime and isn't burned or anything?
DM: No.
PD: OK, now, going to the boy, Poelin, is that his name?
DM: Poelman.
PD: Poelman. Where is the gun that was used to shoot him?
DM: I have no idea.
PD: It's your gun, right?
DM: No.
PD: Whose gun was it?
DM: It was my gun at the time.
PD: What did you do with the gun?
DM: It was, I, I, purchased another one about a year later.
PD: What did you do with that gun?
DM: Well, I traded it in.
PD: To who?
DM: Uh, Beaver Pond. That one out here.
PD: Here in Bozeman. OK, uh, you did see the boy fall and go into the river; is this right?
DM: Yes.
PD: You assumed he was dead; is this correct?
DM: Yes.
PD: I mean in the absence of newspaper stories or anything, you assumed that you had shot him and killed him. Is that correct?
DM: Yes.

PD: Did you stay to see what happened?
DM: No.
PD: How did you leave?
DM: In my truck.
PD: A jeep, right?
DM: Uh, yes, but…
PD: Your older jeep.
DM: Yes.
PD: What year?
DM: '64.
PD: And you returned to your home.
DM: I, uh, no, I went back up through the hills, come out at Logan, and went and talked to a friend of mine. Jim, ah, Jim Gregor.
PD: When you say up into the hills, you went north into the Horse Shoe Hills?
DM: I went Manhattan to, drove to the Lockhart ranch.
PD: By the Lockhart ranch and out of Logan; is that correct?
DM: Yes.
PD: The normal back road through Horse Shoe Hills?
DM: Yes.
PD: OK, going to the Raney boy, was there anyone else with you?
DM: No.
PD: And this is real important. There is another boy very suspect. Was there anyone with you who stabbed the Raney boy?
DM: No.
PD: Was this caused because of problems that happened a day or two before?
DM: No.
PD: What caused you to go to the camp?
DM: Well, uh, I wanted, I wanted to get that little—to get a little kid.
PD: A kid. Did you—you were not looking for the Raney boy. Is this correct? A boy or any child.
DM: Anyone.

PD: [...] Err, I should say, what caused you to stab him, rather than take him out of the tent?

DM: I wanted to, I was going to choke him like I'd done to, like what happened to Susie, but I could [...] around him; I couldn't get in just right to do it, and I was scared.

PD: But you did not hit him.

DM: I did not.

PD: Did you know he was dead until you read it in the paper?

DM: No I didn't; it was three, four days later.

PD: Right. Did you, uh, then leave the area after you, after he was stabbed?

DM: Yes.

PD: Where is the knife?

DM: It's, uh, it should be in my jeep.

PD: Your present jeep?

DM: Yes.

PD: Is this the same hunting knife that you used for Susie and Sandra?

DM: Well, uh, same one for Susie, I think. I used another one, a different one for Sandra.

PD: Where is the knife you used on Sandy?

DM: It should be in the jeep too.

PD: In other words, there should be two hunting knives in the jeep that were used to cut these people up; is that correct? Where is the saw that was used?

DM: Uh, I'm not sure which one it was. There's two in the back of the jeep, in the camper.

PD: What kind of saw?

DM: What kind of saw? A wood saw.

PD: I mean a backsaw or a regular crosscut saw.

DM: It's a crosscut type.

PD: Not, not, uh, anything special.

DM: No.

PD: Just a crosscut saw.

DM: Yes.

PD: Now, David, we have, as you know, come a long way. Is there anything else that we should know now? We have made certain assurances to you. In return, I feel that if there is anything else that you should tell us about, then, because there is nothing to gain by not telling us, are there any other events that have happened that you were involved in that are of concern to families or people?

DM: No.

PD: In other words you definitely, absolutely, without reservation state the only things you were involved in were the stabbing of Michael Raney, the shooting of the Poelman boy on the Nixon Bridge near Manhattan, the kidnapping and killing and cutting up of Susie Jaeger, the kidnapping, killing, and cutting up of Sandy Smallegan. Is this correct?

DM: Yes.

PD: There is absolutely nothing else?

DM: Yes.

PD: Nothing else.

DM: There's nothing else.

PD: Uh, when you talked to Mrs. Jaeger; do you remember this?

DM: Yes.

PD: She felt that when she asked you about a little girl that you had taken to the Disneyland amusement area, that this caused a reaction. Is there any girl in San Diego or Los Angeles that you were involved with?

DM: No.

PD: Who was the child you took to this park?

DM: I never took, I haven't taken any child.

PD: Now, you recall the tickets that I got from you.

DM: Yes.

PD: One of them was a child's ticket—

DM: Tickets to Disneyland are sold regardless of age.

PD: There is nothing else, then. In other words, we have mentioned four very important things. There is absolutely nothing else that, in, in our opinion would be a crime or, or an act that we should know that you have been involved in.

Is that correct?

DM: That's correct.

PD: This is a complete, absolute story?

DM: Yes.

PD: Mr. Olson has made you certain statements in the presence of your attorney, statements that I intend to see are complied with, but if there is anything else, now do you realize, David, there is these promises, these, this assistance, this help that we want to give you. Unless you tell us, we will not be bound by what we have told you. We intend to keep our promise completely, but in turn we expect you to tell us everything that we should know. Is this a complete, accurate story? DM: As far as I know.

PD: Is there anything else?

DM: No.

PD: Nothing else. OK, uh, my questioning is completed. Uh, Mr. Olson, do you have any questions for David?

TO: No questions.

PD: Mr. Dasinger, do you have any comments to add?

DD: None.

PD: This is Pete Dunbar; I am the investigating officer.
The time is 4:00 a.m.—September 29? I need glasses to read this.

TO: It's the twenty-ninth now.

PD: OK, September 29, 1974. We have completed a formal interview with David Meirhofer in the presence of David Meirhofer, present Mr. Meirhofer's attorney, Douglas Dasinger; the County Attorney of Gallatin County, Tom Olson; investigating officer, Pete Dunbar, FBI. All right?

DM: Yeah.

(Tape shut off.)

PD: David, we have discussed these cases. Are you well aware that these cases were worked by the local law enforcement officers in Gallatin County, long and hard, the city-county investigative team?

DM: Yes.

PD: And will you make a formal statement to the city-county investigative team that they can witness? None of them are present here, but would you let one member of that team witness your formal statement, which you are going to execute tomorrow, or today if there is a secretary available?

DD: If he—is sworn to secrecy.

PD: Sworn to secrecy. Uh, you can select the member. I'll, I'll give you the names.

DM: What would be the reason for this thing?

PD: The reason for this, David, is that the people of Gallatin County, I think, have somewhat a feeling that our law enforcement has not done their job, and I believe they have done their job, and I would like their efforts in this case to be known. They will be sworn to secrecy, but when you plead guilty, it will be an acknowledgment that this is the agency responsible. (At this point the tape was turned off with the consent of the defendant.)

PD: Uh, Mr. Meirhofer, we have discussed many things, and you have told me that you do intend to give a signed statement of them.

DM: Yes.

PD: OK, thank you very much. The time is now 4:11 a.m.

David Meirhofer allowed his mask of sanity to be slightly removed in sharing the insanity he confessed to committing. There is little doubt that this was only one incomplete chapter in a life dedicated to violence. When one examines the confession, there are many unanswered questions. There are also many untrue statements. Could he be responsible for any or all of the other crimes alluded to by Pete Dunbar. We will never know.

The confession ended in the early morning of September 29, 1974. The following night, he committed his last murder. David Meirhofer hanged himself with a towel in his cell.

With every such series of crimes, the question of why always is asked. How can an individual who was described by Three Forks Deputy Ron Brown as a likable, young man be a killer? He had many of the characteristics of a likable, young man—bright, quiet, polite, willing to give you a hand, and a talented carpenter. Pete Dunbar had attended school with David Meirhofer's mother and knew David. According to Pete, he made an exceptional soldier while serving in Vietnam. Pete Dunbar and David's mother were both aware that when he was younger, the parents of the Boy Scout troop he was active with expressed concern and had him removed from the Scouts. Dunbar was also aware that as a young man in school, he got into a fight and used a knife. Basically, however, David was able to walk around wearing his mask of sanity well.

The confession and crime scene at the Lockhart ranch left the profilers with much to be concerned about. The search of David's residence unveiled the depth of his insanity. The confession was the end result of law enforcement's first effort in interviewing David about the crimes he was willing to talk about. When carefully examined, David did very little talking about the actual crime events other than admitting to being the perpetrator. There was a scarcity of detail. What the confession did tell us was that his crime progressed from the impersonal, long-distance sniping of Bernie Poelman to the deep, personal killings of Michael Raney, Susan Jaeger, and Sandra Smallegan. Killing became a sport to David. Killing was a thrill, something to be witnessed up close and personal. Conquering and controlling the victim became paramount. Torturing the victim was his matador appearance in life. David stole, by his suicide, the opportunity for law enforcement to further question him regarding additional crimes and the reasons behind the crimes he committed.

The crime scene at the Lockhart ranch revealed more than body parts and blood. The Lockhart ranch became David's execution chamber. In it he sought secrecy, solitude, and an escape from reality. The Lockhart ranch became the place David Meirhofer could take off his mask of sanity and act as the real David Meirhofer, the insane monster. Deputy Ron Brown put it well when he said, "There were two sides to David. One, when he was normal and good, like when you would see him bowling. The other side was the dark side, which I have never seen." Very few people ever saw that dark side. It is safe to say that Michael Raney, Susan Jaeger, and Sandra Smallegan were among those who had the horror of witnessing this side of David. There had to be more, and this we will never know.

Although Marietta Jaeger was never at the Lockhart ranch, she mysteriously visited it in her nightmarish dream. Marietta was given the gift of knowing when her daughter Susan passed from this life to the warm embrace of the beyond. The nightmare Marietta had was the vision of David Meirhofer's execution chamber.

Most interesting of all, in the aftermath of this investigation, was the search of David Meirhofer's house. Finding body parts in the refrigerator was not a surprise. What was a surprise was finding large quantities of blood on various bed coverings. Most intriguing of all was that shoved away in a dresser drawer, a black hood mask with two eyeholes cut into it. This was David Meirhofer's "mask of insanity." There was little question in my mind that this mask was one of the instruments used in the series of crimes David was involved in. There is no doubt that he wore this mask while stalking his victims at night. There is little doubt that this was the mask he wore as he played the matador role in the Lockhart ranch. David was the Matador of Murder.

Howard Teten, Bob Ressler, and I had opened the window to the mind of a very sick killer. This case gave us the opportunity not only to prove profiling a worthwhile tool for law enforcement but also to redefine the most deadly type of killer. For months, we had discussed the phenomenon of the killer with many of the traits of the psychopath coupled with many of the dominant characteristics of the simple schizophrenic. We regarded the psychopath as ruthless, without boundaries when committing a violent act of murder, extrovert, sexual experimenter, braggart, and beyond remorse. Colliding with this pathology was the simple schizophrenic: known to live in his own world, quiet, loner, impaired interpersonal skills, lacking in heterosexual experience, obsessive/compulsive, and regarded as strange. It was our opinion at the time that this combined personality disorder, when directed toward violence, made the very worst of killers. David Meirhofer was that type of killer.

As years went on, in studying violent killers, the list became legendary with the likes of Bundy, Dacy, Dahmer, Kemper, and so on. What was common in these types of killers was that they were not satisfied with just killing. What satisfied them most was the total destruction of the victim through dismemberment. No behavior was beyond these killers. Necrophilia and cannibalism were common in cases of this nature. Saving body parts was another behavior pattern not noted in other types of killing. This was clearly the type of killer who could be among us yet be unrecognized for all practical purposes because of his unwillingness to share his madness.

Marietta Jaeger was the person most responsible for tearing the mask of sanity off of her Susan's killer. Marietta stood in direct contrast to David. The goodness in Marietta overcame the demons in David. Her bravery in confronting Susan's killer was out in the open, not needing the sick shelter of the Lockhart ranch. Her faith in God gave her the necessary courage to continue to look for Susan amid dark despair. David, once revealed, was the matador of his own execution, fearing justice for his crimes.

There were many victims in this crime, as in all crimes across our country. In many ways, murder is like the arborist slashing off a vital branch within a family tree. Had Susan lived, she would be a vibrant mother today, bringing her children to visit Marietta and perhaps Bill. Yes, Susan's life was taken, and so were her children's lives and their children's lives. What murder does is destroy, in great measure, a tree of life that will never be because of a ruthless and senseless act.

While little sympathy will ever go toward the killer, he too, has altered a family tree that should have been a positive contribution to life. Today, an aging woman who used to be Pete Dunbar's classmate, Eleanor Huckert, lives in disgrace for what her son, David Meirhofer, is known for in Bozeman, Montana. She lives with questions similar to those of Marietta Jaeger. Why did this ever have to happen? Eleanor Huckert's questions go even deeper. Where did I go wrong in raising a vicious killer? What happened to that little boy who was so affectionate? What happened to that little baby I held in my arms when he was born? Was he born to be a killer?

Those of us in law enforcement, and all society, ask the same question. Are people born to be killers, or do they develop into killers through the way they respond to their individual socialization process? These questions go back to Cain and Abel. They have not been answered. What we have answered in our American society is that we have more "Jack the Ripper" type killers than any other civilized society has. There is something radically wrong with the way we are raising our children. That is, perhaps, what needs study? In the meantime, modern-day profilers work backward from an ugly crime scene, where inhumanity has been forced on the innocent, to determine the next name to be placed on the wall of mass murderers. Who will be the next "normal" person to have his mask of sanity ripped off in a brave encounter on a street in "Somewhere, USA"?

CHAPTER 5

Mad Greek

IT WAS EARLY TUESDAY MORNING when Richard O. Hall arrived at his office at 129 East Market Street, Indianapolis, Indiana. The weather in Indianapolis was typical for that time of year, cold and somewhat rainy. It had snowed, and patches of frozen snow had not yet melted in the sun. Mr. Hall was the president of Meridan

Mortgage Company. He had no idea what awaited him. Suddenly the door swung open, and a wild-eyed individual walked in looking very upset. He pulled out a sawed-off shotgun and demanded that Hall get down on his knees. Hall recognized the individual as one of his customers, Tony Kiritsis.

Kiritsis had borrowed $110,000 from Meridian Mortgage Company three years earlier, purchasing some seventeen acres of potential retail property, where he had planned to build a shopping center. His plans didn't materialize, and Kiritsis fell behind in his mortgage payments; the original note had to be renegotiated to $130,000, covering unpaid interest. It was evident to Kiritsis that the city planners had not cooperated with him, and his shopping center appeared to be a bad dream. Unable to interest any food chains in developing his land, Kiritsis was faced with his note coming due on March 1, 1977, at which time, if he failed to pay, he would be foreclosed on. Kiritsis felt that Hall had swindled him in leading him to select this property instead of one of several other potential sites.

Once Kiritsis had Hall's attention, he handcuffed him and used a wire to tie the shotgun so tightly around Hall's neck that it cut a mark. The wire around his neck was tied tightly to the sawed-off shotgun, with the wire going through the trigger guard. Any quick movement of the shotgun would cause it to go off. Kiritsis pushed Hall out of his office and started a five-and-a-half-block parade down the center of Indianapolis. During this period, Kiritsis was ranting and raving about his plight, using the most vulgar language imaginable. Crowds watched him as he passed and engaged him in vulgarities. Kiritsis was clearly in a state of rage, and Hall's life was in serious jeopardy.

Kiritsis was heading to the security of his nearby third-floor apartment. One slip on the ice, and Hall's life would end. One trip by either Hall or Kiritsis, and it would all be over.

As a direct outgrowth of teaching criminal psychology and doing many psychological profiles, Howard Teten and I were invited up to New York to lecture before a new class that the New York City police department was conducting on hostage negotiations. We were given a block to lecture on abnormal behavior and how it applies to law enforcement. NYPD Sergeants Frank Boltz and Harvey Schlosberg were in the middle of training two classes of hostage negotiators.

This was being done in the aftermath of the massacre at Olympic Village in Munich and the famous Entebbe raid. Many large departments were readying themselves for terrorism. No one knew exactly how terrorism would affect us in the United States, but preparations were underway. The New York City police department started an excellent program in hostage negotiations. We saw the value in it and reproduced it for law enforcement across the United States. We also began training FBI agents to be negotiators in the various field offices around the country.

On February 9, 1977, the FBI office in Indianapolis relayed a request of Police Chief Eugene Gallagher for the presence of Supervisory Special Agent Patrick Mullany to assist in the ongoing negotiations with Anthony Kiritsis. Tony Kiritsis was holding John Hall in his third-floor apartment at the Crestwood Village West complex in Indianapolis.

Arriving at 6:55 p.m. in Indianapolis, I was met at the airport by police officials and Marion County Deputy Prosecutor George Martz, who transported me to the scene. We arrived at the scene at approximately 7:15 p.m. and immediately had a conference with the top-ranking members of the Indianapolis Police Department, local FBI officials, psychiatrists, acting negotiators, members of the prosecutor's office, and relatives of Tony Kiritsis. Chief Gallagher's summary of what had taken place over the last day and a half was very bleak. He claimed that his men were extremely discouraged by the way things were going. According to Gallagher, a local WIBC broadcast at 5:00 p.m. had triggered Tony Kiritsis into a total state of rage and irrational behavior, nearly bringing an end to the entire episode. It was determined that the 5:00 p.m. news report contained a live broadcast of an army ordinance personnel soldier explaining how he was going to cut through Kiritsis's wall to discharge the reported explosives that he had engineered to prevent entry into his apartment.

From my involvement in past cases, I was keenly aware that when a crisis such as this occurred, there was always the possibility of interagency conflict. This case would prove no exception. It occurred to me that almost every jurisdiction was represented in this negotiation process. Taking the lead was the city police from Indianapolis, headed by Police Chief Eugene Gallagher. He had two counterparts in Marion County: Sheriff Larry Broderick and Indiana State Police Colonel Al Walker. Representing Marion County was the deputy prosecuting attorney, George Martz, and representing the Department of Justice was a local US attorney, James B. Young. While Young never appeared on the scene, his presence was felt very much toward the end of the crisis. Somehow, during the course of this event, Tony Kiritsis ended up with two attorneys representing his interests, Chuck Wilson and John Ruckleshaus, the brother of a former acting FBI director, William Ruckleshaus. There was literally a cast of thousands, and all felt it incumbent upon them to make decisions.

At approximately 8:30 p.m. on February 9, 1977, Chief Gallagher requested that I take charge of the negotiation operation and said that he would handle the tactical issues. The state police had set up a command post alongside Tony Kiritsis's apartment and were actively recording all phone calls being made to the Kiritsis apartment.

From discussion with family members, Kiritsis's psychiatrist, police, and attorneys, there was no reason to question that we were facing a bad situation. Teaching criminal psychology and conducting profiles back at the academy seemed like a piece of cake compared to what I was now involved in. All of these disciplines were coming together. We needed to understand the mentality we were dealing with and come up with a game plan to handle the psychological profile of a person in total rage. The difference between this and what we faced at the academy was that now lives hung in the balance, nobody was dead yet, and death had to be prevented.

Having caught bits and pieces of the ongoing hostage case since its inception, I know it was critical that I master every aspect of the case. From 8:30 p.m. until approximately 9:30 p.m., a review of all the taped activity of Tony Kiritsis, with emphasis on his emotional eruption just prior to my arrival, was imperative. The profile developed quickly, and I concluded that although the police had succeeded in tactically handling the situation, what was happening in the negotiation phase was heading toward disaster. Tony Kiritsis was in an extreme state of rage. His entire complaint was against Dick Hall and what had been done to him financially. It was a waste of time to try to convince him otherwise. What Kiritsis did demonstrate over a day and a half was the ability to control his trigger finger. He had not, intentionally or unintentionally, killed Dick Hall; this was good news.

The telephone inside Kiritsis's house was ringing off the hook. Somehow his phone number was listed or got out, and numerous phone calls were coming into him. One caller yelled into the phone, "You crazy son of a bitch, you don't have the courage to blow his brains out; blow his fucking brains out."

Kiritsis responded to the caller, "You are a lot sicker than I am, you son of a bitch." He hung up on the caller. There was every imaginable type of call coming in to Kiritsis. Most of the callers were upsetting Kiritsis even more than he already was.

The first plan of action was to sterilize the inner perimeter—namely, Kiritsis's apartment. No calls were allowed in, and the police controlled the calls out of the apartment as well. Everything had to be done to get Kiritsis down from his high state of rage...

What perhaps was the most difficult issue for both Kiritsis and Hall was that we succeeded in isolating them by turning off the electricity to the apartment. This gave us the tactical advantage in that he could not watch television and see how the police were setting up or be upset by television programs discussing the case. He became very nervous when the lights first flickered because he felt the bomb technicians were coming through the walls.

We had to verify in some way whether Kiritsis had explosives in his apartment. The military provided bomb dogs to process his car, and they had three makes—one on the trunk and two on the side back doors of Kiritsis's car. We were pretty convinced that his threat of having explosives was real, or at least we had to assume it was real.

For the next two days, we monitored all external and internal events that caused behavioral ups and downs in Kiritsis. We altered his environment, not only by cutting off his electricity but also by having his half-brother cook Greek food in an apartment across the hall, blowing it toward Tony's apartment. We were trying anything to get him to open the door to his apartment. We offered food, medicine, and so on—anything to get him to open the door—and nothing worked. We started to chart his every mood swing as well as the effect it was having on the victim, Dick Hall.

Once Kiritsis's environment was controlled, the police spirit started to pick up. They did not feel as hopeless and devastated as they had in the first thirty hours. Talk of assaulting the apartment started to subside. The authorities could see progress, and no lives were being lost. Great concern was expressed for the victim, Dick Hall. From what we could tell, he was holding up extremely well and was not in a position to do anything stupid. The shotgun was left tied to his head during the entire crisis.

The primary negotiator during all of this was a trusted friend of Kiritsis's named Dutch Sheffer. Dutch was most cooperative, and the link that he provided between the police and Kiritsis was of great value. He made numerous trips between the command post and the third-floor apartment. However, the smell of Greek food, offer of refreshments, and comforting words from his friend, Dutch, all did nothing to convince Kiritsis to move from his barricaded position. The police were getting restless.

That restlessness was being shared all over the city of Indianapolis. Mayor Hudnut showed up at the command post very concerned over when it was going to end. The unknown factor was that Kiritsis was writing the script and had control of the stage, or so he thought. We had long since learned that in a hostage case, time was on the side of law enforcement, and it was important to manage it correctly. If the mentality of getting it over with took over, the weapon of time would be wasted, and the arguments for assaulting the barricade situation would win out.

A very key figure emerged in the late afternoon hours of February 9 and continued into the next day. Fred Heckman, WIBC News director, contacted Kiritsis and struck up a strong trust relationship with him. We requested that Fred Heckman come to the command post for a briefing, where his possible role could be used to assist in peacefully ending this standoff. Heckman was initially concerned that he would be abandoning his role of reporter and getting into an area where he did not belong. However, when the humanitarian function he had in his hands was impressed on him, Heckman wanted to know how he could help. We outlined for him three objectives: first, reduce Tony's fear of the police attacking; second, emphasize the optimistic outcome of this crisis; third, reinforce Tony's sense of self-esteem. Fred Heckman gave his pledge to fully cooperate. His cooperation was a major factor in the successful outcome of this crisis; his role cannot be overstated. Once we had Heckman talking to Tony, we gave Heckman a bone to dangle in front of Kiritsis. Kiritsis grabbed at it, and we turned the lights back on to his apartment.

The hostage crisis moved away from the initial rage and volatility that was experienced in the early hours, and the stabilization lasted until 4:00 p.m. on Thursday, February 10, 1977. Two things took place in Tony Kiritsis's mind: he wanted this whole thing to end, and he was concerned over what charges he would face. Kiritsis initiated a deal with the local authorities on the evening of February 9 and got immunity from local prosecution. This occurred around 8:30 p.m.

Allowing the lights turned on gave Kiritsis a window into what was going on outside his apartment. He overheard the news commentators questioning whether there was an issue with federal charges brought against him, such as kidnapping.

The dilemma of negotiating with a subject who had a shotgun tied to a victim's head turned quickly to infighting regarding a political debate over the issue of immunity. It would escalate all the way to US Attorney General Griffin Bell. How this got into Griffin Bell's office was beyond belief.

Two special agents of the FBI from the Indianapolis division were active on the scene during the negotiations: SA John Mullen and SA William Blackketter. They had been maintaining liaison with the FBI office and the special agent in charge, Frank Louie. While the issue of federal immunity was starting to gain steam, I kept asking what the immunity issue was about; we did not have, in my eyes, any federal violation that required immunity. Mullen and Blackketter told me that on the previous day, February 9, Indianapolis Supervisor James Deegan discussed the Hobbs Act violation of the sawed-off shotgun at US Attorney James B. Young office. At that time, the Assistant United States Attorney rendered an opinion declining prosecution in this matter.

From left field came the bolt of lightning that nearly destroyed all efforts to avoid innocent lives being lost. The deputy prosecuting attorney for Marion County, George Martz, took it upon himself to respond, once and for all, to the federal immunity issue, which he felt was bogging down negotiations.

Martz called the attorney general's office in Washington and spoke to Assistant Attorney General Osgood. According to Martz, Osgood stated that he would immediately have the papers dispatched to the local US Attorney's office in Indianapolis and sent to the scene. By 6:00 p.m., hearing no further word, Martz placed a call to the White House. The ladder was being climbed, and very quickly we had political involvement that was absolutely unnecessary. By 6:10 p.m., the White House responded with the attorney general's position, which was (1) immunity would not be granted; (2) if the subject released the victim unharmed, every consideration would be given toward fair treatment; and, (3) no prosecutive opinion would be given on this case until it was resolved.

What clearly had taken place in the negotiations was that it got politically out of hand, and a decision level was triggered into action that was totally uncalled for. Negotiating with Kiritsis was one issue. Having to negotiate with the attorney general of the United States was quite another. What was very clear was that the Washington position on immunity was very different from that of George Martz's local immunity. There was little doubt that the local prosecutor was playing bluff; there was no such game in Washington because of the precedent such a ruling on immunity could set. All along, I kept asking anyone who would listen—immunity from what? To me it was a nonissue. I was able to convince Ruckleshaus and Chuck Williams but had no luck in convincing the local US Attorney.

At approximately 7:05 p.m. on February 10, I was called to take a phone call from US Attorney Young. He was advised that we were aware of the attorney general's position and that we agreed with it. All during this time, Kiritsis was getting very restless in his apartment. By every indication, the crisis was coming to an end. I told Young that we were not interested in having federal immunity for kidnapping charges, but we were interested in using the declination of prosecution on the Hobbs Act violation that was rendered the day previous. Mr. Young denied having ever rendered a prosecutive opinion the day previous. We were at a major impasse, and it was emphatically made clear to Mr. Young that lives were being held in the balance over this issue. I asked Mr. Young if I could present the matter to him then, over the phone. Special Agent Blackketter had prepared the written document that we were intending to use as bait for Kiritsis. Mr. Young fell into the safe position of stating that he would give no opinion until the entire matter was over. At the time, this decision appeared to guarantee that someone would get killed. I made every effort to impress upon Mr. Young that an unsuccessful outcome could very well rest on his shoulders and that all the good efforts of law enforcement would be wasted. He became incensed at that suggestion and demanded to know whom I worked for in Washington and under whose authority I came to Indianapolis in the first place. He demanded to see me the following morning in his office. It was clear in my mind that this hostile encounter was going nowhere fast. I placed the phone down on the desk and returned to the negotiation process at hand.

Many of the news media people were gathering across from Kiritsis's apartment. Live broadcasts were coming from the lobby, and we knew Kiritsis was watching. Once again, we set the trap with a little bait. We had the feeling that if we set up this media stage in the lobby, within a short walk of Kiritsis's apartment, he might bite and join the show.

Things were really coming to a head. There were numerous heated arguments about what was being offered to Kiritsis and how it would be delivered to him. I remember spending a great deal of time assuring Kiritsis's attorneys that they were perfectly safe in approaching Kiritsis because the shotgun was tied tightly to Hall's head. I convinced them that at most, Kiritsis could get off one shot, and that would be for Hall. There was no chance that either one of them would be shot. It was a little like convincing someone going into a lion's den that the lion had already eaten and would not be hungry.

Meanwhile, back in Washington, the phone conversation I had with US Attorney Young served as the proverbial puncturing of the beehive. From approximately 7:20 p.m. until 9:30 p.m., the night supervisor back at FBI Headquarters was diverted from his routine, and he paraded into the act big time. During this period, he made four urgent calls to me at the scene. They were all less than encouraging and totally void of any concept of what was going on at the time. On his first call, his memorable quote was, "You might have a lot of degrees behind your name, but frankly, you sure don't impress me that you know what you are doing." On another phone call, he commented, "I don't know how many years you have at headquarters or in the bureau, but frankly, you might be looking for a job tomorrow." Supervisor Lee's third call was perhaps best of all when he stated, "You have put me in a real bad spot, and how the hell am I going to write this up?" We were within minutes of Kiritsis coming out when John Lee's last call was put through to the phone we were actually talking to Kiritsis on. His demand was, "I want you to leave this line open." It was impossible to leave the line open; we would have surrendered the last line we had to the person with the shotgun. I hung up on Lee and never heard from him again that night, though I became the victim of his bureaucratic memos to the US Department of Justice.

The negotiation phone rang six times in Kiritsis's apartment, with no answer. I was standing in the command bus keeping an eye on all monitors. Having the phone go unanswered had to mean that Kiritsis took the bait and opened his apartment door to come join the media excitement in the lobby across from his apartment. As I put my head out of the command bus, I heard someone yell, "He's coming down!" Across the parking lot came Kiritsis, with Hall still under the control of the shotgun. As he walked across the parking lot toward the lobby, Kiritsis and Hall hit a large patch of melting ice. Kiritsis stumbled to one knee, and very astutely, Hall crouched down so as not to put pressure on the trigger of the shotgun. Regaining his balance, Kiritsis paraded toward the lobby, all the while screaming obscenities at anyone who would listen.

The lobby was well lit and crowded with media representatives and residents of the complex. Kiritsis barged through the door into the middle of the crowd, screaming, "You do not know how much this son of a bitch has ruined my life, and I am going to blow his fucking brains out." It was approximately 9:30 p.m.

Both Kiritsis and Hall looked worse for wear. They were still in the clothes that they had dressed in some three days earlier. Both were terribly unshaven. Hall had a blank, stressful stare on his face; he looked pale and worn. Hall's striped shirt looked tattered and dirty. The collar was tossed up over the wire that reached to the shotgun. Hall listened very intently to every word that Kiritsis uttered. The handcuffs on Hall's wrists were held chest high, looking very uncomfortable. The shotgun had been tied to his neck for over sixty hours, and it left a deep purple, scarred impression. Hall's energy and bravery were draining from his body.

Kiritsis's eyes were riveted on Hall. He was sweating profusely. His catlike moves reflected the tremendous energy he was expelling. He was on national television, the whole world was watching, and he knew it. This was the performance of his life. His language was vulgar beyond imagination; every sentence contained profane words. We were standing within two feet of Kiritsis but were helpless when it came to disarming him. Even though we could reach out and touch him, there was no way to wrestle the shotgun from him without blowing off Dick Hall's head. Kiritsis's performance would last for well over an hour.

During the tirade before the media, with Hall in tow, Kiritsis went around the crowd and recognized people he knew. Kiritsis was no stranger to the police; he knew many of them by name, and in better times, he was friendly to them. Kiritsis's relatives were present, and he apologized to them. What was noticeable was that Kiritsis's mood began to change. I pulled Chief Gallagher aside and expressed my extreme concern that Kiritsis was going to kill himself. His long apologies seemed to be good-byes. The longer he talked, the more somber his mood became. There was little doubt in his mind that this episode was coming to an end. Kiritsis praised the media, praised Fred Heckman, praised Chief Gene Gallagher, and, in a backhand way, praised his victim, Dick Hall, apologizing to his family

At about 11:10 p.m., Kiritsis signaled that he wanted to get this "fuckin'" shotgun off. He had said all that was to be said to the media, and in his mind it was over. The loud vulgar screaming was over; the stage had to be rid of its actors. At the direction of the chief, Hall and Kiritsis were led into an apartment living room. Kiritsis gave permission for the police to cut loose the wire from the shotgun. Kiritsis still had not surrendered. With the shotgun free, he yelled, "You do not know how much I have wanted to shoot this goddamn shotgun for the last three days." Kiritsis walked out an open patio door, pointed the shotgun skyward, and fired. Coming back into the room, he handed the shotgun to Chief Gallagher. The Indianapolis Police Department SWAT team was set up outside the apartment; it was a miracle they did not take out Kiritsis when he appeared on the patio. At 11:15 p.m., Chief Gallagher placed Tony Kiritsis under arrest.

After the shotgun had been released from Hall's neck, Kiritsis yelled, "Get this fuckin' bastard out of my sight." I grabbed Hall and brought him to an adjoining apartment, where we laid him down on a bed. I remember leaning over him; his body was still trembling, and his mouth was dry. His eyes were glazed in fear, and he was in a state of shock. His neck looked raw, and his wrist showed the marking of his ordeal. I looked straight into his staring eyes and said, "FBI, Dick, you are going to live."

He mumbled, "Thank God."

It was at that moment, leaning over Hall, that I heard the loud shotgun blast in the next room. I had an initial sinking feeling, not knowing at the time that it was Kiritsis shooting the weapon. I turned to Special Agent John Mullen, asking what had happened. He said Kiritsis is gone. I thought he meant Kiritsis was shot and killed by the police, and a sense of defeat and failure came over me. I was saddened, believing Kiritsis had not survived. After further questioning and my posing the direct question of whether Kiritsis had been shot, Mullen cleared up the issue; he was placed under arrest and taken to the police station for booking. No life was lost.

Within two days, the new attorney general, Griffin Bell, was asked at a press conference, "How are you getting along with the FBI?" He responded, in his Southern accent, "I am getting along real well, except one of those young ones tried to make an end run on me, and I am taking care of that." That young one was me.

By memorandum, dated February 22, 1977, the attorney general wrote Clarence M. Kelley, director of the FBI, a short note that read as follows:

I asked John Harmon, Acting Assistant Attorney General, Office of Legal Counsel, to prepare a memorandum regarding the events that took place after I made a decision not to grant immunity to the Indianapolis gunman who was holding a hostage. The memorandum, a copy of which is attached, calls into question the conduct of an Indianapolis FBI Agent. I would hope that you will look into this matter and provide me with a report on it. Signed Griffin B. Bell

The memo from John Harmon clearly had me between the crosshairs. Its last sentence summarized the essence of the memo. "The evidence would indicate that Agent Mulhaney (misspelled) deliberately ignored the Department of Justice instructions on the question of immunity, which he received through the local US Attorney."

Although negotiating for Dick Hall's life was over, negotiating to save my career was just beginning. What had taken place emphasized the reality that negotiating with a subject in a hostage case is often less difficult than handling the authorities who are jurisdictionally responsible for the case.

The Department of Justice was dealing with a lofty concept of immunity, and the Attorney General took the right and only position on the subject. What did not fit was that we were not talking federal immunity during the negotiations. There was no federal violation from which we needed immunity. Perhaps County Prosecutor Martz, however well intentioned, pushed the wrong button that night and brought in a level of decision making that was unnecessary.

Six months later, the Department of Justice sent a brief note concerning this event. It said, in full, after referencing the original note of the attorney general, "In reference to this matter, take no administrative action on this agent; neither reward nor punish him."

A subpoena was issued for me to appear before the Honorable Judge of The Superior Court of Marion County, on Wednesday, September, 14, 1977, at 9:30 a.m., then and there to testify on behalf of the defendant in the cause of State of Indiana against Anthony G. Kiritsis.

At the trial, Tony Kiritsis looked like a different person. The rage and insanity were gone. The filthy, profane language was no longer present. At the break in the trial, he came forward and extended his hand in apology, expressing regrets if he had caused my family or me any hardship. He told me that his family had told him what a nice guy I was and that I really helped him even though he hadn't realized at the time what was happening. Kiritsis was convicted of his crime and spent several years in prison. He was released several years ago and spent several years as a free individual. He died of natural causes, taking to his grave memories of a drama that fell just short of people dying because of his actions.

Dick Hall was given the opportunity to face death and live. His experience changed his life in many ways. His previous orientation to the importance of his business gained new focus. Family, life, and doing good for others became more meaningful. Hall was never one for seeking attention and resisted the notion that he was a hero for having survived such an ordeal. After the incident, he expressed, "I just figured in my mind that God had a plan for everybody. I didn't quite understand why this was part of His plan, but I'd just go with what I had." Hall felt his faith had saved his life.

As hostage cases go, this was a classic, one in which hostage negotiation principles work. Stalling for time, never giving something without getting something in return, controlling the environment, monitoring emotional levels, and dealing directly with issues—it all worked. This was a case of an extremely enraged person acting totally irrationally. It was not a case of a person who was delusional and imagining things in his mind. Kiritsis's personality could be easily managed. While extremely violent at the time, he had enough self-control to allow law enforcement to take control.

Chief Gallagher by letter dated February 23, 1977, wrote Clarence Kelley, Director, FBI, as follows:

Although this situation was finally culminated in a frightening unprecedented live national television conference, it was brought to a successful conclusion, and so much of that credit is directly attributable to the professional guidance of Agent Mullany.

As you know, policeman are rarely impressed or awed by other people, but every man that worked with Agent Mullany was deeply impressed and quickly developed great respect for him. He was commanding in his demeanor and sense of self-confidence, and a source of strength to all involved. The FBI, great as it is, was never held in higher esteem in Indianapolis as it was by those who worked with Pat in this very trying situation.

Kind words are always appreciated after difficult events. As you move forward, you cannot help but look back and wonder what would have taken place had either Hall or Kiritsis lost his life. You realize that the job you are doing has a direct effect on lives, and that is what matters. You leave behind the jurisdictional and policy battles very quickly. You vividly realize that you do not do this job for monetary reward. The rewards you gather, are those that stay in your memory for a lifetime as flashbacks. The memory from bending over Dick Hall and looking into his penetrating eyes, telling him that he will live, is one that no one will ever erase.

CHAPTER 6

When Washington Stood Still

◈

THE POLICE CAR ROARED OUT of Warrensville Heights, Ohio, with red lights and sirens blaring. Corey Moore had just surrendered and released his two hostages, Shelley Ann Kiggans and Police Captain Leo Keglovic. Having been summoned to the next outbreak of hostage taking in Washington, DC, my mind raced in reviewing what I had just left. Corey Moore, a twenty-five-year-old former marine, had held his hostages for forty-six hours, making some of the most outlandish demands yet heard. Moore was clearly suffering from paranoid schizophrenia and was incoherent. He wanted all white people to leave the face of the earth. One demand that he made was acquiesced to—namely, to talk to the president of the United States. President Jimmy Carter honored the request once the hostages were released. That phone call was never recorded, and we were fearful that it might set a precedent. We were most fortunate that it never did.

The United flight from Cleveland had already closed its doors, and the ramp was being slowly pulled away from the aircraft. Fortunately, the uniformed police officer was still with me and yelled to the attendant to get me on board. The attendant spoke with the captain, who allowed the ramp to be reconnected for me to board. Before I left Cleveland, I received only extremely sketchy information. It was made clear that it was a major hostage case.

Still turning in my head was the debacle after Indianapolis and the difficulty I had with the Department of Justice. I was in Jim Adams's office when he told the Department of Justice that he was going to send me to Cleveland. They questioned him, asking, "Isn't that the agent we had difficulty with in Indianapolis?"

Jim Adams came back with a quick retort: "If you read the material we sent over, you will clearly see that you had no problem with Mr. Mullany in Indianapolis; it was with your own people." He was very emphatic, and for the first time, I understood that the FBI was supporting me. Jim Adams was the number-two man in the FBI; he served as associate director, right under Clarence Kelley.

Arriving in Washington, DC, proved interesting. I grabbed a taxi at the curbside and told the driver to head toward the district building on Pennsylvania Avenue. He said, "No way; the whole town is shut down." When I showed him my FBI credentials, he agreed to take me. On the way into town he stated, "I wouldn't do what you do for all the money in the world, no way." The closer we got to town, the more red lights and sirens could be seen and heard in the distance. The taxi driver gave me some insight as to what was taking place. He told me that more than one building was under siege. Aside from the district building, he stated that the B'nai B'rith Building and some temple had been taken over. His words were, "The whole damn town is under siege. At Constitution Avenue and 12th Street, we came to a police barricade. Rolling down the window, I flashed my FBI credentials, and the police allowed us through. At this point, the cab driver got very nervous. He became even more nervous when we got to the corner right next to the district building and he saw a body lying on the sidewalk covered with a white sheet. With a deep sigh and major expression of concern, he let me out where I needed to be but where he wanted no part of. The cab sped off.

I was to learn later that under the sheet was the body of Maurice Williams, age twenty-four, black radio newsman, who moments before had a dream of a life that did not include this ending. Standing close to the entrance of the building was City Councilman Marion Barry in a white shirt with the collar opened. In the center of his chest was a large bloodstain. He had been shot in the chest. Two other individuals were shot, but their wounds were not life threatening.

There were police cars and emergency vehicles everywhere; Washington was under siege, as the cab driver had said.

When I entered the district building, I was impressed by its emptiness and quiet. The shooting had subsided, and the standoff was underway. I quickly made my way to the top floor by using the staircase. On the half landing before the top floor, a huge desk was placed across the stairs, serving as both a shield and a barrier. The police tactical teams were in place. I edged my way past the table barricade and moved quietly up the stairs, embracing the wall. To the left was the office where the two gunmen were barricaded behind office furniture. No shot had been fired since they had positioned themselves in the office. The corridor outside the office was wide and open. About sixty feet from the office door was the outstretched body of a man. The body was motionless, and we assumed this man had been shot and killed. There was no way to get to this person because crossing over to him would mean going into the direct line of fire. Ironically, after the siege was over, this person got up and walked away. He had not been wounded but was petrified of moving for fear of being killed. He was right.

At the district building, much carnage had occurred, but at this point in the crisis, there was a total standoff. I quickly retreated to the police headquarters and joined the command post team, which was busy coordinating response efforts for what turned out to be three sites.

The first assault occurred shortly after 11:00 a.m., when seven Hanafis, led by Abdul Amass Khaalis himself, burst into the headquarters of the B'nai B'rith Building, the nation's largest and oldest Jewish service organization. Moving upward, floor by floor, they seized dozens of victims, shooting some, slapping and stabbing others, shouting that they were ready to die for Allah. The hostages were herded into the top floor conference room and forced to barricade the stairway leading down from the roof with furniture. The stairway was in the middle of the conference room. The conference room had one toilet facility. For the next forty hours, 116 hostages and 7 gunmen would share one toilet.

The second attack came right around noon. Three Hanafis entered the Islamic Center, a showcase for Muslim culture on Embassy Row. There they rounded up eleven hostages. No shots were fired at this location, and no one was injured. The last—and what would turn out to be the bloodiest—attack occurred at the district building around 2:20 p.m. Two trigger-happy terrorists, guns blazing, shot their way to the top floor of the district building and barricaded themselves in a top floor office. On their way into the district building, they killed one and wounded three while taking control of seven hostages.

Seeing the body on the street and knowing that people had been shot changed this hostage-negotiating situation radically. We always knew that when a life had been lost, the stakes were much higher in negotiating. One of the major cards had been removed from our hands: they had already killed, and the charge of murder was impossible to negotiate around. This was clearly the biggest hostage case we had ever faced. What was uncertain during the initial stage of the crisis was whether these cases related to each other. In the early hours of the crisis, it was determined that, in fact, they were. We were also able to determine that the terrorists were an extremely well-connected group with one leader, Khalifa Hamaas Abdul Khaalis.

Khaalis's background was quickly pulled up. Born in Indiana as Ernest McGee, he received a medical discharge from the army during World War II on the grounds of mental instability. Though he was born a Roman Catholic, while working as a jazz drummer in New York City, he changed his religion to the Nation of Islam and rose in that religion to many trusted positions before he broke with the Black Muslims in 1958. In the mid-1960s, Khaalis formed his own group, called the Hanafi. In 1968, he was arrested for bank extortion. Charges on extortion were dismissed after he was found to be mentally ill. In 1972, Khaalis made an extremely bold move for which he would pay a high price. In an open letter, he attacked the leadership of the Black Muslim faith, calling the leader, Elijah Muhammad, a lying deceiver. Khaalis blamed the Chicago-based religion of violence against any of their detractors. He accused them of murdering Malcolm X. Prior to 1958, Khaalis had worked with Malcolm X, but he was not nearly the influence on the Muslim group that Malcolm X proved to be.

Khaalis attracted a modest number of followers. Many of the individuals he attracted were athletes in various sports. One such was Kareem Abdul Jabbar, formerly Lew Alcindor from New York. Jabbar became famous for his basketball talents displayed at UCLA and with the Lakers. Lew Alcindor was no stranger to me; I first met him when he was in seventh grade grammar school at St. Elizabeth's School on the upper west side of New York. Jabbar came from wonderful, devoted Catholic parents. In seventh grade, he was extremely clumsy and awkward, barely able to dribble a basketball. I coached a basketball team at Good Shepherd School and managed to double team Alcindor with someone half his size. We wound up winning the game, but there were not too many more games for which Lew Alcindor would be on the losing side. In 1970, Kareem Abdul Jabbar purchased an impressive brick fieldstone house, where Khaalis was living.

The most important phase in any negotiation is to determine why the person—or in this case, the group—resorted to violent behavior. With an armed robbery that goes bad, the reason people take hostages is simple; they got caught doing what they were doing, and now they want to bargain for freedom. This hostage case was different, and many theories were being thrown around. It was not until a dialogue was initiated with Khaalis that the picture developed, though his main reason for going on this rampage was still unclear.

One early theory seemed to relate to Khaalis saving face; he was extremely upset over the recently released movie titled *Mohammad, Messenger of God*. Khaalis presented a compelling argument that this film was an insult to all God-fearing people, especially followers of Allah and believers in the Koran. The producer of this film was faced with a serious dilemma because of the strict Muslim prohibition against representing the prophet's face or form, much less his voice, through any medium. The producer/director of this film was Moustapha Akkad, a Syrian-born American. He was making two versions of the film, one in English and the other in Arabic. The producer had hoped to counteract the Western belief that Islam is a faith that comes bearing violence and the sword. Khaalis believed the Koran to be revelation and that the life of the prophet was a divine reflection of that revelation. The idea of this religion and the prophet being portrayed by infidels was extremely offensive.

Hours were spent discussing this issue as being the primary reason for Khaalis's actions. Slowly but surely, however, the real cause started to emerge. At the center of Khaalis's violence was a tragedy lived only by him. It was his reality, and it could not be talked away.

We had been briefed that Khaalis, after parting with the Chicago Black Muslims, came home one evening to find his family lying in a pool of blood, massacred. A squad of Black Muslims had invaded the house provided by Kareem Abdul Jabbar and slaughtered Khaalis's family. His ten-day-old son had been drowned in a sink before his mother's own eyes. Three other children, two of Khaalis's and one grandchild, were drowned in a bath. Two of Khaalis's other sons were shot. He had lost all; nothing was left. Khaalis claimed that his family's killers did not get justice. He stated, "The Koran teaches us an eye for an eye and a tooth for a tooth." His demand was clear. Bring Khaalis James Price, Theodore Moody, Ronald Harvey, John Griffin, and William Christian, and he will administer justice. Khaalis wanted to behead the killers of his family.

The voice of Khaalis was coming over loud and clear: "You house and feed them, which is not justice. Bring them to me, and I will do what Allah would command us to do." Khaalis had contempt for the court that convicted the killers of his family. Khaalis went into a rage during the trial in 1973, and he was charged with contempt for his behavior. He mocked the same court for holding him in contempt and fining him $750. He demanded the $750 be returned. This was a concession that was easily granted.

The psychological profiling of Khaalis was a very complex matter. His early mental illness, while he was a young man in the military, had little present-day bearing. His deep attachment to his religion was a force to be dealt with. There was no question that he was the spokesperson for this armed Muslim group of twelve men. Khaalis had never turned to real violence in the past, but that was well before his family was slaughtered. What was clear was his family being murdered had radically altered the equation of murder for Khaalis. Whenever you attempt to negotiate with someone, you must always make an effort to see life as they perceive it. I felt a tremendous amount of sympathy for Khaalis after hearing his family's plight. Khaalis had a heart full of revenge and the anger to carry out that revenge. This was an event that happened, and it was clearly irreversible. I could readily relate to Khaalis's feeling and his desire to become judge, jury, and executioner. The only task not accomplished in our judicial system, according to Khaalis, was the latter—executioner. He was willing and certainly able to perform the task.

What was clear was that talking about this tragedy would only take Khaalis into a deeper depression. To even attempt to talk away his grief was futile. Certainly, it was impossible to discuss this incident as though it had never happened. It *had* happened, it was real, and it was terrible. However, the individuals who had taken the lives of his family were safe in prison, and they could not become bargaining chips to save the lives of innocent hostages.

This hostage case was extremely difficult because we were dealing with a rigid, forceful, intelligent person who had the charisma to have eleven followers willing to carry out his every wish even if it meant killing innocent people. Khaalis did not represent to us the religious fanatic caught up with such strong beliefs that dying for them would bring a glorified martyrdom. Rather, he was the charismatic religious leader, with a strong following, who had been deeply offended. His motivation was to deliver justice as the Koran and Allah would have him do…by beheading the killers.

At the command center, Chief Maurice Cullinane wore the expression of a deeply concerned leader. Although he was a quiet man and did not seek attention from the press, he was strong leader, well respected by his department, and known for handling major crisis events. To Chief Cullinane, this was a major crisis, and it had to be dealt with wisely. Fortunately, he was a believer in not rushing the crisis but rather giving it time to develop on its own. Deputy Police Chief Robert Rabe was a trusted and good friend of mine. We had served together on the State Department's Committee to Combat Terrorism. Chief Rabe had attended our hostage negotiations training session and was street smart. While he never claimed to be the most accomplished speaker, when he spoke, people listened. Bob Rabe knew his people on the tactical squad, and he knew he could rely on them. We had handled two major crises before this one, and we had a strong bond of friendship and trust. It was just two years earlier that we had worked side by side; two prisoners had overcome the US Marshals and held hostages in the federal building lockup. The special agent in charge of the FBI's Washington field office was Nick Stames. An important figure in the command center was a homicide detective who had established trust and confidence with Khaalis during the murder investigation, Captain Joseph O'Brien. Khaalis knew and respected O'Brien and recognized his voice, and we hoped that he would listen to him.

In the early hours of the negotiation, Khaalis made two demands. Primary demand was death to the killers of his family and secondly, stopping the film. Efforts were underway to have the film *Mohammad, Messenger of God* stopped. Actual television coverage of the marquee being dismantled gave Khaalis a sense of accomplishment. We had already determined that this was not the center of his concerns, but cooperating on it gave us time to strategize without him killing anyone. We were also able to have his fine for his outburst in court refunded. The return of $750 was somewhat of an embarrassment to Khaalis. He stressed it was not the money but the fact that the Jewish judge did not give his family's killers the death penalty. Thanks to Captain O'Brien and Chief Bob Rabe, a line was opened to Khaalis for negotiation. Khaalis had selected one of his hostages to serve as his secretary, Betty Neal. Mrs. Betty Neal was a secretary in the personnel department of the B'nai B'rith. For the entire thirty-nine-hour siege, she answered and placed calls for Khaalis. She did not sleep the entire time. She sat opposite Khaalis and kept a complete log of all incoming and outgoing phone calls, placing all the calls Khaalis asked her to make and receiving all the calls from the negotiators. She served as a settling agent for Khaalis, developing a good relationship with him despite the phones ringing constantly. According to Neal, she said she had a degree of sympathy for Khaalis. "He was very nice. He was basically a compassionate person. He was very upset about his wife and children; that is all he talked about." Betty Neal said that Khaalis told her where to hide if the shooting began. He promised her that he would not kill her. Khaalis shared the reason he selected her to help him—because she was not Jewish. According to Neal, Khaalis did not charge long-distant calls to the B'nai B'rith phone bill.

Unlike Indianapolis, Washington, DC, had an excellent US Attorney, Earl J. Silbert. Silbert became actively involved with all decisions being requested by the negotiating team and was an excellent interface between the crisis and the Department of Justice. When demands came for federal prisoners to be released, he found out where the prisoners were and brought in the director of prisons for assistance. His judgment and insight were exceptional.

Toward the end of the first full day, realizing that this was a critical case involving many hostages, I recommended to Chief Rabe that we seek the assistance of two psychiatrists, Robert Blum and Steve Pieczenik. Blum was an independent Washington psychiatrist with whom I had worked before, and I had great respect for him. Steve Pieczenik was deputy assistant secretary of state, and we had known each other from working on international terrorist cases. Both of these individuals were an exceptional addition to our negotiating team. They were of particular help in reviewing Khaalis's medical records. Our strategy was simple. We cut many of the phone lines going into the B'nai B'rith building, keeping open only those that we felt we needed for negotiating. This took a great deal of time to accomplish. In the early hours, the numerous phone calls of people attempting to interview Khaalis and give him information were a major distraction to him. We felt these calls were counterproductive and distracting to our efforts in channeling Khaalis as we planned.

We were making progress toward getting inside Khaalis's head. He was a man in pathological rage and anger. He had a well-developed inferiority complex that was sublimated by his sense of grandeur as head of a religious following. He was a very sensitive man who had loved his family very much. His ego was fragile and could not be abused without him striking out. His code of conduct rested in his following the Koran. His religious beliefs were rigidly established in the faith that he believed Allah would have him follow. He placed a great deal of value on cleanliness, neatness, and order. He despised filth, dirt, and disorder. He ruled his followers by his adopted power, and they followed him blindly. We knew we had to negotiate with him in a manner that would give him an exit out of this event without losing face. We also knew that Khaalis was greatly upset over the fact that the two followers had killed someone at the district building. He was caught in a bind because his original intent was not to kill innocent people but rather to use them to negotiate having his family's killers be brought to him. He was willing to kill them and risk justice because he would have fulfilled what the Koran called for.

Before we were successful in controlling the phone lines, a female television talk show host reached Khaalis at the B'nai B'rith Building. Her interview of Khaalis set the negotiations back a day. We had succeeded in calming Khaalis, but she reversed all of that. The talk show hostess's remarks were all directed at questioning the government's sincerity in negotiating. She reminded him of the promise of immunity in Indianapolis that was quickly withdrawn. She even questioned the sincerity of the removal of *Mohammad, Messenger of God*. She claimed that was a trick and would be reversed as soon as he surrendered.

Khaalis became highly agitated during his next encounter with Chief Rabe, remarking, "You are playing games with me! There is going to be a blood bath. You will understand when we start cutting heads off. Heads will roll."

While all this was going on, separate meetings were being conducted with the tactical elements of the FBI and the metropolitan police. Khaalis had long since had his hostages cover the windows to the top floor of the B'nai B'rith Building. We could see lights on but only shadows of people moving around. The major tactical concern was the B'nai B'rith Building because it had 116 hostages. What became evident from the outset was that there was no easy way to extract the hostages. Don Bassett was the FBI SWAT commander on the scene, and he concluded that there were only two ways to get in. Blow your way into the middle stairs of the conference room, endangering the hostages with the explosion, or rappel from the roof, crashing into the conference room from the windows. This seemed like a suicide mission in which most of the SWAT members would be sitting ducks for the Hanafi firepower. As the frustration of coming up with a good tactical plan increased, so did Khaalis's threat that heads would roll.

We heard Khaalis complaining on the phone about how there was only one restroom. When people requested to go to the bathroom, they were accompanied by a guard and made to clean the bathroom on the way in as well as on the way out. This became a major problem for Khaalis, and the stench of the bathroom was wearing on him. With 116 hostages in all stages of fear, it began to wreak after almost forty hours of captivity. Khaalis was kind to the women and did not tie them up, but he was very dominating to the men. His followers worked over the men with regularity to keep them under control. We knew for certain that the individuals who became the biggest management problems in captivity would be the first to be killed. When Khaalis was convinced that the SWAT teams were readying to assault the eight-floor bunker that he constructed, he had the men stand in front of the windows as shields against any assault.

For the most part, during the long hours of negotiation, Khaalis kept his composure and remained demanding but calm. He became extremely agitated, however, when he saw the tactical teams on the roofs of surrounding buildings. He demanded that they be removed. Instead of removing the teams, we discreetly hid them.

We were able to use up many hours of negotiation while arranging food and medicine for the hostages. We were willing to send food in to the Hanafi members as well. Food and its supply line became a very important instrument. Toward the very end of the last day, when all else seemed lost and it seemed likely that we would see a head or two tossed out the window from the top floor, we were able to distract Khaalis with details. Khaalis had just about given up on his demand to have the prisoners brought to him and was making his threats to kill very real. He yelled on the telephone, "No more talk...we are getting nowhere...heads will roll." At that point, we distracted him with a simple question: "Do you want the mustard and mayo put on the sandwiches, or do you want it put on the side?" Distracted by this question, he turned to his men to find out how the people wanted their sandwiches. This caused a great deal of confusion, and he told Betty Neal that he would get back to us. He got back to us on the sandwiches but did not return to the heads-would-roll issue for some time. Truly, we had bought time.

The technique we had used in negotiating was simple. Bob Rabe, Bob Blum, Steve Pieczenik, and I sat at a table with telephones so that we could all listen in on the negotiating conversation. Chief Bob Rabe had replaced O'Brien as the primary negotiator. It was Rabe who was doing the actual talking on the phone. We all had numerous large, yellow pads. We would actually script the conversation live, writing down questions to be asked and statements to be made. This worked marvelously. Chief Rabe, if uncertain in what he heard, would ask, "What do you mean by this?" Khaalis was never aware that he was talking to a group as opposed to one person in Chief Rabe.

Our plan was simple: keep him talking, avoid controversy, avoid talking about his family, distract him when he talked about his family's killers, keep him concerned about his hostages, and build on his inner tensions of being surrounded by filth. We kept his attention on the uncleanness of one toilet for so many people. Most important, we played to his sense of grandeur; we wanted to make him look important and feel that he was the center of attention. We also were emphatic in stressing that his captors were not just a bunch of Jews but human beings. They were human beings who had families extremely concerned about their well-being.

The telephones were brought under control; we were not allowing calls to go to the eighth floor at random. This took great effort, but it was critical in the negotiating posture we had taken. What became clear to us four was that not one of us had one ounce of knowledge about the Nation of Islam religion or the Koran. Khaalis was quoting from the Koran widely, and we had to accept his interpretation of everything. This, we determined, had to be changed.

At the command center, we received great support from Chief Cullinane as well as Peter Flaherty, the newly appointed deputy attorney general who had previously served as mayor of Pittsburgh. US Attorney Silbert was constantly available to help with any and all decisions. What was working to our distinct advantage was that all the decision makers were involved; they were present and not miles away from the crisis. Thursday morning, March 10, 1977, Griffin Bell, attorney general, and FBI Director Clarence Kelley came to the command center to view firsthand what was happening.

Speaking to the FBI director was somewhat puzzling at this phase of the crisis. His major concern was whether the on-going incidents were related. When I assured him they were, he questioned how we were certain. I shared with him that we were actively monitoring the phone conversations from Khaalis's residence to the district building, the B'nai B'rith Building, and the temple. He was reassured. FBI Director Kelley was a kind and good man. He was a perfect fit in replacing Director Hoover. As we stood and talked, he stretched out his hand and offered me a cracker out of a peanut butter and cheese package. I remembered that very well because the last time I'd had something to eat was on the airplane from Cleveland. I actually took advantage of him and helped myself to two crackers. I guess what most surprised me was that I was briefing the number-two man in the FBI, Jim Adams, about every two hours or so. I was concerned when Director Kelley came to the command center with the attorney general with so many unanswered questions.

At the Islamic Center, a problem started to develop that later became a negotiating weapon. Taken hostage at the center was the Egyptian wife of the center's director, Muhammed Adbul Rauf. Her behavior was less than ideal for a hostage, although we admired her for her bravery. She became belligerent and argued with her captors about Islam. She demanded that they recite the five basic tenets of Islam. They either could not or would not, and she angrily told them that she knew as much about Islam as the number of hairs on her head. Rauf, on the other hand, was smart; he never opened his mouth for fear that they would blow his head off. We became aware that this hostage case had international ramifications, not just domestic ones.

Chief Rabe and I had participated at the state department with Ambassador Douglas Heck on terrorism matters. We placed a call and quickly briefed him on what we were running into. We asked his assistance in finding someone who would help us on two issues: one, dealing with Islam, and two, speaking for the Islamic diplomatic community.

Ambassador Heck was quick to respond. He came up with what first appeared to be an odd collection of individuals to deal with any gunman, much less a religious fanatic such as Khaalis. Ardeshir Zahedi was well known in the United States as being a playboy. He was forty-eight years of age and very engaging. He had a reputation for dating beautiful women, one of whom was Elizabeth Taylor. Zahedi had been married to the daughter of the Shah of Iran. He was an extremely competent ambassador, having been ambassador to the United States from 1959 to 1961 as well as from 1973 until this event. He was famous in Washington circles for throwing lavish parties, where his trademark was excellent caviar. Zahedi was a tall man of dignified posture. His behavior during the crisis was remarkable.

Ashraf Abdel-Latif Ghorbal, age fifty-one, was a man of small stature, perhaps five feet one inch. He was brilliant, had a sense of humor, and was very dignified. He had been serving as Egyptian Ambassador since December 1973. He was a member of an aristocratic Egyptian family. After graduating from Cairo University, he attended Harvard University, where he was awarded both a master's degree and a doctorate. He was one of Washington's most respected foreign diplomats.

Finally, Sahabzada Yaqub-Khan, age fifty-six, was a trim, athletic figure who was a retired lieutenant general in the Pakistan Army and its former chief of staff. Khan was no stranger to danger. He had been twice captured in World War II and escaped both times. Khan was an exceptional polo player and was fluent in English and several other languages. Khan had been serving as Pakistani Ambassador to the United States since December 1973.

While Heck deserves credit for getting the three ambassadors involved in what clearly was a major domestic crisis, credit goes to Ghorbal, who was the first to volunteer once he knew that Egyptians were being held hostage at the Islamic Center. It was Ghorbal who reached out to Khan and Zahedi for their assistance, and although they were a little uncertain of just what they could do, they were both willing to get involved.

Matador of Murder

The negotiators had been given the piece in the chess game that would count: three Arab ambassadors able to enter into a discourse about the Koran and the Muslim faith. This is what was missing. We now had the stage of grandeur that we felt Khaalis needed to stand on to save face. We also strongly felt that the very presence of three ambassadors would honor Khaalis and make him feel elevated from where this crisis had begun—with killing people. The added dimension the three ambassadors gave to this crisis was the deep concern that nothing happen to endanger their lives. From the attorney general to the president of the United States, everyone expressed concern that nothing be done to endanger their lives.

The ambassadors came to the command center with Ambassador Heck and received a complete briefing on what had transpired from the beginning. They were allowed to listen to portions of the conversations that had gone on before. Much of the rhetoric from Khaalis during the early hours was anti-Jewish. These outbursts clearly made the Arab ambassadors feel uneasy. It was indeed a great irony, three Arab-speaking ambassadors negotiating to save the lives of at least

116 predominately Jewish hostages. National affiliation seemed to disappear, and human life took on a new importance. Each of the ambassadors reached out to individuals more familiar with the Koran for assistance. Ghorbal phoned his political counselor, who supplied him with appropriate quotes. Zahedi sought assistance from Mohammad Javad Farzaneh, a Middle Eastern scholar from a religious center in Bethesda, Maryland.

The ambassadors agreed on a strategy that was consistent with the overall strategy in negotiating with Khaalis. The central theme from the Koran related to passages reflecting compassion, forgiveness, understanding the things our Lord orders us to do. They stressed one passage that warned against lawlessness…"O ye who believe, forbid not to yourself the good things that God hath made lawful for you; do not transgress the limits; verily, God loveth not the transgressors." The theme was great, but the question remained… would Khaalis buy into it?

Kahn was the first to try his hand on the phone with Khaalis. At first, Khaalis was honored and somewhat embarrassed. He was not certain he was really talking to Kahn. When quotes started to come from the Koran, Khaalis had the feeling he was being preached to. He cautioned Kahn, "Don't try to teach me, I know the Koran better than you do." In fact, Khaalis did know the Koran, but he began to listen and share his life with Kahn. The centerpiece of Khaalis's problems was being unfolded…the murder of his family. Kahn had great empathy for Khaalis, as we all did.

Early Thursday morning, Ambassador Khan was on the phone again with Khaalis. Our direction for the day was to keep him upbeat and positive. A decent rapport had been established, and the ambassadors were taking the attention away from the prisoners Khaalis had been demanding. What happened on the first call of the day was no surprise; it was predictable for the profile of Khaalis.

Betty Neal answered the phone, and Kahn identified himself. The phone was immediately given to Khaalis. Kahn remarked, "My comrade, it is the beginning of a new day. I would like you, my brother, to join me in a prayer to Allah that it will be a day of compassion, honor, and bravery." Khaalis rejected the offer to pray and told Kahn that he could not pray in a place that was unclean. This told us two things: that the lack of cleanliness was getting to

Khaalis and that, in fact, Khaalis was genuine in his claim to practice the will of the Koran. In the Islamic tradition, a Muslim will pray only in an area that has clean surroundings.

Thursday morning had just begun when we were hit by more strange news. The morning events showed that there was a formal greeting of Great Britain's Prime Minister, James Callaghan, on the mall next to the district building scheduled for 10:30 a.m. At this function, which President Jimmy Carter and his wife would attend, the usual nineteen-gun salute would occur. Our concern was that the Hanafi gunmen in the district building—or, for that matter, at the B'nai B'rith—would see this as an assault on one of their positions and start killing the hostages. Contact was made at the White House with Jody Powell, and we told him of the extreme concern. He agreed that it was not worth taking the chance. The US Army cannoneers were already in position on the mall. Powell got word to them that they would not be used, so they immediately loaded the Howitzers on trucks and boarded their buses, heading back into Virginia and to their military base.

Moments later, as the president was getting ready to leave the White House and make his way to the mall with his wife, Powell briefed him concerning our request. Powell advised that he had dismissed the military and there would be no salute. President Carter was extremely upset at this turn of events, fearing that it would send a message to the world that terrorism altered the US course of action. It was too late; there was no time to call them back, and the ceremony went on without the nineteen-gun salute. Khaalis was advised of our efforts to halt the cannons and was told to advise his men that it did not involve the Hanafi group. He felt we were tricking him and did not believe us. It was fortunate that the guns did not go off that day because nerves were stretched; it is difficult to predict the effect that the nineteen-gun salute could have had on the crisis.

Two very positive events were happening at once, both with a profound effect on the negotiations. With the controlled telephone atmosphere existing at all three locations and negotiations going on only with Khaalis, we could determine that the conditions on the eight floor of the B'nai B'rith Building were getting to Khaalis. We could also tell that the condition of the hostages was becoming more fragile. Anger and the feeling of total discomfort were displacing the initial fear of the hostages. The hostages had not eaten properly in two days. Confrontations were starting to occur. Individuals were trying to manipulate the hostage takers for favors, and a certain amount of whining was beginning to take place. Our concern was that once a hostage became a management problem, the person's likelihood of being killed would increase.

After the cannon scare was behind us, much of Thursday afternoon was spent discussing the Koran but also addressing the issue of feeding the hostages. The hostage takers were very leery of eating any food supplied by us for fear that it might be treated to disable them. Darkness seemed to fall early that Thursday evening. You could readily tell the ambassadors were growing tired of Khaalis's repetition and constant reference to the Koran. While the hostage negotiation team was holding together fairly well and the strategy was paying off in stalling for time, we felt pressured by the concern for the health of the hostages. We knew they could not last much longer. The tactical units of the police department and FBI were growing more restless as the hours went by. They were keenly aware of the difficulty they would have in extracting the hostages, but standing still and doing nothing was wearing on them.

The negotiators were convinced that Khaalis had his fill of the atmosphere on the top floor of the B'nai B'rith Building. He described the condition of the toilet as "filth." We knew filth meant ungodliness. At this point in the crisis, everything and everyone were dirty. The conference room, with over 120 people in it, was very uncomfortable. We knew that Khaalis wanted out no matter what the consequences were. We had a hunch that he did not have the appetite for beheading people who had nothing to do with the death of his family. At the same time, we had discussed in great depth what we would do if in fact a head were tossed from the top floor. The consensus was that if we had a beheading, we would have no choice but to assault and save as many lives as possible.

With the feeling that Khaalis was ready to call it quits, we had the ambassadors suggest to Khaalis that they have a face-to-face meeting. Khaalis liked this idea but was as cautious as a cat. This was a major tactical move in Khaalis's mind, and he wanted guarantees that he would not be shot and killed. Chief Cullinane suggested that Khaalis come down to the street unarmed. What was of immense concern was the safety of the ambassadors. At first Khaalis wanted to speak with Khan alone. We were very reluctant to agree to that for fear that they would take Kahn hostage, improving Khaalis's bargaining position significantly

Khaalis agreed to come down to the lobby of the B'nai B'rith and meet with Chief Rabe, Cullinane, the three ambassadors, and Khaalis's son-in-law, Aziz. A table was set up in the lobby with eight chairs. Khaalis took the elevator to the lobby. He was unarmed. Khaalis greeted the three ambassadors in Arabic with the customary embrace. No such embrace was given to the police authorities, but he was polite in recognizing their presence.

The summit started in a rather hesitating manner. There were exchanges of verses from the Koran used to get familiar with each other and become better acquainted. Unfortunately for the command center and the negotiating team, we had no way of knowing how the meeting was going. US Attorney Earl Silbert, Deputy Attorney General Peter Flaherty, Bob Blum, Steve Pieczenik, and I took up positions next to the B'nai B'rith at the Gramercy Inn. The waiting seemed like eternity, and the tension was high. The longer they met, the more positive we began to feel. As it turned out, a strange set of alliances took place during the meeting. At the outset, Ambassador Khan broke the ice and tried to get a sense of where Khaalis was coming from. As the meeting wore on and Khaalis became more aggressive in bringing up the tragedy of his family, Ambassador Zahedi struck a strong relationship with Khaalis. Zahedi shared with Khaalis some very personal tragedies that he had experienced in life and his method of handling tragic events. Khaalis started to soften and became more accepting of the suggestions of the three ambassadors who, at this point, were doing most of the talking.

When planning for this meeting, we went through an actual rehearsal of the meeting. The ambassadors were coached to cover certain points and stay away from others. No coaching could have brought out the superb performance of these three ambassadors, however. While every department in government feared that anything could happen to them, all were in awe at their willingness to become involved in a crisis that clearly no one felt they were part of.

Three hours into the meeting, Ambassador Khan suggested to Khaalis the freeing of thirty hostages as a sign of good faith. Khaalis surprised everyone present as he looked around the table and quietly said he would release all of them. The ambassadors and police asked the obvious question: "Under what condition." The condition was what we had expected: that he be arrested and charged but allowed to be placed on bail to return to his residence that morning. What was clear was that Khaalis did not want his followers to see him arrested as one of them, and he wanted to have time to put his house in order. He was not looking for immunity or amnesty but for time and a way to save face. The negotiations with Khaalis ended at approximately 11:00 p.m. When the ambassadors, Chief Cullinane, and Rabe left the lobby of the B'nai B'rith, they had no sense whether they could deliver on the release of Khaalis.

Immediately joining those of us at the Gramercy Inn, they presented Khaalis's demand. Silbert and Flaherty were reluctant to make a deal for fear of the precedent it would set. Both of these men knew very well what was at stake: the lives of more hostages than were ever held before in the United States. They were vividly aware of the efforts of the ambassadors and all the authorities. For Peter Flaherty, it was one of the biggest decisions he would have to make in a lifetime. Reluctantly, they called Attorney General Griffin Bell at about 1:10 a.m., asking if he would agree to a bail free release for Khaalis, with his followers arrested and held as charged. Bell agreed on the condition that court approval be obtained. Immediately, Silbert called Harold Greene, a kind and soft-spoken chief judge of Washington's Superior Court. Like Bell, Flaherty, and Silbert, Greene was concerned about the precedent it could set, but he was extremely sensitive to the number of lives that could be lost if he stalled. The chief judge agreed.

The last act in a deadly drama was about to begin. We knew from the beginning that Khaalis was a proud man. We also knew that Khaalis was a man of justice, driven by rigid beliefs, and that he would stand up to punishment for the acts he caused. What we really knew was that justice might have to be delivered on his terms, but it was a small trade-off for so many lives.

The call was placed to Khaalis telling him that he would be charged with the crimes he committed and placed on house arrest. He would be allowed to return to the house where his family had been murdered. His followers were to be arrested and held for the charge of kidnap and murder, along with countless other charges.

The Islamic Center gunmen surrendered at 1:30 a.m. At 1:45 a.m., Deputy Chief Robert Klotz and Officer Joseph Taylor pushed back the makeshift barricade on the stairway of the district building and walked to the northwest corner of the building, where they were met by the two gunman handing over their weapons. Eleven hostages were freed.

At 1:30 a.m., moments after the conversation with Khaalis advising him that he would be charged and released under house arrest, the seven Hanafi soldiers walked out into the handcuffs of the metropolitan police. Khaalis was held until his hearing, which occurred before Judge Greene at 5:10 a.m. He was arraigned for armed kidnapping and murder. He walked out of the courthouse, unmanacled, between two deputy marshals.

The Hanafi Muslims never told their captives at the B'nai B'rith Building that they were surrendering. The 116 hostages were made aware of their survival when the police broke into the conference room that had been their prison for so many hours. The hostages came downstairs using the fire stairs and went out onto the street, where they were able to breathe the cold air of early morning. They were free. Free from the control of the Hanafi terrorists but not from the memory of forty hours facing death. Many looked worse for wear. It had been a long ordeal. The men had sustained the most beating. The women, for the most part, suffered emotional but not physical damage. As word spread of the release of all the hostages, the city took on a new face, no longer strangled by the crisis. Church bells started to ring, and people rejoiced for their freedom. The president of the United States expressed joy over the peaceful surrender. Few criticized the way we were forced to look at the law that night. The negotiating team looked at each other, realizing we had perhaps pulled off the impossible. The three ambassadors, faithful to the end, embraced each other as well as us in gratitude for a successful conclusion to an event they should not have been party to. We all could resume our lives as they were before the shooting began.

Before releasing Khaalis, Judge Greene imposed many conditions on him. Khaalis could not leave Washington. He was made to surrender his passport and all his firearms. He was told to shun all pretrial publicity and, above all, not break any law. Violating any of these orders would be cause for his arrest.

When Washington, DC, woke up that Friday, March 11, 1977, it quickly recovered from the state of siege it had been under. Slowly but surely, the police barricades were removed from around the three centers of activity. Traffic began to return to its normal flow along the wide boulevards. Glass was swept up, and order was being restored. Life would be no more for the young black news reporter, and it would be forever different for each hostage who was held. Life would be different for Khaalis and his eleven followers, who would be spending the majority of their lives confined to the boredom of prison. Life for all of us would change. We now had memories that could have readily turned into nightmares. We all knew in our hearts that the part we played in bringing this crisis to a successful and peaceful end relied greatly on good fortune. We also knew that close proximity to the main decision makers in government made this possible. We looked in the faces of our SWAT members and members of the tactical units of the metro Police Department and realized that we spared their lives for perhaps another event. We were all grateful because we knew it could have been very different.

Very shortly after the crisis, FBI Director Clarence Kelley received the following letter:

UNITED STATES DEPARTMENT OF JUSTICE

OFFICE OF THE UNITED STATES ATTORNEY

WASHINGTON, D.C. 20001

ADDRESS ALL MAIL TO:
UNITED STATES ATTORNEY
ROOM 3138-C
UNITED STATES COURT HOUSE BUILDING
3RD AND CONSTITUTION AVENUE NW.

March 15, 1977

IN REPLY, PLEASE REFER TO
INITIALS AND NUMBER

Honorable Clarence M. Kelley
Director, Federal Bureau of
  Investigation
Room 7176 - JEH Building
Washington, D. C.

Dear Director Kelley:

    I wish to bring to your attention and commend Special Agent Patrick J. Mullany of the Behavioral Science Unit, FBI Academy, Quantico, Virginia, for his contribution to the peaceful resolution of the recent takeover-hostage crisis in the District of Columbia.

    Special Agent Mullany remained with us throughout the crisis until its peaceful resolution. His knowledge and experience in these kinds of situations was invaluable to all of us. He was patient and persevering; his advice and insights were tremendously helpful. He should be commended for his outstanding effort.

    In addition, may I compliment the entire Washington Field Office under the leadership of Nick Stames for its key role in achieving the release of the hostages without harm and surrender of the perpetrators.

                               Sincerely,

                               EARL J. SILBERT
                               United States Attorney

EJS:owt

Additionally, a handwritten note was sent personally to me from the Ambassador of Pakistan, S. Yaqub-Khan. It read as follows:

Dear Mr. Mullany:

I am writing you to express my unbounded admiration and gratitude for the assistance and cooperation we received from you on March 11–12 in the Police Headquarters. Your advice and judgment contributed immeasurably to whatever little we might have been able to do, and the successful outcome of the "operation" owes much more to your wise counsel and cool decision making than to our modest endeavors.

It is a privilege knowing you and working with you, and I cherish greatly the bond of friendship that has been forged between us.

Sincerely,
S. Yaqub-Khan

Strange things happened during the course of negotiating with the Hanafi Muslims. We formed a sense of togetherness while negotiating and also a sense of friendship. When the negotiations were completed and the crisis had passed, everyone involved went their separate ways. What was shared was a real-life drama, each of us playing a part. What was experienced was all of us going to the brink of a near human tragedy and being able to turn around without additional lives being lost. It was, in many ways, being in battle and surviving to tell the story.

The press caught on to this event big time. The FBI was being pressured to tell the story of the Hanafi Muslim negotiating plan. Homer Boynton was in charge of the press office and urged me to make myself available to the media. He had lined up a few media venues that had an interest in the story. *The Washington Post* was one, and *The New York Times* was another, along with one or two magazines. Needless to say, the press coverage was wide because this was an event that had grabbed the country's attention for a week. One such article started with my recounting the trip from Cleveland and arriving in Washington, commanding a taxi to get into the district. Everything went well until the number-three man in the FBI read the papers. Jack McDermott was a very bright man and extremely well respected, but it did not sit well with him that someone other than a special agent in charge speak to the media. I was summoned to his office and received a rather thorough dressing down. One of his comments stayed with me. "Do you tell everybody what you do for a living?" He was directly referring to the lead into *The Washington Post* story and my conversation with the cab driver. At the time, it had been clear to me that the only way to get a cab driver to take me where I needed to go was by identifying who I was. I politely took the dressing down and was excused. It appeared to me that I had a pretty decent reputation as a negotiator but was doing rather poorly with the politics of a bureaucracy.

Shortly after this case ended and before Khaalis appeared in court, I was on a road trip out of town when I received a call from Jack Steward at the FBI academy. According to Jack, the Washington field office had received information that Khaalis had made a reference about me in a conversation. It was not clear whether this was a telephone overhear or words from an informant. What was at issue, and obviously grew out of the press coverage, was Khaalis's remark: "Let's see how well he can negotiate for his own family." This concerned the FBI to the extent that Jack Steward made a visit to my home and left a shotgun with my wife. She was cautioned to be observant of any strangers hanging around and, if she was concerned, to immediately let both the police and FBI know.

My wife and a shotgun was enough to chuckle about. Had they left a fishing rod, it would have been more useful. I returned the next day and was comforted somewhat by having the shotgun available. Fortunately, nothing ever came of the threat. Khaalis's gang never got out of jail, and ultimately, Khaalis was convicted and sent to prison in Atlanta.

The Hanafi Muslim case taught us many lessons. It truly was one of the first hostage cases involving many elements of the US government. It was an interface between federal and local law enforcement. The State Department was at the center of the negotiations. The federal courts were also involved. The lesson learned was that having all these branches of government in close proximity greatly enhanced the ability to make policy decisions in a timely manner, aiding in the crisis. While there were moments of distrust and hesitancy, at the end of the day, all elements worked toward the most important goal of saving lives. In theory, it is easy to state that the primary goal of negotiating is to save lives, but in practice, saving lives can disappear behind imaginary precedents being established.

Driving home early that Friday morning in March, I looked back on a week of madness. In many ways, I had a sense of sadness for both Moore and Khaalis. At some point in their lives, they intended to serve their country by being in the military. They were good people who allowed bad things happen to them. Cory Moore's causation, undoubtedly, was a mind that suffered serious mental illness. The demons and voices in his life led him to believe all white people should leave the face of this earth. On the other hand, Khaalis was trying to lead a good life. He had dedicated himself to God and had a following. He broke away from what he viewed as badly motivated people to form a more just following of individuals heeding the words of Allah. What happened to Khaalis was unforgivable. It was difficult to imagine where any of us would be if someone slaughtered our family. Clearly, a person's sense of revenge and hatred would need the greatest set of controls not to strike back. For Khaalis, Allah and the Koran led him on a course of self-justified revenge. There was no doubt in my mind that Khaalis would have beheaded the killers of his family. Where does the blame go when the equation of murder within a person is so radically upset? Khaalis lived with terrible memories until he died several years ago in prison. Most unfortunate for Khaalis, his memories were not the product of his sick mind but rather were the deeds of very sick minds that turned to slaughtering the innocent for the purpose of delivering a message.

Thirty-seven years after this event, my greatest reward came in the form of a phone call. Paul Green reached out to me and thanked me for being instrumental in saving his life during the takeover of the B'nai B'rith Building. He credited me with contributing to the successful outcome of this hostage case. He stated that he felt his life had been given back to him, and he had the reward of seeing his daughters grow up into womanhood. Paul was one of the hostages who was held and severely beaten. He feared for his life during this terrible incident and was grateful that he was spared.

CHAPTER 7

To Touch a Saint

As a direct outgrowth of psychological profiling and the way it was applied to hostage negotiation incidents, attention was being placed on what happens to a victim of a hostage or long-term kidnap case. Every kidnap and hostage case handled gave clear indications that victims of these type of events behaved differently.

Dick Hall, while saying very little in a negative way about his captor, Tony Kiritsis, had a rather dramatic change in life after facing death. Many of the hostages exiting from the B'nai B'rith Building expressed gratitude for the treatment they received while being held captive. Betty Neal expressed words of compassion for Khaalis. There are many well-documented cases, including that of Patty Hearst, in which captivity has led to compliance with the captors. In the early 1970s, a bank robbery that went bad in Stockholm, Sweden, gave birth to the phenomenon called the "Stockholm Syndrome." In this bank robbery, the gunmen held their hostages in a bank vault. During the tense hours of negotiation, the robbers became acquainted with their victims, and relationships developed—to the authorities' surprise.

While it was more popularly referred to as the "Stockholm Syndrome," what was happening was actually far more involved than someone falling in love with the bad guy. What was taking place was critical for anyone handling a hostage or kidnap case to fully understand because the behavior of a victim has a direct effect on the outcome.

After studying the effects of captivity on many individuals, we came to understand that the captivity phenomenon was based in large part on the will of an individual to survive. What happens to a captivity victim occurs in stages or events that seem to be present in most cases. What was central to being a victim was survival identification and transference of feelings with one's captors. Many factors entered into this, and there were distinct differences in very case. Victims who were blindfolded or hooded had greater difficulty developing meaningful contacts with their captors. Victims held in total isolation were also at a great deficit.

At the time of being grabbed as a kidnap victim, the greatest concern is whether you are going to be killed. In most cases, the act of kidnapping is violent, sudden, and well planned. This is the period of the highest risk to the victim. It is the time when the victim realizes that death is a reality. If the person being taken is physically beaten or shot, the realization of death is reinforced. How the victim behaves at this point is very important. Behavior at either extreme—cowardly or heroic—can precipitate violence. The best advice for a potential kidnap victim is (1) do not resist, and (2) try to escape only if you are sure you will be successful.

The life/death experience is very real and can linger in a person's mind forever. It will be present in a victim's mind for the entire duration of a kidnapping. Once the victim is stored in a secure place, such as a halfway house or a safe house, an incredible sense of isolation takes over. The isolation can be real or imagined. Kidnappings in Colombia are well known for their length of time, and the holding of a victim is in an isolated part of the jungle. What is most important is the mental frame of mind of the kidnap victim. The victim could be surrounded by a dozen foreign-speaking individuals and still have the same feeling of isolation as the person left in solitary confinement. Many prisoners of war, especially during the Vietnam War, were left in solitary confinement for very long periods. How the victim handles solitary confinement is critical to survival. The victim must remain mentally focused and must use the long hours and days of confinement profitably, staying mentally active. Mental activity might include recollections of happier times with one's family or setting up imaginary vacations for the future. The victim must stay mentally alert, even if mental activity is limited to learning the names of the captors.

Isolation can play very hard and real tricks on your mind, causing the mind to concentrate only on the fact that you will be killed. Isolation can shut out the possibility of surviving this terrible crisis. If isolation is accompanied by environmental deprivation, such as darkness, it can be very disorienting. Every effort should be made to keep track of the time of day and the day of the week. Total isolation will deprive you of the ability to do that. In some manner, the victim must set up a scheme or system to substitute for the sun coming up and going down. Sleep deprivation can add to a sense of isolation. Enough sleep deprivation will also lead to delusional thoughts, which can be based on either real or imagined events. The more professional kidnappers of the world know how to work isolation on a victim. Many kidnap groups will have little or no contact with their victim. During the limited times they have contact, they will do so masked or with their faces hidden in some manner. This type of isolation makes it impossible for the victim to establish a rapport with his/her captors. Establishing a rapport with one's captors is critical. The more a victim is able to portray himself/herself as a human being, the more difficult it becomes for the captors to kill the victim.

Real or imagined isolation leads to mental confusion. A total absence of any reference point in life is an incredible burden to live with. When hours, days, weeks, months, and even years run together, a sense of disorientation sets in. When the victim does not know when a week begins and ends, time becomes irrelevant and burdensome. The victim will grow angry not knowing whether it is winter, fall, spring, or summer. The inability to converse with someone because of the captors' unwillingness to converse or because of a language barrier hastens the mental sense of disorientation in a kidnap victim. Many victims will catch themselves talking out loud to themselves just to hear someone. Many victims will wisely set up a calendar system, so they can stay in touch with the reality of passing time. Captivity can bring an increased disorientation as to whether they are eating breakfast, lunch, or dinner, simply because the captor chooses to feed them only once a day.

It is during this period that the victim loses all confidence in those responsible for his/her release. The more time goes by with nothing happening and no signs of rescue, the less faith the victim will have in his company, country, and family. The victim will be convinced of the impossibility of anyone helping him. If the victim is not allowed to maintain personal cleanliness, his sense of disorientation increases, along with a restless sense of hopelessness. During this period, if punishment is introduced, the mental state of depression is virtually impossible to control. Punishment can occur as physical beatings or in the form of environmental elements, such as blaring light twenty-four hours per day, the total absence of light, constant loud radio, or noise such as screams of torture.

If such an atmosphere is allowed to continue for weeks or months, the victim will reach the lowest point of captivity. It is at this point that thoughts of suicide will occur. It will become more difficult to think positive thoughts about family and happier times. The imagination will not be as vivid as it once was. The person held in this manner will come to a crossroad and will choose to either give up in captivity to despair or continue to take as much control of his captivity as he possible can. The crossroad is almost predetermined. What a person carries into captivity bears fruit in captivity. The president of Italy, Aldo Moro, when captured and held by the Red Brigades in the early '70s, totally came apart in captivity. His conduct in captivity confused the Italian government and increased the level of difficulty of the attempted negotiations for his release. On one occasion, Aldo Moro's wife went along with the government's strategy, pleading with the captors to give Aldo Moro vital medicine—only to be contradicted by Moro and chastised for their foolishness. Aldo Moro as president was the architect behind the policies of no negotiating with terrorists and no ransom payment to terrorists for kidnap victims—only to castigate his country and political party when they refused to pay a ransom for his freedom. Before captivity, Moro was a rigid, inadequate personality who fell prey to hypochondria. In captivity, his true personality came forward, and captivity brought him down to defeat. In many ways, the Italian government, while saddened when he was discarded, dead, on the streets of Italy, was spared the difficulty of rehabilitating him as president after captivity.

The preconditioning of a potential victim of kidnapping is critical. There are many examples of individuals, captured for long periods, who survived to lead productive and positive lives. Senator John McCann is an excellent example of an individual who faced death, isolation, despair, and disorientation but still survived these most difficult times. There are countless examples, both from the military and from the private sector, in which survival was not a surrendering of all that was held dear. What has been a constant factor in the outcome of kidnap victims was that character played a vital role in how the person survived. Individuals with strong character had what it took to survive the worst kind of treatment under the most difficult of circumstances. After hitting the low point of captivity, marked by despair and disorientation and sometimes thoughts of suicide, the strong of character decide to depend upon themselves for survival. They are able to muster up the strength to make the most of their captivity, even if they are in a seven-foot-square cell. They become determined, no matter what, to get the upper hand. They learn how to survive day by day, hour by hour, and minute by minute. These individuals, while they would welcome a safe rescue attempt, spend little time on the fantasy of such events but take control of everything around them to survive. They master control of their feelings, thoughts, and actions and become less threatened by their captors. In many ways, they take control of their captors without the captors being aware of it.

At this point in captivity, the survivor is willing to risk forming relationships with those who have control over the confinement. This happens in very subtle ways. Talk of one's family, children, home, grandchildren, and so forth—directed at presenting the victim as a human being—make the captor see the victim in a different light.

As mentioned earlier, however, if the victim is kept totally isolated and hooded, it is almost impossible to convey human feelings to the captors. Claude Fry, in his captivity, was highly successful in communicating to his captors and was able to share his medical situation. Fry had a heart condition and convinced the Tupamaros Guerrillas that he needed medical attention. The Tupamaros kidnapped a doctor and brought him to Fry, attending to his medical needs.

It is at this point in captivity that, to the outsider, strange things seem to happen. When all the stages have been passed through—facing death, isolation, disorientation, despair, and self-dependence for survival—the victim becomes the controller.

It is incomplete to simply say, "This is the Stockholm Syndrome." What is taking place is an emotional transference within the hostage/kidnap environment. If allowed to "eyeball" his captors, the victim on many occasions, even with the most hardened terrorists, is making it more difficult for the terrorists to kill. The simple reason is that the captor now knows his victim. Very sophisticated groups and even countries are aware of this happening. If a decision is made to kill the victim, someone other than the "jailer" will do the killing. The emotional transference with a captor is not viewed as a negative in a kidnap case but rather a positive. In many ways this identification with the captors increases the likelihood of the victim surviving. There have been documented cases in which the captors and victims have entered into agreements to meet each other at a prearranged location some years after the event was over. In other documented occasions, criticism has been directed at victims who refused to talk negatively about their kidnappers after they were released. There have been documented cases in courtroom testimony where victims were able to give only positive testimony about those who held them in captivity.

Being held for a short or long period as a kidnap victim or hostage can have serious effects on an individual. The most obvious short-term effect is the victim's loss of objectivity. It is not practical to rely on a victim's unverified assessment of the situation. The victim is impaired in the perception of reality, and often the victim will show complicity with the captor. The biggest area of complicity is the lack of trust for the authorities handling the crisis. The victim feels safer and more under control with his captors than he does with any plan to assault where he is being held. Risking letting the victim know the tactical plan is very chancy. The hostage takeover of the DC jail in Washington was an exception to this very rule. We secreted the key to the cellblock in a female sanitary napkin. The risk was taken, and the secretary never revealed the plan to her captors. She was able to unlock the back door of the cellblock, and all the hostages escaped safely.

Being held as a hostage or kidnap victim can result in short-term or long-term psychological problems. These problems are compounded by what has taken place in the crisis. If someone has been killed in your presence, guilt for lack of action can haunt a person for a lifetime. If your conduct as a victim was less than admirable, second-guessing your behavior can become a lifetime sport. Witnessing the death of the captors can be an experience that causes the kidnap victim to question the wisdom of the authorities for years to come. The trauma of facing death and surviving can be a nightmare that requires years of professional help. The inability to concentrate after such an experience can become a characteristic of the victim. Sleeplessness is a common short-term effect that needs to be dealt with.

The most puzzling of effects after being a victim to a hostage or kidnap case is the family's or organization's rejection of the victim after the incident. Many times a kidnap victim comes home in a rather fragile condition only to face immediate media scrutiny. On occasion, the victim can become a short-lived celebrity of sorts. The family members, on the other hand, feel that they, too, have been victims, especially if they have paid a large ransom for the victim's release. While the victim was being held, the family became very independent in decision making and getting on with life during a difficult time. The reentry of the victim into the family is a major disruption from the normal chaos they had become used to. The dynamics of this event and its aftermath can be an enormous strain on a marriage. Professional care can act as a wise counsel for a family experiencing this posttraumatic stress.

Stranger yet is the rejection an organization can show to a released victim. The number of months or years the victim has been missing compounds this rejection. In the absence of the victim, the organization was forced to continue business as usual. The replacement for the victim resents the return. Many times the organization blames the victim for being caught, very much holding the victim responsible for the large ransom it was forced to pay. The organization will also try to distance itself from the negative impact the crisis had on its company. It is not uncommon that once the victim has been returned from a long period of captivity, he is never able to reach the high level of trust he once had before captivity. In many ways, the victim is damaged goods, never to be fully trusted again. Years ago, the US Military had a black colonel who was held captive in the Middle East. At the time he was the highest-ranking black colonel in the military. He was blamed for his captivity and was even criticized for assisting his captors in making a tape recording of his plea for release. Upon his successful release, he returned to the military but never made rank beyond where he was. He was damaged goods.

Not all organizations look upon released victims as damaged goods. William F. Neihaus was employed by Owens Illinois in Venezuela during the 1970s. On a Friday in February 1976, a terrorist group operating out of the jungles of Venezuela kidnapped Niehaus. Neihaus was held for some forty months. He was released June 29, 1979. Neihaus was welcomed back to his job with Owens Illinois, where he had been a regional vice president. His experience in captivity could make an excellent textbook on how to successfully survive a kidnapping. Not only was Neihaus a well-educated and forceful business executive, but he had been in the US Military, serving in Korea. He was well disciplined and structured. He made good decisions in life before captivity and made excellent decisions during captivity. Upon his release, many were amazed at the physical and mental condition he was in. In his own words, "It was no wonder I was in good condition upon my release because for the last forty months, I lived out in the open, did not smoke, and drank very rarely. It was in many ways a forced campout with guns." Speaking before a security conference after his release, his comments were well put. Niehaus admitted that had he been offered a course on kidnap survival before his kidnapping, it would not have interested him. In his comments concerning captivity, he presented five main objectives. The first was to be human. Second, communicate with your captors. Third, establish individual goals to achieve. Fourth, eat and exercise as much as your captors allow. Fifth, have faith.

Niehaus admitted that he was not overly religious before he was captured, but he claimed that captivity gave him the time to reflect on where he was in life. That ability to not give up hope and to have faith that somehow he would survive this ordeal was vital during captivity. Niehaus very concisely summarized the important issues facing a kidnap victim: being mentally, physically, and spiritually strong before captivity goes a long way once captured.

One of the most interesting domestic cases in the United States was the kidnapping of Patricia Hearst in 1974. There was an inordinate amount of hostility toward Patricia Hearst when she was first captured by the Symbionese Liberation Army (SLA). The SLA was a tight-knit group of radicals, predominately female, and led by a black male called Cinque. Cinque was by no means an intellectual but rather was a typical criminal of the time. While he was regarded as the leader of the SLA, the group dynamics defied his leadership role. The real leadership rested in the strong females who made the plans and called most of the shots. Patricia Hearst was stereotyped as the rich heiress who was wasting her life in a perpetual college environment. Little media sympathy was directed her way, and from the very beginning, serious questions arose regarding whether she was originally part of the SLA. Nothing could be further from the truth. Patty Hearst had no prior knowledge of her captors and no part in her own kidnapping.

To assist the prosecution in this case, I journeyed to San Francisco in an effort to brief the prosecuting attorney on what was regarded, at the time, the phenomenon of being held as a kidnap victim. Vincent Pugliosi, of helter-skelter fame, was also asked to assist on the preparation of this case. After my presentation on what happens to a true kidnap victim, the prosecution team all but had me escorted out of town for fear the defense in the case would get wind of such radical thinking. I felt that my purpose was to prepare them to hear some of this theory in court in defense of Patricia Hearst. However, it was clear to me that the prosecution wanted no part of these concepts and certainly did not feel it would hear them in court from F. Lee Bailey and his team.

It turned out that the prosecution had guessed correctly: F. Lee Bailey never came close to understanding or presenting what actually happened to Patricia Hearst. Patricia Hearst was a genuine kidnap victim, no different from most kidnap victims. She was violently captured, hustled into a hiding place, which consisted of a locked closet chained shut, and tied to a chair. Twenty-four hours a day, she was victim to a loud blaring radio. She was harangued and abused by Cinque. She was poorly fed and forced to listen to the radical barrage of the SLA. Patricia Hearst was like most college girls in the mid-1970s. Her mind was full of lofty ideals. She had been the product of a wealthy family environment that had lavished her with material wealth. She was a good person perhaps seeking direction in life. She had never been trained to survive a kidnap and was not a person with a fully developed personality that could withstand the pressures of a kidnapping.

While she was in captivity, the SLA concocted a plan of releasing recorded tapes of Patricia Hearst. These tapes would document the progression of events surrounding her kidnapping. Tape number five would prove to be the most interesting, when Patricia Hearst announced to the world her conversion to the SLA and referred to herself as Tania.

Dick Gallagher was the assistant director of the criminal division when Patricia Hearst was kidnapped. An individual by the name of Dr. Murray Miron contacted him. Dr. Miron was on the staff of the University of Syracuse and had a strange discipline: psycholinguistics. This was the study and identification of word usage. According to Gallagher, Miron had closely analyzed the first four tapes released by the SLA and predicted that in tape five, Patricia Hearst would join the SLA, announcing her membership with them. Dick Gallagher did not have the time or background to fully hear out Dr. Miron's work, but he thought it would be of some value to the behavioral science unit. We met with Dr. Miron and started what would be an interesting but confusing relationship. Dr. Miron's efforts on the Patricia Hearst case very closely paralleled the work we had been doing. Howard Teten and I firmly believed that from tape one to tape four, there was a marked degradation in Patricia Hearst's mentality. We felt strongly that she was being influenced by the SLA, and we believed there was a high likelihood that she would become compliant with them. Our tape analysis was based on a pure psychological assessment. Dr. Miron's was based on word usage. We both arrived at the same point, and in fact, tape five had Patricia being very critical of her family, denouncing them and their efforts, and joining ranks with the SLA, taking on the name Tania.

I have always been torn by what happened to Patricia Hearst in the trial that would ultimately convict her of bank robbery. The reason I was torn was that I felt very few among the public accepted the fact that she was a victim to violence, mental torture, and true kidnapping. In my mind, Patricia Hearst was a very malleable personality, easily led and swayed. With the pressure of violence and ultimate death, her personality would conform to that which would allow her to survive. When she became Tania, she reinforced what most believed to begin with—that she was part of the kidnapping. Even if a logical case were presented in her defense, portraying her as a credible victim with diminished responsibility for her actions might not have swayed a jury's verdict. I always had the sense that had a convent of nuns kidnapped Patricia Hearst, she would have become a nun. I found it fascinating that she would later marry the police officer who served as her bodyguard. What has been rewarding in all of this is that time would heal her wounds of being a victim and that she would mature into a well-rounded woman whom people respect. Her pardon for her actions was well received and just.

Murray Miron, on the other hand, did what very few people were able to achieve. He became a consultant to the FBI in the area of threat assessment. For at least three years, I had the responsibility of coordinating his efforts. He became an institution within an institution. It was most unfortunate that he was ever introduced to the behavioral science unit because what happened from that point would be his eventual downfall. He became fascinated in the work we were doing on psychological profiling and allowed himself to melt into pure psychological profiling while still using the structure of word usage. Had he stayed with his original concept of identifying people and their potential by the words they wrote or spoke, he would have survived. Instead, his analysis of many documents and tapes in the 1970s disintegrated into a form of psycho-garble. He overextended himself, using the same research base for many branches of government, all the while picking up separate contracts. Perhaps the worst insult was his attempt to write a book on hostage negotiations in which he used, as examples, four cases we had been involved in. He never once spoke to me about these cases, and his book reflected this shortcoming with many factual errors. I thought it ironic that, as a word specialist, he misspelled my name throughout the book.

The psychology of what happens to a victim of kidnapping has to be rewritten upon the release of every new victim. While there is a body of theory that graphically charts what takes place in a kidnapping, no firm body of information exists on how each individual reacts to a kidnapping. One of the most impressive victims I have ever interviewed, listening to his story of captivity, was Father Martin Jenco.

On January 8, 1985, the Shiite Muslim extremists in the residential section of West Beirut abducted Father Martin Jenco. He was held for nineteen months before he was released in the Syrian-controlled Bekaa Valley in the eastern part of Lebanon on July 26, 1986. Father Jenco was a member of the Servite Order, a religious order in the Catholic Church. He had been assigned as director of the Catholic relief program in Beirut and lived near the American University. Father Jenco was well aware of the difficulty that was going on in the region. What he was not well aware of was that he would be taken as a kidnap victim through mistaken identity and held against his will for so long. He found himself a victim to a brutal Shiite Muslim group that had great animosity for anyone and anything non-Muslim. Father Jenco was held with fellow American hostages, Terry Anderson and William Buckley. On two occasions, as I sat and listened to Father Jenco recount his agony in captivity, I had the sense that in shaking this man's hand, I had touched a saint.

The Shiite Muslims who held Terry Anderson for almost eight years and beat to death William Buckley were by far the most vicious and terrible captors for anyone held in captivity. The Shiite behavior toward victims would make those held in Colombia by the ELN feel that they were in a five star hotel. The Shiites were known for their cruelty and bloody treatment of their hostages. They had little or no regard for their victims, often leaving them to live in their own filth, sweat, blood, and tears. They showed little care for them and didn't give them medical attention or the basic needs of life: food and water. Their cruelty was marked by extreme sadomasochistic behavior when they tortured their victims, and they demanded that their victims remain hooded in their presence. They kept them chained to the floor with not even a cot to rest on. They kept them in solitude for the most part and would punish them severely if the victims were caught conversing with their fellow hostages. The Shiites had perfected cruelty, all under the shadow of the rigid god they claimed to follow.

Father Jenco described his captivity at a security conference on November 14, 1991.

⊗

This morning when I was getting ready, I watched CNN, and as you know, there are meetings going in Madrid concerning a Middle Eastern peace initiative. As I recall in Friedman's book, *From Beirut to Jerusalem,* in the last chapter of his book, he writes this: After all, there has to be something more to Middle East politics than that which we see, or at least God intended that there be. Surely there is a meaning to a critical portion of the book of Exodus, when God commands Moses to liberate his people from bondage in Egypt. Meant to be saving was a sign from the Lord, when Moses asked God a simple question: what is your name? How should I identify you to my people? God gave Moses an intriguing answer. On the one hand, he tells Moses to tell the children of Israel that he the Lord is the God of their ancestors, the God of Abraham, God of Sarah, God of Isaac, and the God of Jacob. Some modern rabbis have interpreted this as God telling Moses, I am the God of your past, of your memories, of your historical roots, of your ancestors. All of which I know are important to you. I was with you in your suffering and in your joy, wherever you were. On the other hand, though, God tells Moses to tell the children of Israel that he, the Lord, is also someone else. God says, "Tell the people, I will be who I will be." The rabbis interpret this as saying, "Although I was with you in your past, I am also the God who invites new possibilities for the future. Your past, while essential in your identity, does not exhaust all you can become, either as individuals or as a community." For I tell you, then, there is a balanced land out there, I tell you, then, that the future can be different from the past for you, and your community can become something different. How exciting it is, for as I was watching this morning, this should be for all of us, to know that tomorrow can be different from yesterday. Also on television this morning, they had a group of children, Arab children, and they were talking to the children about what is happening in Madrid. It was Christmas Eve, and I had been in Beirut, and they said it was not safe for me to be in West Beirut and that it would be better if I went into the Christian side in East Beirut. So I went over to celebrate midnight Mass, and I walked to this home, an elegant home. We had just come from a Christian Palestinian campfire party, and I walked into this house and the table was set with food; they had five servants waiting on us, and Papa Noel was giving out gifts. They were a group of old people, young people, and middle-aged people celebrating the birth of the servant of peace, Jesus. I looked around that room and said to myself, "I am not going to talk about the infancy narrative of Jesus; I am going to speak with them about a sermon on the mount that is very costly and very demanding because it requires an adult conviction to the Gospel. In the kiss of peace that we say at Mass, I could have said, "Absolam," which would mean, "Peace be with you." Instead, I said, "Shalom"; peace be with you, thank you. Jesus was a Jew. Shalom was a marvelous word of peace, and I went around the room and said "Shalom" to people, and at the end of Mass, the woman of the house came to me and said, "Where, American, do you get the right to use this Jewish word in our home?"

I said to myself, "Oh, what a tragedy." Perhaps recent events in the Middle East are as recent as Cain and Abel. I was very discouraged by that, and I sat on the floor with the children. I was reminded of that this morning when I saw the little kids on CNN speaking to their interviewer about their world, and these little ones were telling us about a world of peace that you would not believe. I sat on the floor thinking that perhaps we pass this on to our children, and we pass on our bigotries and our prejudices and our hates. I spoke to the children on the floor, and I asked them what they wished their world would be. Like the children today, you would not believe the world of peace they spoke of. The adults were listening to their children, and I looked up and said to them, "Does anyone ever listen to the children?" The old folks later on came up to me and said, "Father would you hear my confession?" The old and the young were very much caught up in this peace initiative. The middle-aged group seemed not distracted.

Sunday was Terry Anderson's seventh birth date as a hostage. And I am reminded that I had hoped, when I was a hostage, that the guards would say, that the other Americans would say, "It is Father Jenco's feast day," and they would bring a cake in. "It is Father Jenco's birthday," and they would bring a cake in. "It is Father Jenco's anniversary of priesthood," and they would bring a cake in. With the other ones, when their birthday would come up, we would hope for some extra food or a birthday cake. I remember when it was Tom Sutherland's birthday, they brought in cupcakes. Sutherland said, "How come Father Jenco gets birthday cake, and I only get cupcakes?" But they [hostages] would use me to get things out of the guards. Sunday, Terry Anderson celebrated his seventh birthday as a hostage, and I thought, "Wouldn't it be marvelous if Terry Anderson could celebrate his forty-first birthday with candles on top of a cake and celebrate that in the light of freedom?" I know that soon this man will be out and able to celebrate his freedom.

It was July 4, 1984, and I was associate director of the Catholic relief services in Indochinese refugee camps in Thailand—what a marvelous ministry that was—when the phone rang and the question was asked, "Marty, would you be willing to go to Beirut, Lebanon, as the program director of Catholic relief services there?" Their idea was that, being British, I would be safe and secure in that part of the world. My response to it was first an internal response s, speaking to God, and I said, "My God, they understood that going to the Middle East was not going to be an easy position there," so I asked for permission to go to the Middle East before I would accept the position there. Then July 10, I flew to Larnaka and went by plane to Beirut. It was very strange because that was the first time the airport was open in a long time. I went to Beirut and spent ten days there, and had a chance to see what it was all about there. I went there in 1976 to participate in a new relief organization with food and clothing and medicine, and then we expanded to a program of reconstructing hospital, schools, orphanages, and homes. We even had a place for the old women who were former prostitutes whom we found living in these bombed-out shelters, and we opened a community for them. I had the chance to meet the heads of religion, Roman Catholics, Greek Catholics, Syrian Catholics, Maronite Catholics, now the Greek Churches, the Protestant churches. I had a chance to meet the heads of the churches of Islam, Sunnis and the Shiites, the Drews. As you know, there are one billion people of Islam in the world. Many people think that Islam only belongs to Northern Africa; the majority of the people of Islam are not in Northern Africa. Eighty-five percent of the people of Islam belong to a people called Sunni, and 14 percent belong to the group called Shiite. The great division of the people of Islam takes place early in the history of Islam. The question is who is the rightful successor of Mohammad? The Sunnis will say it is them; the Shiites will say no it is blood lineage. And that division comes down to this day. Among people, it is a marvelous thing to see.

After ten days, I said yes. I went back to Thailand to pack my bags and off back home to Joliet, Illinois, to celebrate my twenty-fifth anniversary as a priest. I arrived there on October 1.

It looked like what was involved in all the peace initiatives was taking root and the government was finding meaning, so I said yes. But when I got back at the setting of the sun, once again violence came upon Lebanon, and particularly the city of Beirut. I lived in an apartment building that was adjacent to the American University, which was on the west side. Some of my Christian brothers would complain that I was on the west side and not on the Christian side. In fact, I remember receiving a letter from one of my fellow priests saying, "Remember, you have a responsibility to the New Testament; you are a tour guide for the household of the Lord first." But my mandate was not that at all. My mandate as director of the Catholic relief services—I was destined to serve the poorest of the poor, and the poorest of the poor were the Shiites; it was the Shiite community. They would live at one time in Beirut, Lebanon, and because of their trade in the kingdom of charity and because of the absence of so many of the others, the Sunnis and the Christians fled the country, and as you know, the government of Lebanon was a government that was given to them in a very unique way with a constitution that had tremendous factions once; the president had to be Maronite Catholic, the prime minister a Sunni, and the parliament Shiite. The Drews and others, you know, were given minor offices in government. When the Shiites began to say, "We are the majority now," they wanted a piece of the action. And I think rightly so. They were the poorest of the poor. Perhaps you have had the chance to see the buildings of southern Beirut and see where the Shiites lived. They lived in huts and shanty homes. They do not have the advantages that the others have. My mandate was to touch the poorest of the poor.

It was the morning of January 7, and I was not feeling well. The violence around my building was so phenomenal. My dad died at the age of fifty-three of a massive heart attack and I was having chest pains and a lot of stress, so I said to Madeline Trays, an American sister I had met, "Do you know a good doctor around here?" And she designated one up the street, and I walked there. He did a series of tests for me and he said that he would call me that evening to tell me the results of these tests. "And tomorrow, I will see you for another test."

So I went back to my office and told my staff that I would not be there in the morning. At about noon, I went home. My suspicion is I should have been kidnapped that day, that afternoon. That evening, I called a priest brother of mine who was a Vatican diplomat. His name is John. I said, "John, do you know every day, when I go into work, I see the Muslim women standing on a green line. And they ask the Christian sentry, those that they have kidnapped, 'Please John, ask the Holy Father to intervene on their behalf to set them free.'"

His response to me was, "Father, I do not know too much about that."

And I was angry when I heard his response, and I asked, "What do you need to know?"

The doctor called and said, "You have a blood condition we need to look at." That is how the evening ended. Early in the morning, as usual, I got up and went out, celebrated Mass, and came back to prepare myself; my van was coming by to pick me up at 7:30 in the morning. I was to go to the Lebanese government for what we used to call a signature ceremony. We designated institutions that fell within the mandate of needing moneys, but the Lebanese government had to agree with them. They would say yes to that, and then they would signature it. That was on my mind, and on my mind was to go to the doctor.

Sahib picked me up, and I was in my car. I was going through my notes, and we were in a very congested area, in the business section, and I looked to the right and saw four policemen directing traffic that morning. The owner of the grocery store was directing traffic, and I said to Radii, "That seems very strange; four policeman standing on the corner, and this man up here, the owner of the grocery store, he is directing traffic. Doesn't that seem strange to you?" I just finished that conversation, and all of a sudden I hear this tremendous violence. Automatic weapons being shot in the air, and I looked up. I saw men rushing to my car, I heard the same violence coming from behind me, and I turned around and saw them rush the car with automatic weapons fired in the air. I turned to my driver and said, "I am going to be kidnapped." Within seconds, they were in the backseat of my car, and I find myself with Radii and two other men, three other men up front. The crowded streets were completely empty now. That morning was very strange now, for I was carrying a document in my folder that the American Embassy had given me when I had arrived there: "What to do when kidnapped." None of it made any sense now.

But because of the violence, we were quickly separated off and went down to an area on the corner; they threw my driver into a trunk of a car and then took me out of my car and put me on the floor of their car. Later my driver escaped somehow and let my office know that I had been kidnapped. They drove me to an isolated area near the airport, took me from the floor of the car, and threw me in the trunk of another car. As I was getting out of the first car, I was wearing a chain and a cross that was given to me on the occasion of my anniversary of my twenty-fifth year as a priest. It was something that came from Jerusalem, and I absolutely treasured it, and it came from beneath my collar, and the guards took it away and never gave it back. They threw me into the trunk of the car, and as you will recall, there was a young Polish priest by the name of J. J. Komieisko who was kidnapped a few weeks before my kidnapping. He was shoved into the trunk of a car and was killed.

So the first thing you think about, in the darkness of the trunk of a car, is that you are going to die. At one time in my life, I taught a course at St. Mary's Hospital in San Francisco on death and dying. I used Elizabeth Kubler Ross's book, *Death and Dying*, and there are stages you go through in the process of coming to the ultimate stage, which is the acceptance of your own death. I recall, when I was telling Pat, "I don't have the luxury now of going through those four stages. I quickly moved to the ultimate stage of accepting my own death now." Those reflections, even now, surprise me a little bit. One, in dying I thought I would be telling God how sinful I am; instead, I was telling God how beautiful God is. In every instance when they threatened me with death, I found myself speaking to God differently than I thought I would be now speaking to God.

They led me off to another place, where they transferred me to the trunk of an old junk car. And you know, in that part of the world—you see it on television and you read it in the news—what they do to old cars is they lace them with bombs, and they become terrible vehicles of violence, where innocent men, women, and children die. Once again, you think about death.

They moved me to the southern suburbs of Beirut to a one-story building that was under construction. They brought me in and sat me down on cinder block. They kept bringing people in to interview me, well-dressed people, people who spoke English impeccably. They would ask me, "Are you Joseph Kertin?"

I would say, "No, I am not he; I am Father Jenco." They kidnapped the wrong person. I thought that since they kidnapped the wrong person, surely they would set me free. Once, around 4:30 in the afternoon, I was chained but not blindfolded, and there was a young man sitting next to me. I was cold then; the sun was setting, and it gets cold there at that time of year when the sun sets. And I turned and looked into the eyes of the young man sitting next to me. I looked into the eyes of hate. He said, "You are dead."

And I said, "Why did you say that?"

He didn't respond to that question. Interesting to know, his name is Macmoud. In the course of my nineteen months, he was one of my guards who remained for the entire period of nineteen months. He doesn't know that I know who he is. There are times he used to beat me and say, "I will kill you." On the eve of my release, I stood in front of an elevator on July 26, 1986, in a building in the southern suburbs of Beirut. A man stood behind me. He was massaging my shoulders. It was not a touch of hate; it was not a touch of violence. It was a touch of compassion and love. For that was Macmoud. I wish I could have lifted my blindfold and turned to look into his eyes. I am sure that after nineteen months, it was not a look of hate anymore.

I had a young driver by the name of Abdul Ali who turned and said, "Here, Buddha," and he handed me a cross. It was so strange. I will share with you that story at the end. How that cross became so important for me and what I was all about at the end.

They bedded me down in a mud patch there, put a headset on my ears, and plugged it into a cassette player so all night long all I could hear was Arabic music. I could hear their conversation. They wanted to hear, perhaps, what CNN said about my kidnapping.

Early morning they woke me up and brought me to a toilet. I came out of the toilet, and they put an old sweater around my head, and they began to tape my body up to the tip of my nose. And I said, "Oh, what are they going to do? In the Arab world, they have to save face. What they are going to do is save face and drop me off at a hospital nearby." What they were doing was preparing me to move.

Once again, I am in the trunk of a car. They drive me to this building, and I can't see anything now. And later, I won't be able to watch because I have broken the gauze several times. They stand you up and put your ankles very close to one another, and they do a very tight taping of your body, like a mummy, and it goes all the way to the top of your head. They put a piece of cloth in your mouth and seal it shut with a piece of tape. It is only through your nostrils that you can breathe. And then they lift your body up and slide your body under the truck where the spare tire goes. I don't know where that is. I thought they were placing my body in a hearse, and for some strange reason, I could even smell flowers.

They moved me from the southern suburbs of Beirut to the Bekaa Valley. It took about three hours. When they hit a bump, my body flew up, and I hit my face on the bottom of the truck and my nose began to bleed. And it coagulated. I was having such a difficult time breathing. Experiencing such difficulty, I recalled the prayer of Jesus I used to teach my students at Berkeley; it is a prayer that rushes to me, that the desert foxes, the saints, used to say, a simple prayer of breathing in and breathing out, inhaling and exhaling while saying, "Lord Jesus, Son of David, have mercy on me."

And that is the prayer I prayed beneath that truck. It put me very much at peace. So when I finally arrived at the first of many places, I was out of it, though. The fumes came in there, and they had to drag me out. They dumped me on the side of the road there. Then they stood me up, and I couldn't stand. They had to lug me up four flights of stairs, and then they stood me up and cut the tapes off. They came to my mouth, and when they pulled the cloth out, I said in Latin, "Resurrecit sicut dixit, alleluia, alleluia: He has risen from the dead, alleluia, alleluia."

I was too naive to be a hostage. I took my blindfold off and gave these two young guys eyeball-to-eyeball contact, and these young guys looked into my eyes and said, "Oh, please, if someone comes into this prison, you must put your blindfold back on." And I was very sad, for when someone would put a key in the door, I put the blindfold back on. But for the most part of that first month, I could see.

There is a Jewish proverb that says when you get caught up in situations like these, the first thing you do is cry. The second thing you do is you sing. The third thing you do is you remain silent. I cried, I looked out the window, and there was snow there and birds, and I found myself singing, "Somewhere over the rainbow." And the next six months, I would live in total isolation and remain silent. From day one, I had to remind God of something now. I was chained to a radiator in a kitchen, and I had the sense of being a puppy dog. I ate off the floor. They allowed me to go to the toilet when they decided that I needed to go to the toilet. And I needed to tell God, "I am not an animal. I am a person of worth; I am a person of dignity. I am loved, and I am redeemed, and I do have a destiny."

People say, "Do you ever get any feedback, or do you have any flashbacks about this?" Sure, when I see somebody wearing cowboy boots with a copper tip.

When I was in another prison, chained to the wall and on the floor, blindfolded, I could see out from my blindfold a man standing next to my mat. He wore cowboy boots with copper tips, and I remember saying one day, "What hate inside this man." But then he stood on my forehead and squashed me. That was extremely painful. I said to him, "I am not an insect; I am a person of worth. I am a person of dignity. I am loved, and I am redeemed, and I do have a destiny.'

From day one, what I would do, because I am a priest, I would try to recall God's revealing words in the Hebrew and Christian covenants. What did God say about love, patience, and kindness, and gentleness, and forgiveness? And I would take a piece of bread, and knowing the Eucharistic prayer by heart, I would celebrate Eucharist. And I would retain a piece of the Eucharistic Christ, so when things got lonely or sad or frightening, I would hang on to the Eucharistic Christ. In one of my prisons that was going to be closed for two months, one day the guard said, "What do you have in your hand?"

I opened my hand, and there was the piece of bread, and I said, "That is Jesus." He didn't comprehend that is Jesus at all.

It was the morning of February 14, and I looked out the window and saw that the guards were very agitated and angry about something. I was allowed to go to the toilet, and I came out of the toilet. Instead of bringing me back into my kitchen prison, they brought me to this room, and there was a man. The man had two legs tied together. It was Jerry Levins. On February 14, Jerry Levins escaped. I got his room for a couple of hours. And for some unknown reason, they gave me a pencil. There I was writing on the wall: "Today is February 14, the feast of St. Valentine's Day."

I couldn't stay there very long because Jerry Levin had escaped. He would be able to tell people where we were. So once again, I am in the trunk of a car, and they drive me higher into the mountain, and it is frigid cold. And they kept me there about three hours. Then they finally got me out and brought me into this room where there were four cubicles. It was dark. It was so cold in that place that your urine would freeze. And when the guards left, I heard someone say, "Who are you?" It was William Buckley, the American diplomat.

I said, "I am Marty Jenco. I am a priest."

Then I heard the man to the left of me say, "I am Ben Weir. I am a Presbyterian minister." We three Americans were in that prison together, and next to me on the right were a man and a woman. They were from Saudi Arabia. They were diplomats. They do kidnap women, too.

It was on the morning of February 17, and I knelt in front of Ben Weir. Now Ben Weir had been a Presbyterian minister in Beirut for thirty years. He spoke Arabic, he read Arabic, and he was fluent in Arabic. Haas, the man who had me kidnapped, had me kneel in front of Ben Weir, and he tells Ben in Arabic what I am to write to my family. I choose to write to a famous American, and I choose Cardinal Bernardine. I wrote, "Dear Brothers and Sisters and Cardinal Bernardine, I shall be held hostage as long as the seventeen in Kuwait are held in the prisons of Kuwait." These were the seventeen Shiites who did violence to the American and French Embassies in Kuwait. And I had to continue to write, "If the American government would intervene on my behalf, I would be hanged." In my heart, I was saying to myself, "Oh, I prefer being shot." And then I said to Ben, "Is the correct English hanged or hung?" It is amazing what kind of questions you ask in those kinds of situations.

For some reason, they wouldn't give me any water. And Ben would push his water bottle around the cubicle, and he would share his bottle of water with me. We never talked after that. I took a piece of an orange peel—the young Shiites were very religious, and they would pray five times a day. Every time they addressed their prayer to Allah, I would address mine to Abba, my dear Father. And I took a piece of orange peel, and with the oil from the orange peel, I wrote on the wall in the cubicle, "Abba, dear Father, I love you very much, and Jesus is Lord." The guards would find these little bits of calligraphy I did, and they used to challenge me about them. And I would say to them that they gave me tremendous encouragement. Ben Weir would find them in other cells, and he said to me that I would not believe how much encouragement it gave him when he looked up and saw, "Abba, dear Father, I love you very much, and Jesus is Lord."

March 14, they said they were going to move me to another prison, and once again, I am in this room, and they said, "Stand up." And I am standing up, and again they start taping me, and they came to my mouth, and I said, "I cannot breathe when you do that." And because I said that, they whacked me on the head, put the cloth in my mouth, and sealed it shut. They were throwing me in the trunk of a car. There was this gentle person, though. He pulled the tape back and pulled the cloth out of my mouth. It was an act of love.

This time, they lace my body with explosives, and they tell me they have a triggering device in the cab of the truck, and if I make any noise, they will just blow me up.

They drove me through the southern suburbs of Beirut again, and this is where I end up in my clothes closet. Two feet by six feet, and now they blindfold me with a plastic bag over my head. I am chained hand and foot. I used these chains to cool off the extremities of my body; it was so hot in there. I used the chains also as a prayer form. When I was in the Bekaa valley, I formed a rosary out of a string from a potato sack. The young guards saw me praying, and from around his neck, he gives me his prayer beads. Because the people of Islam also pray with beads; they have thirty-three beads for the ninety-nine names they have for God. They touch a bead and give God a name. It is a marvelous prayer.

When I was in this new prison, I had a frightening experience once. They opened the door. They said, "What are those silver things in your mouth?"

And I said, "Those are fillings."

They said, "They are not fillings. You are a CIA spy. And those are transmitters. We might have to take them out."

And when they closed the door, I said, "Oh, dear God, they are not serious. You see what happens in that part of the world and many parts of the third world, they send lots of these crazy videos of Rambo, and we shouldn't be sending any of those. We should only be sending the best of our cinema, not the worst of ourselves. They believe that. These young guards who were holding me hostage, they gave up their formal education at the age of ten. Sometimes it was very difficult to talk to them because their academic background was so limited. It is like when I was in India, sitting on a beach, the children would say, "Is it true that the American landed on the moon?"

And I would say, "Yes it is true."

"Oh, that is American propaganda."

It is amazing, even when they don't have the intelligence, you can't hold a conversation, you can't tell them, and you can't convince them. I could not convince them that those were not transmitters. They believed that.

They move me to another prison, and now they build cubicles. I am in one cubicle, the other corner Terry Anderson is in, and in another room is William Buckley. There are times I complained to God. I would tell God, "Listen, for I am not Job, I want to go home now." Then I heard Mr. Buckley tell God...he is dying now, very, very sick. And he said, "Dear God, why, why this now?" And I recall Jesus, in his own dying, asking God why. "My God, my God, why have you forsaken me?" It is a complaining question, I believe, taking a chance on the audience.

They move me out of there, oh, March 15, I was in the closet, and I could see through a crack and see a man chained to a bed. That is Terry Anderson; I don't know it is Terry Anderson. I just know it is a man who weeps. He is traumatized. Later on in the passage of time, I will get to know who this man is.

They move me out of the room and chain me to a wall. And they are carrying Mr. Buckley to the solarium. He is so sick. He is delirious. He is sitting on the floor in there, and the last words he would speak will be, "I would like some poached eggs on toast, please." And then, that evening, he dies. And they carry him out. The young guards, especially Sieb, he was so overwhelmed by Mr. Buckley's death. He grieved his death; he really did.

They forgot to close the window, and I stood up and I could see out. And I saw a tree. And I started to cry. Because of Mr. Buckley's death, they would kidnap a Jewish doctor, whom they would later kill on Christmas Eve. Because of him, they designate that I have this tremendous eye infection. He designates that adults need guards, and this man has a tremendous eye infection. My eyes would just weep with a white liquid. And, ah, I have high blood pressure. So he said, "He is not to wear the blindfold." I could not function without the blindfold. Have you ever tried to keep your eyes closed for twenty-four hours? I went and searched the garbage for the blindfold so I could put it back on.

They will move us to another prison. Then they said, "Once the door is locked, you may lift your blindfolds, but when the key goes back into the door, we demand that you put your blindfolds back on. Because if you see us, we will kill you." So, it was a new blue light, and I am chained to one wall. There is a man chained to another wall. And we lifted blindfolds. We had not washed since February, and this is July now. I had a long beard, and I looked across and saw this man with a long beard. We just looked at each other.

Wherever you are, you give praise and thanks to God for the marvelous gift of sight; it was Ben Weir. Then Ben whispers to me, "I think this room is bugged."

"But why do you say that?"

He sees something against the wall, and I stretched my chain and picked it up, and it was a room deodorant, and we burst into laughter. We gave praise and thanks for the marvelous gift of laughter.

And he would say, "How did you cope?"

And I would say, "My nourishments were God's words, God's table, and then this gentle God gives me the nourishment of Ben Weir." My point of nourishment that I reflect upon later in life is that God gave me a marvelous sense of humor. I think you have to have a marvelous sense of humor to get through it all.

At the end of July, Tom Sutherland shows up. He, like Terry Anderson, is now into the seventh year as a hostage. And because of them, we find out who our neighbors are. My neighbors are David Jacobson, Huntington Beach, California; Terry Anderson, Associated Press Bureau Chief; and a Kuwait diplomat. We, as American, were allowed to come together to pray. Ben had a Bible, and I didn't have my glasses. I cannot read without my glasses. But Ben's glasses worked for me. So Ben and I, when we were together, we would come together and be nourished by each other in the nourishment of God's Word and the nourishment of God's table. And then we would go over and celebrate with David and Terry and the Kuwait diplomat. Terry Anderson was the only Catholic in the group other than Marty Jenco. And Terry would say to Hodge, "I am a Catholic. I would like to confess my sins."

Hodge would say, "You don't need to confess your sins to a priest; you confess your sins to God."

Terry was adamant. "Well, my tradition is to confess to a priest."

Hodge will reference that, and he will pull everyone out of the room and allow Terry and me to be present to each other. And once again, it is the lifting of blindfolds. It is the most beautiful sacrament of reconciliation. When I looked into the eyes of this man, it was such an emotional time for me and it was for Terry.

End of August, they say—oh, end of July—they say, "We are moving Terry and David down to a prison called the 'stalls.'" They kept accusing us of being CIA, and you could do all the challenging you want; we are not CIA. On that day I told Hodge, "If anything, I am VIA."

He said, "What do you mean by VIA?"

I said, "Vatican Intelligence, Hodge." And, they never accepted my humor.

They didn't move them to the prison called the stalls; they moved them downstairs. Ollie North was already selling arms, and we were to be released because of the sale of arms. But, somehow all that fell through. August 14, we five Americans were all put together, and we were allowed to go to the summit to go home. We could vote for Ben Weir, David Jacobson, or Marty Jenco. We refused and we prayed, and we voted for Terry Anderson. Then they told us we could not vote for Terry or Tom. Then we told Hodge of our vote, and he told us because we did not follow his directions, he would tell us who would go home.

On September 14, a month later, Hodge came in to tell us, and he spoke to Ben in Arabic, and I could hear Ben go, "Oh my, oh my." And after Hodge left, we asked Ben what happened. Ben said, "They told me I am going to go home tonight."

Because of Ben's leaving, we were all allowed to write love letters to our family, and Ben took them with him. And because of Ben's release, we asked if it would be possible to follow Ben's release and be allowed to have a radio and a newspaper, so as to follow his pilgrimage home. And they did. They occasionally gave us a newspaper and a radio, a little portable radio. A Sony. We did not want to wear it out because it was battery. So we would only listen to the *Voice of America* to see if we could find out what was happening. And because of that, we heard Ben on *Voice of America* saying that he had met with Terry Waite and that Terry Waite would be willing to go to Beirut, Lebanon, to negotiate to secure our release. It was Christmas Eve, 1985. And Terry Waite was in the country, and we thought we would be going home for Christmas. We heard that he had faltered in his negotiations, and we were not going to go home.

I celebrated midnight Mass with these Americans. It was a difficult midnight Mass. We sang Christmas carols. The next day, the guards were saddened by the fact that we were not going to go home. And they go out and move us to another room; they brought in this beautiful cake. On top of the cake were candles, and written on the cake was, "Happy birthday, Jesus." And they sang that to us. They allowed us to write a love letter to our family, which none of them were ever sent, but on the eve of my release, that love letter would be read to me.

"I assume you know that if I were to die, I would hope to die with the words of Jesus on my lips. 'Father, forgive them, for they know not what they do.' Please, do not hate them. If you want to know where I am spiritually, read Psalms 116, 117, and 118."

It was hard to live in a room with four other Americans, twelve feet by fifteen feet. Perhaps, if ever a book is to be written, it should be written on how we five Americans survived each other. We were all allowed out ten minutes a day to go to the bathroom, and after a while, you get on each other's nerves; you can't believe it. And they gave us a journal, we all had a journal, and I remember writing in mine, "Oh, dear God, I am so glad that I am not married to any of these men." When I got out, I met their wives, and I said, "Were they always this way?"

And their wives said, "Yes, they were always this way."

Terry Anderson used to fashion out of the covers of paperbacks decks of cards for us to play. The guards would catch us, and they would take them away. And Terry would recreate another deck of cards. If you ever get kidnapped, somewhere around the world, I would suggest that you don't play Hearts. It is a very vindictive game. Terry Anderson also fashioned, out of aluminum from the cheese swatches, a chess set and they would catch us doing this, and they would always confiscate them. They felt what we were doing was evil. And I remember one day with the guard, Sieb, one of the young guards, reflecting on what we were doing, and he would say, "Cards are evil, chess is evil, music is evil, and certain foods are evil."

And I said, "Oh, Sieb, all these things are evil, but kidnapping is not evil, Sieb?" He never responded to that question.

Matador of Murder

About three months prior to my release, my teeth were falling apart. The fillings were coming out, and my teeth became like chalk. I had made a videotape, and I could speak to my family, and I could speak to the American government. I do not know if the tape was ever shown. In the videotape to my family, I said, "If ever I get out of here, I will need to see a dentist." Then when Hodge came in one day, I said, "Listen Hodge"—the filling had fallen out, and it was extremely painful—"Hodge, could I get a dentist?" And he said maybe.

Then one night they pulled me out, and they blindfolded me. So you never know when they touch you whether it is going to be a touch of violence or a touch of compassion. You just have to wait for it. No sooner did I hear them say, "Open your mouth," and I opened my mouth, and I felt hands in my mouth, and I felt a needle and I fainted. Then they picked me up off the floor, and they said, "Oh no, we are going to pull your tooth." Then they did. I got a picture of the young doctor. They pulled the tooth.

He was a marvelous doctor. He said, "Take your blindfold off; I could care less if you see me." And he was searching the tooth and gave me antibiotics. So when I came back into the room now, the dentist came, and I said to my fellow hostages, "He pulled my tooth."

And he asked them how their teeth were, and they all said, "They are excellent."

When I think about that young doctor they kidnapped, when we were in one of our prisons, adjacent to the French hostages, the doctor was basically taking care of Michel Sedam, who was dying, and he did die. Within his pants pocket was his love letter to his wife, and it was almost like a love letter that St. Paul was writing. "I will be home, I will be home, have courage, have hope, and I will be home." A couple of years ago, I was in France, and I met his wife. And she had this look you would not believe, and it was this look of *why, why did they kill him?* And it is one of those questions that will go into eternity before it will be answered.

Three months prior to my own release, I was sitting there, and one of the guards sat next to me, and his name was Sahib, the man who was most violent to me. I have a 20 percent hearing loss because of Sahib, over a stupid stone. And Sahib said to me, "Abbuna"—which is interesting in the evolution of a name. Because in the beginning it was Jenco, then it was Lawrence, then it was Abbuna, which means "dear Father." He said, "Abbuna, do you remember those first six months?"

And I said, "Yes Sahib, with tremendous sadness and grief for what you did to me and what you did to my brothers."

And he said, "Abbuna, do you forgive me?"

It was a shocking question to hear. And I said to Sahib, "Oh, Sahib, let me tell you something. There was a story on a mountaintop that Jesus gave, and it was a story that I was never to hate you but that I was supposed to love you. But I am so sorry, Sahib, to tell you that I hated you. So I need to ask your forgiveness, Sahib, as well as God's forgiveness. It was very strange that night; enemies became brothers, and I was very much at peace.

On the eve of my release, they came in and said they were going to move me to another prison. They were going to move all of us to another prison. And there is a process of leaving the room: you get blindfolded, taking only the clothes they gave you in February, and you do not take your journal, do not take your books, do not take your water bottle, do not take your urine bottle, do not take your prayer missal, and you only wear the clothes out and the old clothes they gave you in the plastic bags. I stashed my Bible between my clothes.

Process: go to the elevator, stand, get in, take the blindfold off, go down, get into a van with the blindfold back on, and they were already to go. The door opened up for David Jacobson; we all stood up, and they took David, and then five minutes later, the door opened up. We all stood up, and they said, "Please sit down." They took Thomas Sutherland, and then five minutes later, Terry and I were the only two left in the room. The door opened up, and we both stood up, and they said, "Abbuna, we told you to sit down."

And I gave Terry Anderson a hug and a kiss and said, "Good-bye Terry."

He said, "Why are you saying good-bye?"

I told him, "I am not too sure that I will be in the same prison with you." And he left.

Five minutes later, the door opened up and I stood up, and they said, "Abbuna, we told you to sit down." I sat down. And I remember looking at the floor because I was blindfolded.

Hodge was there, and I said, "Hodge, are you going to kill me?"

He said, "No, Abbuna, you are going to go home tonight." And I started to cry. The rule is you are not allowed to cry.

When Ben Weir got a love letter from his wife, for the first time after a year, he started to sob. Then Hodge said, "We will never give you any information if you cry." Then I heard Hodge say, "Oh, I think I am beginning to understand the tears."

Then Sahib, the man who asked for forgiveness for being so violent to me, said to me, "Abbuna, take your dyazide pills for your high blood pressure."

I said, "Why, Sahib? They are not going to put me under a truck again, are they?" See, my dream was that they would drop me off in Beirut, and I would walk to a hotel. I would call my family and say, "All right, I am coming home." That is the way I wanted to get out. He did not respond. I stood in front of the other guard, and Macmoud massaged my shoulder. I heard someone say, "Here, Abbuna…here, Abbuna…" and he hands me a cross. And they put me in a car, and they drive me to a garage. I am sitting on this piece of cardboard in the darkness of the garage. I am still blindfolded, and I heard them say, "Please stand up."

And I stood up, and they started to tape my body. I said, "Oh, God, no."

I put the cross in the palm of my hand as I was requested to do, and they did this real tight taping like a mummy. As they came to my mouth, I heard someone say, "Open your mouth." I was expecting the cloth. Instead, the two dyazide pills. It was Sahib's final way of saying, "I love you." He wanted me to survive.

They lift my body up and slide me beneath the truck. I was going to Damascus under a truck. Then I didn't know where I was going.

The only thing Hodge said to me, because I was carrying a videotape that David was making—they never went anywhere; they were across the way, and David was making the video that I was to carry out. Then Hodge said, "If the Syrians confiscate it, we will kill the Americans. This videotape has to be given the *Associated Press* and it has to be viewed this day." I was clinging to that videotape, and they taped my body up, sliding me under the truck. I used the cross like a knife to cut all the tapes off so I could move my body up and pressure myself against the base of the truck. My knuckles were bloody when I arrived. They pulled me out and put me on the side of the road, and it was a nice little spot.

As a hostage, they would ask, "Is there anything you want?"

I would say, "Yes, I want a taxicab to go home."

And that morning, over my head, they said, "Here, Abbuna, take these five Lebanese dollars and catch your taxicab and go home."

And I said, "Which way is home?" And over my head, they pointed to the left. I had to wait for fifteen minutes after they left, and then I could take my blindfold off. Now for almost seventeen months, I had not seen God's creation. So I lifted up my blindfold, and for the first time in seventeen months, I could look at a sky; I could look across the way and see a lake. I found myself reciting this prayer, an old Jewish covenant prayer. "The sky, bless the Lord; earth, bless the Lord; flowers, bless the Lord." I didn't rush; finally I got up and started to walk. I came to a mother and father and a couple of children on the road. I asked them in Arabic, "Is there a church?" They said yes, and I asked where, and they pointed. I started walking there.

Now I had cotton hanging off my head, I had tapes hanging off my body, my zipper was broken, and I was carrying a little plastic bag with a videotape. I tried to act very normal. Finally someone picked me up and drove me to this village. Someone said, "Why did you want to go to a church?" I wanted to go to a church so I could leave through the Vatican Embassy. I did not want to identify myself as an American. But I realized that I was in a Shiite community. And a Christian doctor pulls up in this beautiful Mercedes Benz, and I told him who I was, and with tremendous sadness, this man said, "Abbuna, I am so sorry, I cannot help you." And he left.

You have to understand their pain; he could be hurt, his family could be hurt, and the grandchildren could be hurt. A young man says, "Follow me," and took me down to the police station. I went down there, and as soon as I sat down there, I realized my zipper was broken, and I leaned over and grabbed his stapler from him and stapled my zipper shut, and then I had to go to the toilet. I got up and went to the toilet and saw what I looked like. How frightening I must have been to these people. Came back, sat there. There was no way to communicate. They just could not comprehend what it was all about. After nineteen months of this, I just gave in to my own sadness, and I began to cry. Arabs do not like men to cry. They can't cope with that.

They brought in this beautiful woman, and she spoke impeccable English, and she said, "Abbuna, you don't have to worry; you are safe." And within five minutes, the Syrians were there to pick me up. I was about twenty minutes away from Damascus. And the first person to meet me as we pulled up was a woman, and her name was Peg Seigh. She lived in Damascus trying to secure the release of her brother, Terry Anderson.

A gentle God, as I went to the American Embassy. When I drove up, there was a man standing there, and he said, "Hi, Marty!" When I was in Yemen for two years, I baptized his children.

I will share with you today; one of the things I dreamed about when I was a hostage was pickled herring. They had a picnic that night, and on the table—and no one knew my dreams—was a big bowl of pickled herring. And as I got to Wiesbaden and my family was there, lots of kisses and love. We got down at the end of the day to give praise and thanks to a gentle God for my release.

And I walked up to the altar—that love letter, on the eve of my release, Hodge would read that love letter to me. I asked on the eve of my release, "May I please take those three letters that I received as a hostage home? May I take my notes home?"

They said, "No, Abbuna, and now we strip."

As I was naked in front of Hodge, he read my love letter to my family: "Dear Brothers and Sisters, if I am to be killed, I would hope that I would die with the words of Jesus on my lips: 'Father, forgive them for they know not what they do.' Please, do not hate them. If you want to know where I am spiritually, read Psalms 116, 117, and 118."

There are many ways God touched my life; one night, they forgot to give the radio to the French hostages. And I turned the radio on, and it was *Voice of America*. It was my nephew David speaking to me. I got to Damascus, and the first person I met was Peg Seigh. I was welcomed to the embassy by a good friend of his family. I got to Wiesbaden, went down to the chapel, and walked up to the altar, and on the altar was a Bible. And the Bible was opened to Psalms 116, 117, and 118.

And I turned to my family and said, "Did anyone touch the Bible?"

And they said, "No."

The windows were open, and the wind blew the pages. This gentle God is always there for me. There are times when people say, "Ah, it is easy to forgive," and there are those who do not want me to forgive; they want me to hate, but in my life right now, I know. The last reading I read in scripture comes to me, and my time as a hostage comes to me, and I asked God to never let me forget that last scripture reading I prayed in prison; I make it my own now. "I shall give you a new heart and put a new spirit in you, wash the heart of stone from your body and give you a heart of flesh instead, and may you keep my laws, and sincerely respect my ordinance."

Dear gentle God, give us all new hearts, especially this day, as we come together in the Middle East in Madrid. Let us reconcile; give us new hearts, new spirits, and let us love as you asked us to love, unconditionally, and let us forgive as you asked us to forgive, unconditionally. For then, will we be your people, and you will be our God. Amen and thank you.

Psalm 116 is the shortest of all the psalms, a brief hymn of praise calling on all mankind to glorify the Lord for His kindness and fidelity to His promises. It reads, "Praise the Lord, all you nations; glorify him, all you peoples! For steadfast is his kindness toward us, and the fidelity of the Lord endures forever." Tucked away in Psalm 118 are the words, "I am attacked by malicious persecutors who are far from your law. You, O Lord, are near, and all your commands are permanent."

Perhaps one could argue that for Father Jenco, it was his faith that acted as the opium for his survival. There is no doubt that his humanity was tested, and all the feelings of despair, hate, and anger that he entertained in captivity came to bear on the remainder of his life. A mistaken hostage, held for nineteen months, left him deeply scarred and changed. He witnessed death and despair and looked into the eyes of both. Yet through it all, he reached into the innermost part of his humanity and survived.

Nineteen months of captivity took a major toll on Father Martin Jenco physically, mentally, and spiritually. When I first met Father Jenco, he looked beyond his years in age. He was soft-spoken and deeply spiritual. When we met, Terry Anderson was still being held hostage. Father Jenco grieved for Terry Anderson and had an inner sense of guilt that because he was a priest, he had gained an earlier release. Terry Anderson would spend 2,454 days as a hostage under the terror of the Shiite Hezbollah group. Father Jenco had vivid memories of his treatment for nineteen months and anguished at the thought of Terry Anderson's long ordeal.

Terry Waite, an advisor to Robert Runcie, the Archbishop of Canterbury, got caught in the web of intrigue, and his efforts were negated by the actions of Oliver North. He was kidnapped in January 1987 and not released until November 1991. Instead of negotiating the release of the Beirut hostages, he, too, became a victim of their sordid torture.

When he was being held chained to a wall in a dark, dismal cell, lying on a floor, hooded, in some godforsaken prison in Lebanon, Father Jenco had to bear witness to the torture of his fellow hostages. He witnesses, firsthand, the torture and beatings of William Buckley, all the while unable to give assistance. This was worse than the physical beating he had to withstand. This was to be at the heart of the mental anguish that these men would never forget.

The most amazing thing that happened under these vicious zealots was that in the end, they would be unsuccessful in breaking the American hostages, including Father Jenco. In captivity, they were brought to tears, moaning, and sobbing. They journeyed to the edge of their sanity and sometimes beyond. But, in the end, they turned hatred into compassion; anger into kindness; and brutality into caring.

The hostages held in Beirut were among some of the most mistreated hostages in history. In many ways, their treatment paralleled the mistreatment of many of our soldiers who were held captive for long periods.

While I have told, in his own words, the story of the captivity of Father Martin Jenco, there are many similar stories. Terry Anderson, David Jacobson, Ben Weir, Tom Sutherland, Brian Keenan, Frank Reed, and William Buckley all have separate stories to tell. Their stories would ring similar. Initial fear of death, long hours and months of isolation, despair, mental and physical suffering, suicidal thoughts, moments of insanity, sickness, and a terrible sense of loneliness. Though they were not in a grave, in many ways their experience was like being buried alive and living to tell about it.

William Buckley would not live to tell about it. The Shiites had been convinced that William Buckley was CIA, and he received the most severe treatment of all. His final days and weeks were almost beyond imagination. His cry to his creator, "My God, my God, why this now?" were not the words of a broken man but the words of a man unwilling to retreat from his beliefs.

William Buckley's death had a profound effect on those who witnessed it, even from another room. Hostages who are forced to exist together are deeply affected when they lose one of their members. Father Jenco was terribly troubled by William Buckley's death. He was forced to lie helpless nearby, chained to a wall. Father Jenco gave witness that the Shiites were deeply affected by Buckley's demise. Not so affected that it caused them to release their hostages.

Very few hostages have had the benefit of knowing beforehand what it is like to be kidnapped. I am not too sure it would make any difference if they did. What is true is that each victim is affected differently, and how severely they enter into each stage of being a victim often depends on how they are treated.

Father Lawrence Jenco was held for 564 days before being released and allowed to return home to the United States. He died in Illinois on July 19, 1996. Before his death, he wrote a book titled *Bound to Forgive: The Pilgrimage to Reconciliation of a Beirut Hostage*. The title of the book describes the life he led. A life of forgiveness.

The fifty-two hostages who were held in the American Embassy for 444 days, or 14.5 months, all reacted differently to their captivity. In 1980, I had the privilege of attending the senior seminar at the US Department of State with two of the released hostages, David Morefield and Victor Tomseth. Both of these individuals reacted very differently during captivity. Morefield absolutely refused to converse with his captors and buried himself in reading for 444 days. Tomseth was not held with the majority of the hostages and got better treatment than the rest. Tomseth, who was a quiet man and very intellectual, stayed the course and remained silent and inquisitive throughout the ordeal.

During the 444 days, I was assigned to the State Department, along with a CIA psychiatrist and a State Department psychiatrist, for a twofold purpose: first, to open telephone dialogue with the captors, and second, to pass on medical information about our hostages.

It turned out to be a most interesting assignment. We had the floor layout of the embassy with all the extensions to the telephone lines going into the embassy. Phone by phone, we called and recorded what part of the embassy we were in and who answered the phone. It became somewhat of a game for the Iranians because when they answered the phone, they would always identify themselves by X, Y, and Z. It took a few days to come up with sufficient background noise to identify X, Y, and Z by their real names. When X would question how we got his name, we would tell him that Y or Z gave us the name. We did this until we had identified each one of the captors as they would answer the phone. This upset them very much because they were given orders not to identify each other, much less themselves.

They would always answer the phones in Farsi. They would switch to English as soon as they heard English. When they spoke to each other; off phone, it was always in Farsi. We had good medical information on the personnel being held in the embassy compound. In some cases we tried to get the message to the Iranians that one or more hostages had high blood pressure and needed medication. The Iranians actually made an effort to see that the hostages received the medical attention they needed. What became difficult was that the hostages, as a group, bonded together and refused to give any insight into their medical needs.

Much intelligence was obtained from these contacts, and we were able to determine that the hostages were alive and generally well. Being in such a large group, the stages that individual hostages go through in captivity for the most part never occurred. If the attitude and profile of the hostages in Iran were to be summarized, it would be marked by boredom and anger that their situation remained static for 444 days. Very few of these hostages had deep-seated psychological problems that needed long-term treatment after they were released.

Thomas R. Hargrove was held as a kidnap victim for eleven months deep in the jungles of Colombia. He was the victim of being in the wrong place at the perfect time. He had an agricultural job in Colombia representing the International Center for Tropical Agriculture (GIAT) near Cali, Colombia. When they first kidnapped him, his captors were certain that they had a high-ranking CIA official. Hargrove was the victim of a terrorist kidnapping, with all the trimmings of death threats, isolation, loneliness, despair, distrust, disease, and general lack of a good diet as well as hygiene care. He was held high up in the mountains in such a remote place that, had he thought of escaping, he would have been at a loss to find his way out of the jungle. Hargrove also became a victim of his employer, who never admitted that he was a true kidnap victim and refused to bargain in good faith for his life. For all practical purposes, his company abandoned him in captivity.

Had it not been for Tom Hargrove's wife, Susan, and his two sons, he would never have come out of the jungle alive. They took it upon themselves to negotiate with the terrorists for his release. Susan Hargrove was fortunate in attracting the assistance of Michael Bagley, who was an expert on kidnap matters. Kroll Associates, one of the foremost companies involved in kidnap/ransom matters, employed him. After weeks of negotiations, Hargrove was released in the jungle and walked out to his freedom.

Tom Hargrove's experience correlates closely to that of other victims of kidnapping. He was initially fearful of being killed. This fear lasted throughout his captivity because his captors were heavily armed, poorly educated, and frequent users of drugs. The leader was severely prone to depression and in fact committed suicide during Hargrove's captivity. Clearly, Hargrove was dealing with personality types that would not think twice about killing him. His long months of captivity led to deep bouts of depression and suicide thoughts. Hargrove had serious doubts that anyone was doing anything meaningful for his release. Where he was kept was very vulnerable to weather conditions. His food was meager, at best. The days grew long. He had a distinct language barrier with his captors.

On one occasion, I asked Tom if he reflected on his life much or reached out in his thoughts to God for comfort. His answer surprised me; he said that religion never was a critical part of his life, and in captivity it did not play a critical role.

It was my feeling that Hargrove, in his own way, mastered the technique of kidnap survival. I had a sense that the baggage he carried out of captivity was heavy. His wife, Susan, had played such a major and dominant role, and did it so well, that it was difficult for her to surrender this position once he was released. Tom enjoys lecturing about his captivity, and perhaps it is his way of releasing the demons inside of him that were allowed to grow in captivity.

Some years back, I had the honor of listening to a former navy jet pilot, Charles Plumb, who was held prisoner in Vietnam for over seven years. After seventy-five combat missions, his plane was struck by a surface-to-air missile and destroyed. Plumb ejected and parachuted into enemy territory and was captured. Plumb's survival story was extremely interesting in that he found himself in a prison cell that measured seven feet by seven feet. This became his world for almost seven years. He was held in total isolation, without windows, without light. He lost track of time, and like most POWs, he hit rock bottom. Rock bottom, to him, meant that he was convinced he would be killed, lose his mind, or die of natural causes while in prison. He had little hope of being released. What kept him alive was his belief that you have to deal with the cards God gives you. It was his belief that God had given him these difficult cards, and somehow he must make the best of them. He established a daily schedule of exercise; he would eat the food they gave him, no matter how distasteful; he would spend hours recalling meaningful family moments; he tried to sleep regular hours, as much as possible. As strange as it would appear, he was able to conquer his environment, a seven-by-seven cage. Every inch of that cage was memorized. With long encounters with depression and despair, he became the victor over his environment and captors.

The remarkable point made by this captured navy pilot was that his captivity was no different from life. We are all given a deck of cards to deal with; we cannot change that. We must deal with the cards that are dealt. It was remarkable how Plumb was able to conquer the small prison cell he was confined in. There are many forms of prisons: the sick person, confined to bed for life; the cancer patient spending long hours on the other end of a chemo needle; the paraplegic sentenced to a wheelchair for the rest of his life; or the web of mental sickness. In Plumb's words, many of us are confined and given bad choices in life. While it might not be a seven-by-seven prison cell, it is the cards we have been dealt, and we must accept them. Not accepting the reality of where we are is what makes us unable to survive.

There are so many wonderful examples of victims to long periods of captivity, leaving us with remarkable models of survival. Captivity for any length of time can leave indelible marks on a person. The marks left on Father Jenco, and no doubt on his fellow prisoners in Beirut, were significant. Father Jenco had the cross of Christianity to hang his suffering on. The single most common trait exhibited by kidnap victims was their faith in being able to survive. Whether that faith is directed to a higher order or not, it is absolutely necessary in saving not only one's life but also one's sanity.

CHAPTER 8

Murdering Nurses

It was a very quiet evening; the patients for the most part were lying in their beds, watching television. Dinner had been served, and the last medicine run had been completed. All visitors had long since left the wards. The hospital was getting ready to go into shutdown mode for the evening.

This was a very large hospital, and it housed patients of all sorts. It was the Veteran's Administration (VA) flagship hospital, and they were proud of it. The people of Ann Arbor, Michigan, were also proud of the hospital because it was a good neighbor and a good source of employment. It was an extremely large hospital where, from time to time, quality research had been conducted. Like most VA hospitals, it did carry the reputation of being a government hospital, and with that, suspicion as to its level of excellence was always present. However, it was a place where veterans of our military looked to in times of medical difficulty. They had ultimate confidence in it, and it was considered their best choice when in medical need. Many who chose to use the hospital had a high expectation threshold for its services and generally complained very little.

It was about 9:35 p.m. when John Brophy caught himself nodding off and feeling pretty much ready for bed. He was in a two-man room, and next to him, behind a curtain, was Philip Kelley. Kelley had been a veteran of World War II. He drank heavily since his involvement in World War II, and it was not known whether he had turned to drink as a result of his experiences. There would be days when Kelley would tell you nothing of his experiences, and then there were other days when he would lift up his pajama leg and show you scars from when he was landing on Normandy. Kelley was a bright and cheerful person who normally got along well with everyone. His demands on the nurses were few, but when they ignored him, he could be very vocal. Kelley was already sleeping, and his overhead light was on nightlight. John Brophy did not recall Kelley being on much medication. He felt that he was in the hospital for liver failure, and while they were keeping him on a strict diet, he was certainly not overmedicated.

As Brophy was fighting to keep his eyes open, a young nurse came into the room. She pulled back his curtain, asking, "Do you want me to turn off your television?" He remembers telling her, "You might as well." According to Brophy, the nurse turned off his television and went to the next bed, where Kelley was already sleeping. Brophy felt that it sounded like she fixed his bed covers for the evening and left. Kelley had a busy day with visitors, and there was good reason for him to be tired—to the extent that he never heard this young nurse at his bedside.

In less than a minute after the nurse left, Brophy heard Kelley let out a terrible moan. Kelley appeared to be thrashing in his bed in a very frightful manner. It appeared that Kelley was gasping for air. Brophy very quickly rang his emergency buzzer for the nurse to come and check out Kelley. The same young nurse entered the room, this time pulling the curtains shut around Kelley. Brophy could hear the nurse, in broken English, talking on the phone. She said in a very calm voice, "Code 7...code 7...code 7. Room 543B."

The next thing Brophy remembers is that all hell broke loose in his room. The lights overhead were turned on, and the curtain around his bed was drawn. A male orderly stuck his head in and told Brophy, "Do not worry; everything will be ok." Machines were being rushed into the room, and from the sounds of it, they were trying to revive Philip Kelley. He could hear them say, "Do you have a pulse?"

"He is not breathing."

"I have an irregular pulse."

"But he is having difficulty breathing."

"Give him oxygen."

"Should we shock the heart?"

"Does he have a history of these attacks?" No history.

After approximately twenty-five minutes, with at least a dozen medical personnel working over Kelley, one of the doctors pronounces, "I think we lost him; he is not breathing on his own, and his heart has stopped. Let's get him out of here, and transfer the other patient to an open room." Brophy remembers it being a few minutes before 10:15 p.m. when Kelley was wheeled out of the room, and within five minutes, they moved him to Room 417A, one floor below where he had been.

Weeks later, the autopsy report on Philip Kelley was shared with Kelley's family. It revealed nothing to alleviate their grief and shock at his death. They asked the hospital, "How could it be possible, when we visited him that same day and he looked so good and was in such good spirits? His hospital stay was supposed to last between seven and ten days. He had been in the hospital six days, was getting good reports, and expected to come home within two days."

The hospital simply stated that while there was no history of heart failure, nor did the autopsy indicate heart involvement, they must conclude that his heart gave out. The autopsy did show mild to severe liver damage but not to the extent that it would result in a sudden death. The Kelley family accepted the hospital's conclusions but with a high degree of skepticism. They had no choice but to believe the unbelievable. Philip Kelley died April 5, 1974.

The VA hospital in Ann Arbor was very large, and the administration of such a large hospital was a significant task. In the mid-1970s, most hospitals were feeling budget cuts across the country and a shortage of good personnel. There was high competition for good, qualified doctors and nurses. One way to bring an out-of-control hospital budget into line was to slow down the rehiring of doctors and nurses when vacancies occurred. Because this was a federal hospital, the administration in Ann Arbor was not always in total control of its hiring policy. The controlling force came out of Washington, DC, and the natural approval procedure would slow things down considerably.

April 17, 1974, Larry Dolan was admitted into the VA hospital. Larry did not have a long history of physical problems, but his military records indicated that he received a medical discharge from the US Army, having served nineteen months in Korea. Unlike Kelley, who was in his late sixties, Dolan was in his mid-thirties. Dolan had seen some action in Korea and had received a wound in his right side. The longer he stayed in Korea, the more he suffered mentally. He was listed as having paranoid schizophrenia and given a medical discharge. Since his release, he had been treated for schizophrenia and hospitalized on three separate instances. On one occasion, he held the police at bay and threatened his family. He had been drinking for a long period and admittedly had not taken his medication. When Dolan would stay off drink and on his medication, he would have fewer episodes of delusions or hallucinations. Starting the week of April 12, 1974, Dolan went on a long drinking spree and talked about killing himself. He signed himself into the VA hospital on April 17.

Dolan was assigned to Room 323B in the east wing of the VA hospital. He was given a private room, which had additional security modifications made to it, such as a monitoring camera. It was April 23, 1974, and Dolan was making excellent progress in his bout with alcoholism and schizophrenia. Dolan's mental condition had not worried the doctors in the past because they felt he was not self-destructive. His activity before entering the hospital this time concerned the physicians, however. It was the first time that he actually verbalized suicide. Dolan was kept on a strict diet as well as the usual medication that he had been assigned when he was first treated for schizophrenia. He was ambulatory and had only one restriction: to remain on the third floor of the east wing. Dolan had been in good spirits most of the day and was not making any trouble in the ward.

It was about 11:10 p.m. when Dolan dozed off to sleep for the night, and he noticed the bright lights from the corridor illuminate his room. Dolan had the habit of leaving his door slightly cracked to get air circulation and also to give the nurses easy access when they conducted their routine bed checks. A short, young, Philippine nurse came into the room. She was carrying something. Dolan was very groggy and asked her what she wanted. She said, "The doctor put this on your chart, and I forgot to give it to you earlier. It is a vitamin B shot." Not questioning the doctor's order, Dolan offered the nurse his arm. It took seconds for the injection, and he rolled over in his bed as the door was shut, darkening the room.

No sooner had Dolan rolled over than he began to sweat and feel a burning sensation in his left arm. He was having trouble breathing. He reached down, and pinned to his bedsheet was the emergency alarm button. He pushed it and lost consciousness. An orderly changing bedclothes two doors away heard the emergency call button and rushed to Dolan's side. Dolan was in respiratory arrest. The orderly immediately picked up the phone and ordered a code 7.

Within moments, a half dozen nurses and doctors rushed into the room and started to revive Dolan. Fortunately, he had a strong heart and was in decent physical condition. It took the emergency staff forty-five minutes to stabilize Dolan. After Dolan's vital signs were normal, he had little or no recollection of the moments that led up to his "seizure." He was unable to establish the connection between the vitamin B injection and his reaction shortly thereafter.

There had been a considerable amount of discontent and grumbling among the nurses and their assistants at the VA hospital during this period. Many of them were denied the annual leave that they had requested. The requests for nurses to work overtime had increased measurably in recent months, and the routine day shifts were now being scheduled as ten-hour shifts as opposed to the eight-hour shifts of the past. When people would leave the employment of the VA hospital, seldom were they replaced. If they were replaced, it took weeks to get the replacement on board. The fact that they were being overworked was not contested by management, and on numerous occasions, the supervisory nurses would complain. When the supervisory nurses heard complaints, there was very little they could say that would give hope.

Otto Winkler had been a longtime patient of veteran hospitals around the United States. When he was in his early sixties, he spent three weeks in the VA hospital in West Los Angeles. Otto had lost his wife five years before this most recent hospital admission on May 17, 1974. He moved from Los Angeles to live with one of his daughters in nearby Lansing. Otto had a long history of diabetes that had its onset at middle age. Most unfortunately, Otto's diabetes was difficult to control, and its side effects were ravishing his body. Otto's eyesight had suffered greatly, and his recent hospitalization was caused by severe infection in his left leg. Otto was eighty-four years of age, and since his wife's death, he had slowed down considerably. He looked every bit of eighty-four. He was grossly overweight and had major difficulty walking. Otto was hooked up to an intravenous feeding tube, which was keeping him hydrated while delivering antibiotics meant to attack the infection in his leg. There was a real possibility that Otto's leg would have to be amputated. His daughter, Helga, visited him at least three times per week, and Otto was always cheerful in her presence. There was little doubt, when talking to Otto, that he was aware life would not be a long journey from where he was.

On Wednesday, May 21, Otto's daughter visited him. Helga commented to the nurses that she thought her father looked much better and that he was in good spirits. She also knew that the good spirits meant the leg pain had subsided somewhat. Helga went home from her hospital visit feeling very positive about the care her father was getting. Visiting hours had long been over, and the ward on sixth floor east had settled down for the night. Phones no longer rang in the rooms, and television sets had been quieted for another day. It was approximately 11:25 p.m. when a shadowy figure walked into Otto Winkler's room, 619A. The shadowy figure was that of a nurse, approximately five feet one or two, and slightly built. She checked the intravenous feeding bag and proceeded to run her hand down the length of the tube. In her other hand, she was holding a syringe. At the wide connection in the IV tube, she inserted the contents of the syringe, which looked to be 4cc.

Instead of leaving the room, the nurse remained, and within the space of a minute, Otto was gasping for air. He could not breathe. The nurse picked up the phone and called, once again, "Code 7…code 7…code 7 for Room 619A, east wing." Because it was late at night, there was only one doctor available for this code 7. Accompanying the doctor were three additional nurses and two nurse assistants. They worked over Mr. Winkler for one hour and ten minutes but to no avail. The hospital records would show that Otto Winkler deceased at 12:27 a.m., May 22, 1974. The cause of death was cardiac arrest complicated by general poor health as a result of advanced age.

A call was placed to Helga Volker, Mr. Winkler's daughter, at 2:00 a.m., advising her of her father's passing. She was shocked and sought an explanation as to how it could be so sudden after noticeable progress. The same day, when she went to the hospital to make arrangements for her father's burial, she questioned the hospital personnel but to no avail. Stunned in disbelief, she had no choice but to accept the reality that her father had died.

In the early stages of these events, which had patients dying without good medical reasons, the VA hospital did not question the cause. The killings, or mysterious deaths, continued for the remainder of 1974 and well into 1975. There is no fixed date of when exactly the VA hospital became concerned, but in the summer of 1975, the hospital authorities contacted the Detroit office of the FBI and invited them to visit the hospital for an open discussion of what was happening.

The FBI was shocked at the hospital's findings. They suggested that there could be as many as fifty-eight suspect deaths over the period of almost two years. According to the hospital, the deaths almost always occurred late at night, and the cause of death was similar. A few suspicious deaths occurred in the morning hours, but predominantly it was in the late afternoon or evening hours.

The FBI's very first request was for a medical explanation for the deaths. The hospital authorities could only speculate because they had no witnesses to the acts that precipitated the deaths—only a strong belief that it was the drug Pavulon that was being used.

Pavulon has a generic coding called Pancuronium bromide. Pavulon is a drug normally administered for paralysis when someone is in a ventilator or for someone who is undergoing surgery. It is an extremely fast-acting drug that responds in one to two minutes, depending on dose and age of patient. It is never administered to a patient whose breathing is not being controlled in an artificial manner. This is the same drug that is used with a combination of drugs for lethal injections. The most common form of lethal injection uses a combination of sodium pentothal, Pavulon, and potassium chloride. The sodium pentothal relaxes the muscles and depresses the central nervous system while gradually bringing on unconsciousness. The Pavulon blocks the interactions between the nerves and muscles, thereby suppressing the respiratory system and initiating the stoppage of the heart. The potassium chloride stuns the heart to stop it altogether with an electrolyte imbalance. Clearly the use of Pavulon to create a medical emergency or to kill someone not in a ventilator is a well-conceived plan of attack.

In recent criminal history, there have been two other documented cases in which Pavulon was used as the killing agent. Respiratory therapist Efren Saldivar claimed in 1998 that he was responsible for the possible deaths of between one hundred and two hundred patients at the Glendale Adventist Medical Center in California. Saldivar was subsequently charged with the murder of six patients. Saldivar described himself as an angel of death. When this case broke in the late

'90s, the California investigators turned to a case on Long Island, New York, for help. More than a decade earlier, Richard Angelo was arrested by the Suffolk County Police Department. Richard Angelo was a nurse at the Good Samaritan Hospital in West Islip, Long Island. He injected his patients with Pavulon so he could resuscitate them when they went into respiratory arrest. He was convicted in 1989 and is serving a life term for killing four people and inflicting bodily damage on five others. In the case against Angelo, the Suffolk Police had to exhume thirty-three bodies. Although many of the victims were buried for months, Pavulon tracings were found in body organs.

In the Saldivar case in Los Angeles, 171 patients' deaths were deemed suspicious. The victims died between 1996 and 1998. Many of the victims were buried over a year. Of these suspicious deaths, 54 bodies had been cremated, and 117 were left to be reviewed. Twenty bodies were exhumed. It has been well documented in recent times that Pavulon will remain in both living and dead human organs for a long period of time.

As recently as April 2001, ten bodies of elderly patients were exhumed in a rural part of North Texas to determine whether a stolen drug was used to kill them. This incident occurred in a sixty-eight-bed hospital in Nocona, Texas, about 105 miles northeast of Dallas. The stolen drug used was mivacurium chloride, a powerful muscle relaxant very similar to Pavulon.

Although there have been at least three similar cases since the Ann Arbor case in the mid-1970s, at the time the FBI was unable to turn to a case that was already established. It was clear that to prove that any patient was injected, you would have to prove it with the physical evidence that Pavulon was in the body. There was no existing protocol that established in 1976 that Pavulon could be isolated in human organs. In the very early weeks of its investigation, the FBI requested to exhume almost a dozen bodies of suspect death victims. The courts granted permission for the exhumations. Now it was up to the FBI laboratory in Washington, DC.

The bodies were exhumed, after much debate and hesitation among family members of the deceased. What motivated the relatives of suspect victims was that they had questioned the deaths right from the very beginning and never received a satisfactory response from the hospital. The FBI was up against a huge task—whether the FBI laboratory could determine if Pavulon was in the body organs of those exhumed. It had never been done before, and serious doubt existed as to whether Pavulon in fact lingered in body organs after death. After three months of intensive laboratory investigation, however, the FBI came back and told its Detroit office that Pavulon was definitely present in the body organs of those persons whose remains were exhumed. This ignited this case. It gave physical proof that somehow, someone injected these patients with a drug that they had no reason to have. The method of killing was clearly established.

While the method was determined without a doubt, the investigators were having a difficult time establishing motive. The psychological profiling process established in this case met with great difficulty. A quick review of motive had it narrowed down to very few possible motives. The most obvious one was a person who was involved in mercy killing. Second, we looked at the motive of revenge; and third, we looked at the possibility of it being a simple mistake. None of these seemed to fit, especially mercy killing. A profile of the victims would indicate that medical condition had no bearing on who was selected. Certainly, Brophy and Dolan were not cases for a mercy killing. Winkler was old, but he was not in failing health to the point that he would be selected as a target for a mercy killer. A review of the over fifty suspect cases clearly established that the victims were a random sample taken from whomever was available.

Normally, when the FBI takes on an investigation, a meticulous crime scene investigation initially takes place. This was the case in Ann Arbor. We had to get a full listing of where every patient was; how they were injected; when it was that they were injected; who was working that shift; and how the medicine used was being accessed.

To our amazement, most medicines, though at control stations, were never kept under lock and key. There was ready access to most medicines. This seemed to be the case out of convenience and not any other motivation. There existed no log account of a particular medicine's usage. Simple put; there was no control system in place to evaluate where the medicine was going on any single day. The FBI immediately suggested to the VA hospital authorities that all medicine be kept under lock and key. They complied.

The VA hospital had an excellent record of when and where its employees worked. With this tool in hand, and after a great deal of manual work, we were able to determine who was working during each of the fifty-plus medical emergencies under question.

What was very much to our surprise was that two names were common to all the suspect events over the last two years. The two names were Laticia Pilo and Fatima Nunez. Both of these employees were excellent, hardworking nurses with no history of trouble or even absenteeism. They were known for making themselves available to work overtime or to substitute for others. They were regarded as very competent and hardworking. Both were from a Philippine cultural background. They had claimed to be Catholics in good standing with their church and had good, strong family ties.

The time charts were compelling circumstantial evidence. How could you have over fifty incidents that were suspect, with them having been the only ones present—knowing that the delivery system for the drug Pavulon had to be from someone with medical training—and not point to them? However compelling this evidence was, we still had to deal with a fact: no one ever saw Pilo or Nunez inject anyone or anything.

Midway through the investigation, I was requested to assist the Agents in Ann Arbor. The case had long since been given the name VAKIL, for VA killings. I had a twofold purpose—namely, profile the prime suspects with an eye toward interviewing them; and second, suggest a way to maximize the interviews of the surviving witnesses.

On the first evening after my arrival, the gents were working on the eighth floor of a wing that had been vacated for them to use as a command center. It was approximately 7:45 p.m., and the lights were dimly lit on most of the eight floors. There was one section that was in total darkness. Suddenly appearing out of the dark was Larry Dolan. He was dressed in his hospital clothes with a bathrobe over his pajamas. His hair was disheveled, and he looked troubled. There were about six agents sitting in a group discussing the case and the results achieved to date. Larry came over to where we were sitting and asked if he could talk with us. For someone who was suffering from paranoid schizophrenia, he made a lot of sense. His basic comments were that our presence in the hospital was making the nurses very nervous, and he felt the treatment of the patients would suffer if the nurses continued under the pressure of suspicion. He claimed that the whole atmosphere of the hospital had changed since the FBI had arrived and started conducting such an intense investigation. Dolan said he sensed the stress even in the supervisory nurses as well as the regular nurses. He felt our presence was creating a very dangerous environment for the patients.

Larry Dolan's comments were very much on target. He was assured that we would do everything possible to lessen that effect on the hospital staff. What was sure was that since the FBI had arrived at the VA hospital, the killings had stopped. There was no code 7 of a suspicious nature. As a matter of fact, the code 7s had virtually stopped. This was encouraging because it meant that whoever was responsible for injecting patients with Pavulon did not have the courage to continue these injections in the presence of the FBI.

Interviewing hospital personnel was a difficult challenge. Everyone interviewed, especially the nurses and doctors, were angered by the fact that they were under suspicion and that they had to be interviewed. After poring over hospital records, it was extremely time consuming to come up with two suspects, Pilo and Nunez, but it gave us a suspect focus that was not available in the earlier investigation. The work records were compelling in that only two people had a common connection with all the incidents recorded to date.

The hospital personnel files on Pilo and Nunez gave very incomplete insight into who these people were and what motivated them. They were mature women in their late twenties or early thirties. They came from a culture that was far different from the typical American culture. They were children from large families, well educated, and hard working. Pilo and Nunez had no prior criminal records. Their personnel files were replete with awards for excellent work and letters of commendation for their performance. There was no indication that either one of these individual was emotionally involved with her patients. While they were not regarded as overly friendly with their patients or coworkers, they were regarded as dependable. Both did have a history of questioning management. They were both very vocal concerning the staffing problem of the hospital. The old adage in psychological profiling, that present and future behavior is greatly determined by past behavior, gave us very little to go on.

It was indisputable that Pilo and Nunez had a common presence at all of the incidents of suspicious death or near death. There were relatively few survivors of these incidents. As many as forty people died as a result of sudden, unexpected medical reversals. It was confirmed that for those forty, there existed proof they were administered Pavulon when it was not called for.

The preparation for the interview of Pilo and Nunez was painful. What was known were that people were dying for unexpected reasons. The weapon was Pavulon. All nurses in the hospital had access to the drug. We had dismissed the possibility that we had two angel of mercy killers on our hands. Studying the selection of victims led to us dismissing this possibility quickly. The health condition of some of the victims was relatively good, and there would be no reason to put them out of their misery. Pilo and Nunez did not fit into any neat package of pathology. We were not dealing with hardened psychopaths or with a personality driven by the thrill of seeing someone die. We concluded, in our interview preparation, that these individuals were for the most part normal, and we had no idea what motivated them to do such a terrible thing. We were certain that whatever pathology drove these actions was unusual in that two people appeared to be involved.

The interviews of Pilo and Nunez were remarkable. Both totally denied involvement. During both interviews, the nurses presented a very stoic demeanor. There was no indication that they were willing to cooperate. Never at any time did either one of them come up with a plausible explanation as to how all these events could have happened. They gave no insight into, much less agreement with, our analysis that it happened on their watch and only their watch. Nunez, when questioned, would always answer a question with a question. Her response to every question was, "How could I do something like that?" Both Pilo and Nunez spoke English very well. Yet during the course of the interviews, they both sought refuge in English as a second language, constantly asking for questions to be explained. Both gave the appearance of cooperation but insisted they were innocent. They showed absolutely no emotion at any question directed at them. When presented with the hard fact that there were no cases of suspicious death other than the ones where they were scheduled and working the wards, the response was always, "How could that be?"

When one interviews a hardened criminal for a prolonged period, the story always yields contradictions. Many hardened criminals' interview readily because of their desire to brag about what they accomplished. The depressed person, in an interview, will often open up and share her grief. The common criminal, once detected and caught, will readily admit to his involvement in a crime. The two nurses targeted in this case were most unwilling to talk of their activities and gave no impression that they would as much as give a clue to their involvement.

The only emotion that was scratched from the long interviews of both Pilo and Nunez was anger. Their anger was directed at the management of the VA hospital. They felt that the administration did not listen to their complaints at all and that nothing was ever done to address them. The central complaint that came forward was that they were terribly understaffed. The management, when questioned about this situation, agreed. They claimed they could do nothing about the hiring of new employees, and it was their charge to make sure the wards were staffed on all shifts, even if it meant that many employees would have to sacrifice vacation time.

What was developing as a motive was bizarre. After interviewing every nurse, doctor, orderly, and maintenance person associated with the operation of the hospital, it became clear that what was behind all these suspicious events was nothing more than a job action. Unfortunately for the victims, this form of job action caused death.

Pilo and Nunez had concocted the idea of creating code 7s for the purpose of demonstrating how severely understaffed the hospital was. Whenever a code 7 was called in, instructions were clear: drop everything and report to the patient's room involved in the code 7. A code 7, poorly staffed, would clearly demonstrate the serious staffing problems at the hospital. We questioned this motivation; did it not create more work for them? Would they not have more feelings for the patients? Were they concerned about being caught? How would they benefit? Nothing seemed to add up.

We clearly had an excellent circumstantial case. People died, bodies were exhumed, Pavulon was miraculously discovered in victims' body organ parts, and only two people were common to fifty-eight suspicious deaths under investigation. Yet we were missing the smoking gun.

The only conceivable place to find the smoking gun was in the interviews of patients who had either survived or were witnesses to an attack. It was impossible to bring together a worse gathering of potential witnesses than those who survived an attack in the VA hospital or were possible witnesses to a late hour visit by a nurse hell-bent on killing someone. For the most part, those in the patient pool we had to select from were so totally out of it that they could barely recall yesterday, much less weeks before. Larry Dolan was a good example. He had lucid moments, and on numerous occasions he seemed credible. However, we knew a cross-examination of him in court would be devastating based on his medical record of mental instability. As we looked at the potential pool of witnesses, we became very discouraged about how to achieve a desired outcome. As a last-ditch effort, and to maximize the outcome of our interviews of patients, I suggested using hypnosis.

About a year prior to this case, I studied the use of hypnosis as an investigative aid at the University of California at Los Angeles under William S. Kroger, MD. I knew enough about hypnosis to know its use was not without peril: garbage in, garbage out. The maximum expectation in using hypnosis depended greatly on the person you were hypnotizing. At the VA hospital, we were not starting with a great cast to expect maximum results. I was also aware that I would not qualify easily as an expert witness in any upcoming trial. We had to turn to an expert.

Herbert Speigel, MD, was both a medical doctor and a world-renowned expert on the use of hypnosis. Howard Teten and I had established a good relationship with Doctor Speigel, and we knew that he would make a formidable witness in his field. Speigel had conducted many early studies on behavior, especially as it applied to prisoners of war. One of his areas of interest was studying why some prisoners of war choose not to attempt an escape while others go to great lengths, even risking death, to escape. Speigel was an intense man—slight of stature, riveting eyes, personable, and somewhat "Kojack" looking. Speigel was a proponent of the eye roll method in evaluating one's susceptibility to hypnosis. His theory was simple. You ask the person being hypnotized to look straight ahead, with eyes opened, and ask the individual to roll their eyes upward. Those most likely to accept hypnosis would have their eye disappear under the upper eyelid. Those less likely to succeed with hypnosis would have little or no refraction of the pupil under the upper eyelid. Spiegel's research had established a high degree of correlation with the eye roll technique.

Spiegel's approach in the use of hypnosis as an interview technique was very straightforward. He was acutely aware that the surviving patients were not an ideal group with whom to use the technique of hypnosis. Speigel did have a sense that accepting hypnosis at trial could be difficult. It was with this in mind that he suggested every interview session be videotaped. The videotaping would start the moment the person walked in, through the explanation of hypnosis, and during the course of the entire interview conducted under hypnosis. While this was a tedious process, it was necessary. Any future review of the use of this technique would be able to see the clear documentation. This would offset any allegations that some piece of information was placed in the mind of the witness. For the most part it worked, but it had its shortcomings.

In theory, hypnosis enables the witness to recall in greater detail specific facts about a witnessed event. Hypnosis is not entering into a trance and allowing control of yourself to be given over to the hypnotist. Hypnosis is the process whereby a witness is brought to a greater level of relaxation and concentration. It is a process in which, as much as possible, the individual will put aside all other thoughts and focus on a specific event that he or she has witnessed. Great caution must be taken not to believe everything a person says while under hypnosis. Whatever is revealed under hypnosis has to be verified for accuracy. If the witness was very distracted when observing an event, hypnosis might serve to enable a clearer, more focused recollection of the event. However, if what is sought is not within the person's grasp or recollection, nothing can resurrect that from the mind. There have been many very dramatic uses of hypnosis—perhaps none more dramatic than the mass kidnapping and bus burial in California, where a witness was able to recall, under hypnosis, the full license plate of a vehicle. Many treat such a dramatic result as developing a film in the mind, but in fact it is nothing more than sharpening recollection.

Equally difficult, when administering hypnosis, is what the law enforcement officer and psychiatrist carry in their minds to the interview. During an interview of one of the surviving patients, we had a clear example of this. The FBI had briefed Dr. Speigel, and we had studied the case very closely. Going into the interview, we had a picture in our mind as to what we thought had happened in this case. We had studied the time charts for hours, and only two people were common to all incidents: Pilo and Nunez. This fact alone, coupled by our frustrating interviews with them, led us to believe we had the right people in focus. During the interview of Larry Dolan, we felt that he was in a pretty relaxed state and was making a sincere effort to concentrate on what happened the night he was administered Pavulon. Mindful of Dolan's fragile mental condition, we proceeded very slowly with him. We had him focusing on the night as he was lying in his bed asleep, and suddenly he was awakened by a nurse and given an injection. We asked him several times, "What do you now see?" His response was that the room was dark and he saw two people come into his room. Very slowly, we reached deeper, trying to get a description of who was in the room. "Do you know who is in the room?" We moved ever so slowly with one question at a time.

Dolan suddenly responded, "Pancho."

"Where is Pancho standing?"

"By the door, away from the bed."

"Who is he with?"

"A Philippine nurse."

"Do you know her name?"

"No."

"Can you see her name tag?"

"No."

Our questioning continued for many more minutes, making every effort to have him identify Pilo or Nunez. Dolan was unable to do so.

What we had done, very unintentionally, was inject our thoughts into the interview. We were convinced that Pilo and Nunez should be within Dolan's memory somewhere. We had never factored in Pancho, who had been employed as an orderly in the hospital. Our line of questioning ushered Pancho out of the picture and pointed out one of the weaknesses in the use of hypnosis. The hypnotist, or questioning law enforcement representative, must never lead the witness, intentionally or unintentionally.

Endless hours were spent interviewing surviving patients under hypnosis. At the conclusion of this process, we were no closer to a smoking gun than when we had started. Not one of the survivors was a credible witness who would be able to endure testifying in a case of this magnitude. What was clear was that we had what we'd had before the interviews began: physical evidence that Pavulon was used in the killings and was present in the nine bodies that had been exhumed and that two nurses were common to all of the events under suspicion. What was also very certain was that there was no hope of reaching either one of these nurses for a full confession of their activities when responding to the patients who were killed or entered into a Pavulon-induced seizure. The case would proceed to court based on very compelling circumstantial evidence.

The circumstantial evidence was strengthened by the fact that once the FBI arrived at the VA hospital and started to investigate these mysterious deaths, the killings stopped. We had made great preparations for the interviews of Pilo and Nunez but had not succeeded in breaking them of their story. Their story was not in the manner of an alibi but rather a denial that they could be involved in such activities. In the end, it would come down to whether the jury would pay attention to the mounting circumstantial evidence placed against the nurses or buy into the innocence of two people who had never committed acts like this before in their lives.

This case had clearly written a new chapter in understanding the criminal mind. There existed a dichotomy between past behavior and proven current behavior. There was an absence of pathology in both of these nurses. What was present was very compelling. It was the ability to compartmentalize behavior and deny responsibility for the results of their behavior. It was my strong belief that in the beginning of their work action against the hospital, they did not intend to kill the victims. Initially, they operated with a belief that code 7 with the inflicted patient would bring the patient back, and no one would be the wiser. When patients started to die as a result of Pavulon being administered, there was a mental disconnect, and they failed to see the connection that Pavulon was the death-causing agent. What was more readily accepted was that patients were dying because the hospital was terribly understaffed.

When you step back and closely study this behavior, it becomes more chilling than the killings of hardened serial killers. From all practical measures, you are dealing with normal people who live rather normal lives but make totally irrational decisions and show no element of remorse for their actions. This behavior is not new to society. People justify their behavior at all costs. They justify their actions as necessary and acceptable because they have convinced themselves that the end justifies the means. They question punishment for their actions because they have operated since youth without accepting or being held accountable for the outcome of what they do. What becomes more important is that they have been wronged, and no matter what it takes, they will bring attention to that wrong. The tragedy in this case was that people died, and two nurses never felt the consequences. They simply did not care. Certainly, if you dissect the components of what happened at the VA hospital in Ann Arbor, the explanation is simple. Pavulon administered to individuals in a non-controlled medical environment causes total muscular collapse, resulting in death by failure to breathe. It is also a known fact that medically trained doctors and nurses are well aware of the effects of Pavulon and its consequences. It is true that in certain situations, the effects of Pavulon can be reversed medically in a patient, but the patient's condition has a bearing on this reversal. The VA hospital identified fifty-eight mysterious incidents at its hospital in 1974 and 1975. The two nurses common to those incidents were Pilo and Nunez. The incidents stopped once the FBI initiated its investigation.

This case has lingered in my mind as one of the most baffling cases I have ever reviewed. What makes it so baffling is how very different it is from other murder cases. Most will admit that murder is a grizzly topic and that it involves brutality. The brutality is often at the end of a gun or the sharp slash of a knife. It can be poison or simply blunt traumatic force. Nevertheless, it is remarkable by its force and brutalizing of another person. The killers fit neatly into the mentally deranged, psychopathic thrill seekers or the momentarily enraged individuals. Killing does not fit neatly into the white garb of a nurse who has dedicated herself/himself to caring for people. Killing does not suddenly erupt in a personality that is marked by normalcy for so many years. Killing is seldom shared in its mission. It is normally the act of one mentally driven by a failure to seek rational solutions to everyday pressures. How do you then fit two nurses from traditional backgrounds who have dedicated their lives to studying nursing and caring for people, and with no previous history of violent behavior, into being monstrous killers of potentially fifty-eight people? The answer will never be fully understood. What is clear is that they shared the anger they had against the VA hospital and that they let that anger grow to immense proportions. Their anger was only increased by the VA's inability to deal with a real problem in real time. The VA's lack of support for those working a poorly staffed hospital increased the anger of those left behind to deal with the problem on a daily basis. There was a disconnect between management and the everyday staff managing the wards. This led to a sense of autonomy on each shift. Pilo and Nunez struck back in a very deadly way. They could have chosen sick leave or work slowdown, but in a strange way, doing so was against their character. They prided themselves in doing a good job. The more they witnessed the nurse's role suffer, the more their anger grew. Pilo and Nunez chose a course of action that turned out deadly. It was a job action to demonstrate how incapable the hospital was of dealing not only with everyday events but also with emergency events. Cold blood was the course they chose. It was not an accident that they chose to use Pavulon. Pavulon was quick, basically beyond detection, and complete. If the patient was resuscitated, he survived. If not, he died, and nobody would be the wiser. At the outset, death was probably not intended, but once it occurred, it did not deter them from their course of action. Death occurred often and early in the actions triggered by Pilo and Nunez. In many ways, they traded guilt, and neither ever accepted responsibility.

 Pilo and Nunez killed the way they knew to do so; they killed with an injection of a drug available to them, Pavulon. The weapon was no stranger to them, a syringe. On many occasions, they did not have to touch the victim, only his feeding tube. There was nothing personal; the victim was not the cause of the rage they suffered. When death did occur, it was often well after they struck, lessening their connection to the event. Guilt was not a problem for them because they had not caused what was taking place. It was, of course, the VA hospital. When patients died, they had no real emotional connection with them because they were trained not to become emotionally tied to any patient. Death for a patient was perhaps viewed as being better than living in an environment where care was not good.

It took months of intensive planning and preparation for the government to have its case ready for the federal court where Pilo and Nunez were to face charges. They were officially charged with nine counts of murder and countless attempted murders. When they appeared in court, they seemed relaxed and confident that they would prevail. The government proceeded with its case still missing the smoking gun. The prosecution felt confident that it could present its case in a compelling, logical manner, which would lead to the conviction of Pilo and Nunez. The case was tried before Federal Judge Julius Pratt. Judge Pratt was a very serious man who ran a disciplined courtroom. He had little patience for nonsense and was concerned that justice prevail in his court. He made little effort to befriend either the defense or the prosecution, clearly portraying a neutral position. The prosecution knew him to be a fair judge but one who was somewhat unpredictable. He was by no means a judge soft on any form of crime.

The case took weeks to unfold. In many ways, it did not differ from most cases, with physical evidence laid out, time lines demonstrated, and motive displayed. The defense was clearly aware that the government did not have a compelling witness to testify, "Yes, I saw Pilo/Nunez inject me with a needle, and moments later I could not breathe." That testimony never came because there was no one to deliver it with perfect recollection of what transpired. The available witnesses were far short of the caliber needed in a case of this nature. Despite the lack of a compelling witness, the government successfully presented testimony that spoke to the important issues mentioned earlier. There was no question the weapon was Pavulon. There was no question that the nine bodies exhumed had Pavulon in the body tissues. There was no question as to the list of victims at the hospital. There was compelling testimony in charting the nurses on duty when the suspect episodes occurred. There was evidence presented that demonstrated why it was impossible to bring forward a witness to testify as to what had happened, because they were either dead or incompetent. The defense did little or nothing to dismiss the government's argument. The jury listened intently and seemed to work patiently in wading through all the evidence presented before them. The end came, and the case was turned over to the jury. The future of Pilo and Nunez was in their hands.

After three days of deliberation, the jury returned its verdict. The verdict was guilty on all charges. The prosecution felt very accomplished in that an extremely delicate case, which was very circumstantial, stood up to the test. The individuals charged with this crime were found guilty. The defense, on the other hand, was somewhat shocked that a conviction was returned on evidence that was predominantly circumstantial.

Laticia Pilo and Fatima Nunez sat motionless and without expression when the jury returned the verdict. It was as though it was expected. While their facial expressions did not betray the inner feelings they were going through, after days their anger turned to the streets in the form of mass demonstrations. Seldom in the history of crime were two accused and convicted killers able to turn loose on the streets across the country loud, boisterous demonstrations claiming their innocence. From Detroit to San Francisco, sign-carrying supporters of the two nurses took to the streets, claiming that Pilo and Nunez were wrongly convicted. Demonstrations even occurred in their homeland, the Philippines. One could argue the effect these demonstrations had on public opinion and what political pressure was made on Washington by the Philippine government in behalf of its two "children." For the most part, the demonstrations were noisy but orderly. The one I witnessed in San Francisco was not widely attended, but the banners nevertheless carried the message that justice was not served in Judge Pratt's courtroom.

During the trial, Judge Pratt was very contained in his feelings as to how the case was progressing. Pratt knew this to be an extraordinary case and was aware of the sensitivity based on the nationality of the two accused. Much to the surprise of the government, very shortly after the case was completed, Judge Pratt threw out the conviction of Pilo and Nunez. The reason he cited in taking this action was based on "the outrageous conduct on behalf of the government when prosecuting the case." Most were stunned at this decision because they saw no indication of it during the trial. The decision was final, and the only action the government could contemplate would be an appeal. Based on the nature of this case being formed around an intense amount of highly circumstantial evidence, the government decided not to appeal. Judge Julius Pratt was well within his prerogative to make the decision he made, but it was clear to me that two people got away with murder—not once, but many times over. The FBI saw merit in this case, the mysterious deaths did occur, Pavulon was the proven weapon, and the two nurses were present…circumstantial, yes; but the jury saw it also.

In taking the journey to understand the criminal mind, I have come to understand what makes this case so profound. It is that Laticia Pilo and Fatima Nunez came much closer to being like us than the monsters we read about so frequently as our mass murderers. What makes us reflect on them is their ability to shut guilt down, to disavow the actions they were accused of, and to continue a course of activity knowing death would occur. This compartmentalizing of behavior has become more commonplace in our society. In this case, it entailed injecting a patient lying helpless in a hospital with Pavulon and, when the shift ended, returning home to feed one's children, kneeling down to say night prayers, and tucking the babies in with love.

When people lose touch with the consequences of their actions, society suffers greatly. If the consequences are ignored and the only thing that matters is how we feel when we act, we have surrendered ourselves to less than human behavior. Society will than become a place run on instincts alone. If our instinct is anger, lust, revenge, hatred, bitterness, destruction, or violence, without any sense of inhibition, the consequences are too far down the road to matter. That is when the "normal" among us do not-so-normal things, such as murder.

CHAPTER 9

The Spy Who Couldn't Spy

❦

AUGUST 1984 WAS AN EXTREMELY hot month in northern Virginia. I spent most of that month preparing to move back to Los Angeles, California, where I had been assigned in the mid-60s. Moving back was going to be very different because now we had five children and a golden retriever to be concerned with. Being transferred by the FBI was always an exciting time. The transfer itself meant immediate change and getting used to everything being turned upside down. Neighborhoods, schools, churches, and doctors were all out there as a new adventure.

The FBI was in the process of making transfers less traumatic on families by initiating a program familiar to corporate America. In the program, the government would buy your house if you were not able to sell it on your own. The contract had not been settled on this program, and it would not be fully operational until well into 1985. The secret to a successful transfer was to not fight it but look upon it as a vacation period.

My wife and I packed up five children and a dog for the long trip. Leaving Virginia after twelve years of calling it home was difficult on the children. It was especially difficult for the oldest, who was approaching her senior year in high school. Her senior year had been laid out; she would be head cheerleader and captain of the soccer team. Transferring was not good news to her, but she gave it a valiant try. The younger four took on a positive attitude and seemed to enjoy the vacation-like atmosphere of driving cross-country. In many ways, our trip was much like the movie *The Vacation*. The only exception was that we did not have Grandma with us. Traveling under government transfer made you keep up a pace of at least three hundred miles per day and follow a route plan that you were made to lay out. The routine would soon set in: up early in the morning, drive most of the day, and get to a hotel around four or five o'clock, just in time for a swim.

A well-planned trip would of course give you enough time to see major sites along the way, such as the Grand Canyon. Toward the end of our trip, we left enough time to rent a boat and take a most pleasurable swim in Lake Powell. The next day it was on to Las Vegas for an overnight stay, leaving us within striking distance of Los Angeles.

Pulling into Los Angeles was exciting. The wide-open plains were behind us and the magnificent Grand Canyon a memory. The vastness of the desert where we moved cautiously in our 1976 Ford Club Van and Datsun B210 was a new sight for our children. As we crested the San Bernardino Mountains, descending into the Los Angeles basin, the dense smog that clung to the city struck us. It was not appealing, and the children voiced their opinions: "Dad, this stinks." This helped me make a quick decision to take the 10 Freeway to the end and journey to Camarillo, California, on the Pacific Coast Highway. My decision worked; one view of the Pacific Ocean set their imaginations running wild. Now they felt that this transfer might be fun and have new adventures.

The adventures started from day one. We moved into temporary lodging in a house located on Elma Street in Camarillo. All of our furniture was back in Virginia, and the only furniture we took with us was our fifty-inch projection television and a microwave oven. Our first project was to locate rental furniture to make the house livable. We arrived toward the end of August, just in time to register the five children for school. The house on Elma Street would satisfy the very basic needs of living for the next six months. It took six months for the government to work out the real estate portion of the new transfer policy, and we were one of the first to take advantage of it. When March came, we were more than anxious to have a place called home, with our own furniture, leaving the mysteries of Elma Street behind us.

One of the very first things I did, after arriving, was place a phone call to the Los Angeles office of the FBI, advising them of my arrival in Los Angeles. When I called, I was immediately transferred to Jim Fox, whose position I was filling. Jim stated on the phone, "Pat, you have got to come right in."

My response was, "You got to be kidding me; we just got off the road after driving over three thousand miles."

He responded, "Pat, I wish I were kidding, but we cannot discuss on the phone what is going on. You have to come in now; come as you are."

I was dressed very casually in white slacks and a white shirt when I strolled into the FBI office. I knew Jim Fox would be waiting on the seventeen[th] floor. As I entered his room, he had a very tired and determined look on his face. We had spent a few years as inspectors and knew each other very well. I could tell when Jim was serious and when he was expressing a lighter side. There was little question that he was very serious. As I was sitting down, after greeting all in the room, Jim first explained that it was necessary to call me in because he was scheduled to report to New York on Monday and had to leave by plane tomorrow. He further went on to explain that Richard Bretzing, the special agent in charge, had taken a much-deserved vacation in Hawaii. Bretzing would not return for a number of days.

Sitting quietly in the corner was an individual from Headquarters in Washington, Don Stuckey. Don was from the intelligence division, and it was clear to me when I was advised to report immediately that what had transpired related to the intelligence field. Jim Fox had a very calm way about him. In many ways, he resembled the movie actor Robert Mitchum in both looks and manner. As he started to speak, I was astounded at what he had to say—that we had a defection of one of our agents to the Soviets. The agent's name was Richard W. Miller. Miller had worked in the intelligence side of the office and was currently assigned to monitoring a technical installation. What was clear in Jim Fox's mind was that Miller had just initiated his contacts with the Soviets. Fox was unaware of what material, if any, Miller had compromised to the Russians.

The realization that an FBI agent would betray his country was overwhelming. It had never happened before, and every agent was proud of this fact. For it to happen the first time sent shock waves of anger through our minds. What was more important than the emotions we felt was that we had to prove Miller was intentionally betraying his country. We had to investigate one of our own.

The game plan had been well discussed before my arrival in the Los Angeles office. Although after today I would be in charge of the office until the return of Bretzing, FBI Headquarters would be calling the shots on the investigation of Miller. Already on its way into the Los Angeles territory was the San Francisco surveillance team, equipped with air support. The decision was made very early that the Los Angeles agents would be kept in the dark about this investigation for fear that word would get back to Miller before probable cause was established to arrest and convict him.

This could not have happened at a worse time. Los Angeles had just closed the book on a very successful handling of the Olympics in 1984. Years of preparation had gone into the security strategy for hosting an Olympic event due to the concern about a terrorist attack on the athletes or on some facility remotely connected to the Olympics. Not only did nothing of this nature take place, but the Olympics were a huge success in every way, including financially. The city of Los Angeles was proud of itself, and every participating law enforcement agency breathed a sigh of relief while congratulating itself for a job well done. The FBI was no different; it was basking in the sunshine of praise. However, Richard W. Miller gave it very little time to enjoy the post-Olympic high.

Richard W. Miller was a complex personality to understand. Many of the traits he perfected in his mature years as an FBI agent stood in sharp contrast to what an FBI agent was expected to be. He was extremely overweight, very much a loner in the office, and basically lazy. The most common question asked about him was how did he ever survive without being fired? What Miller had perfected most was the ability to be marginal at best and the ability to survive numerous pressures put to bear by his supervisors. He was somewhat of a castaway and was never a popular choice for serving on any squad. If a special investigation took place in a resident agency, the agency preferred receiving no help rather than having Miller assigned. His current assignment at this time was one way the office had to keep Miller out of the public's perception as much as possible. Miller worked in a small office monitoring a technical installation. He was never out of the office, with the exception of lunch or some personal emergency. Miller was a Mormon and had a large family of what I recall to be eight children. Because of the high cost of housing in the immediate area around the FBI office in West Los Angeles, Miller, like most agents, traveled far to get to work. During his assignments, he lived in both Riverside and Orange Counties.

From all outward appearances, Miller's family members were good, practicing Mormons. They enjoyed the strict traditions of their religion, coupled with an intense loyalty to the United States. There were reports that Miller did have a hard time making ends meet but that on several occasions he received help from the Mormon Church. There were numerous reports, especially after his arrest, that he sold Amway products out of the back of his FBI car. Miller's career in the FBI went nowhere, and in 1984, it was going nowhere fast.

The most intriguing puzzle in Miller's betrayal was who initiated the contact between Miller and Svetlana. One theory is that when Svetlana was being operated as a source of information by the FBI, the handling agents might have given her enough information to know that Miller was a very marginal agent and one she could compromise in the future. The theory that Miller put forward at his time of trial was that he contacted her in an effort to resurrect his staggering career by opening her as a source of information. This theory seemed not to hold up. His fellow agents regarded Miller as a disaster waiting to happen. There was evidence from the telephone traffic within the Los Angeles office that on more than one occasion, Svetlana had called Miller, indicating that Svetlana initiated the contact.

In 1984, Svetlana Ogorodnikova had passed her years of attractiveness. Early pictures of her would indicate that at one time she was an attractive woman capable of seducing someone. The years had treated her very harshly. She was an alcoholic and was known to go on severe drinking binges. During the course of the investigation, while she was under surveillance, an ambulance came to her residence. It was later confirmed that she was rushed to the hospital as a result of drinking cleaning fluid. There was little doubt from the profile on Svetlana in 1984 was that she was no longer useful either to the Russians or to US intelligence because of her lack of dependability; she was emotionally unstable. What drew her to Miller, and what drew Miller to her, was somewhat of a mystery. Miller's reasoning that he wanted to restart his career was baseless, especially when factoring Svetlana into the equation. Perhaps Svetlana was the one who really wanted to prove her importance by bringing in a prize catch of an FBI agent as a defector.

What Miller brought to the encounter with Svetlana was the personality of a beaten man. Miller never accomplished anything in life and was clearly aware that he hung on the ropes as an FBI agent. He was bored of his married life and worn out because of the responsibility all his children brought to him. His Mormon faith did little to bolster him up, but that was his choosing. Miller was ripe for being compromised because he was looking for excitement in his otherwise dull existence. His motivation was none other than greed for money and sex. The match between Svetlana and Miller was very even—both were has-beens in life. Regardless of how they viewed their importance before the summer of 1984, life had now passed them by. The issue of what Miller saw sexually in Svetlana or what Svetlana saw sexually in Miller was baffling. Miller made the conscious decision to betray his country based on selfish needs and the appetite for money. The only question remaining was whether he would perform as poorly as a spy as he did as a special agent. It was now up to the FBI to prove that Miller had betrayed his family, church, country, and the FBI.

From the very first day after arriving in Los Angeles, I sensed that the Los Angeles office of the FBI was under tremendous pressure in many areas. The Olympic Games had just been made a part of history, and the FBI felt very successful in their peaceful outcome. They, along with their counterparts in law enforcement and the city's officialdom, had reason to celebrate. Immediately, however, the defection of Miller fell into our laps. In addition, before the Los Angeles office was aware of what was happening concerning Miller, many other situations had begun to unravel.

With the intense preparation for the Olympic Games, a number of personnel matters were left unattended. The most serious one that demanded attention concerned how the Hispanic agents perceived the way they were treated. Matt Perez had held the position I was filling before Jim Fox took over for the short interim period of three months. Perez and Bretzing never got along, and it was common knowledge in the office that hostility existed between them. In 1982, I inspected the Los Angeles office and was witness to the hostility between the number-one and number-two men of the division. Perez was a very colorful individual, well-liked by many in the office. He was both personal and engaging in conversation. In his earlier years, he had studied for the priesthood for a very short period—but long enough to give him a strong desire to study the arts. Perez was far more comfortable reading a third-century manuscript than reading an FBI report, and he had a habit of procrastinating with issues, especially issues he deemed not important. The job he had as top administrative assistant special agent in charge of the office demanded quick resolutions of numerous problems on a daily basis. Perez, from his early years, had pushed his career along. While functioning as a supervisor in Los Angeles, he clearly let it be known that he was interested in administrative advancement. He was assigned as assistant special agent in charge in San Juan, Puerto Rico, during some very difficult times of terrorism. When the special agent in charge of San Juan was transferred, Judge William Webster elevated Perez to that position. In many ways, this was a critical mistake, and Perez, while satisfied, did not realize that he had missed the most important rank of inspector, which would have provided him with much greater knowledge of running a field division. Perez's temperament and lack of experience worked against his efforts when he was assigned under Richard Bretzing.

What grew out of this negative atmosphere was one of the darkest periods in the long history of the FBI. Perez took his personal fight with Bretzing to a different level—the courts. It became a battle where equal employment opportunity was used as a shield, in somewhat of a masterful manner, to carry out a personal vendetta. The Los Angeles office was divided into two camps. The split-off camp, inspired by Perez, consisted of the Hispanic agents.

Within the first few months of assignment, what also became obvious was the existence of seven long, festering personnel issues. All of these personnel matters had to do with the psychological fitness of special agents. Each of these cases had to be addressed with a great deal of sensitivity and alacrity. It was clearly a period when my early training in psychology was of critical use. All seven were dismissed for medical reasons. Each case was different, but each case was adjudicated for the best interest of the individual as well as the FBI.

Coupled with all of this was a growing unrest among the female FBI agents. This tension grew to the point that the *Los Angeles Times* carried a front-page account of the grievances being aired. Many of the grievances had little merit but were issues that were allowed to grow in the climate of unrest that was being experienced.

There was a tremendous amount of adjustment going on within the FBI, and it continues to this day. The effort to recruit women into the ranks of the FBI was not an easy institutional change for anyone involved, especially the women. In addition, the emphasis on recruiting minorities caused great concern for the lessening of qualifications.

Despite all of what was underway, the news of having a spy be one of us in the FBI was most devastating. This was not the pains of an institutional change in direction or the mistreatment of a class within the organization. This was treason, pure and simple.

The San Francisco surveillance units were in position from day one. It was late August, and the number of daylight hours was decreasing. The difficulty we had was keeping the SF units from being detected by the Los Angeles agents. This was no small task. Simple things, such as where to bed them down and where they should eat, all had to be considered so as not to compromise the investigation. Miller's activities originated from Orange County to the federal building on Wilshire Boulevard in West Lost Angeles. Would someone detect the air surveillance near the office? Certain precautions had to be taken within the office to ensure they went undetected. There had been a relatively close relationship between the FBI field offices in Los Angeles and San Francisco, so the agents knew each other well. Shortly after the surveillance began on Miller, an FBI agent came into my office and asked, "Are you aware of any reason a surveillance plane would be operating around our office?" I was forced to play ignorant, but it was clear to me that the task of keeping this operation outside the knowledge of the Los Angeles agents would not last for very long.

One of the major concerns in a defection of this nature is the integrity of the FBI files. We were extremely concerned that Miller would attempt to copy the files and turn the material over to the Soviets. A camera was installed late one night over the copy machine on the fifteen[th] floor. From all observations, the camera had been secreted as well as one could expect. It would take a great deal of looking to detect it. One week after the installation, however, the clerk operating the copy machine went to her supervisor and reported that she thought a camera was installed over her work area, and she questioned whether it had anything to do with her. She had to be reassured that it did not and that in fact there was no camera over her work area. Whether she was convinced or not, the camera stayed and did the job expected of it.

Following Miller every moment of the day turned out to be an interesting study of his behavior. For the most part it was very routine, but in our early days of following him, he gave us moments of great concern. One such moment was when he showed up to work in his orange Volkswagen beetle carrying a shopping bag. We were confident that the shopping bag was full of FBI files. Miller was allowed into the federal building without a search of the shopping bag based on his recognition of the security guards and his FBI affiliation. Once he was in his work environment, the camera installed over his desk picked him up unloading the shopping bag. We were not quite shocked, but certainly relieved, to see him unpack the contents of the shopping bag into his desk: cookies, chips, and candies. What the camera revealed was his tendency to snack all day, adding to his major problem of being overweight. At this point, we were a whole lot less worried about Miller's weight problem than about what he was back-dooring to the Russians.

As the days and weeks went by, great pressure was on the FBI to have a case that would hold up in court. From the information gathered, we determined Miller had turned over to the Russians certain intelligence security manuals. While these manuals were classified as secret, they were not of a nature that would severely damage US security. At this point in the investigation, the most damaging aspect was that for the first time in the history of the FBI, a special agent betrayed his country and the oath he had taken. Working in the field of intelligence always brought one close to the concept of defection because much of the effort against the Soviets and others related to that very same issue—to get them to defect. The harder we attempted to target someone in the hostile intelligence community, the more we realized the same was being done to us. This was the business we were in, and we were well aware of it. The longer we went without a defector, the greater the pride grew that we were the untouchables. Now that was no longer the case.

A great deal of Miller's contact with Svetlana occurred in Miller's car. During the course of the surveillance, it was documented that Miller engaged in sex with Svetlana while in the Volkswagen (VW) Beetle. A study of Miller's weight problem and the inner space of a VW Beetle left the investigators in disbelief. It was critical in the investigation to broaden the scope of the surveillance by bugging his car. This was no small feat. Miller was unpredictable during the business day. He would often leave his work area and wander down to his car to retrieve something. We needed at least two solid hours to install a bug in a secure manner, and our technicians had to be guaranteed that Miller would not interrupt them. My suggestion was that I would call Miller to my office to fully discuss his serious problem with weight.

When Miller arrived in my office, he appeared very relaxed, knowing that the topic would be his battle with weight. Miller had a very condescending manner about him. He had an answer for every question you would throw at him and a willingness to talk about peripheral matters as long as you were willing to listen. Down through the years, Miller was no stranger to inspectors grilling him about his poor performance, so one more session on the weight matter was of no great concern. What Miller did not know was that I had knowledge of his every move over the past three weeks. Miller went on to explain that in addressing his weight problems, he had gone to a counselor. He claimed his counselor was extremely helpful in stressing that he needed a more positive attitude in setting realistic goals for weight loss. What Miller did not know was that I was aware of how much candy and food he stuffed into his mouth during an eight-hour shift. All the good words of a counselor would be to no avail in such a case.

What Miller did demonstrate was his ability to lie, and lie with conviction. Miller was clearly aware that the SAC, Richard Bretzing, would seek his dismissal from the FBI if he failed to medically qualify. Miller was extremely close to the age requirement for retirement, and that was a major concern. Miller had a way of sweet-talking people. In many ways, he sweet-talked the Los Angeles nurse into feeling sorry for him and for his inability to maintain an acceptable weight standard.

Miller talked for well over two hours on issues ranging from weight to what he planned to do in retirement. He did not hesitate to engage on any topic. The one topic he failed to bring up in almost two-and-one-half hours of discussion was his contact with the Russians. Looking back, he must have felt very good after our meeting. Good that he was not severely threatened by the weight issue but even better about how much I was in the dark about his contact and cooperation with the Russians. When the installation of the bug was complete in his VW, my secretary rang me, serving as a signal that all was clear. It took me fifteen more minutes to wind down and end the conversation with Miller. It was all I could do to keep my feelings of disappointment and anger from showing. Miller sat before me as a very dissipated individual who, because of a lack of personal discipline, allowed himself to be compromised by the Russians. He let down everyone he knew, and he destroyed a tradition that had been held with immense pride.

At his many trials, I was cross-examined with the question, "Were you not deceitful with Mr. Miller in your discussions of his weight problem, knowing that the real purpose of your meeting was to give time for the bug installation in his car?" My answer was clear. I was honest in my discussion of Mr. Miller's weight problem because we felt that if we could not establish a solid case against Mr. Miller, we would still be in a position to terminate him for his failure in fitness for duty. I further testified that Mr. Miller had no right to be advised of our tactics against him; he had surrendered that right when he betrayed his country.

It was natural for me to wonder, as Miller left my office, what motivated him. What was the psychological profile of this spy? This was the first spy I had personally encountered, and in many ways, he seemed not to fit into a neat psychological profile. There were certain indicators that seemed to stand out, but to claim that these indicators led him to the decision of betraying his country was a bit of a reach. Clearly, the trait that stood out the most was Miller's lack of maturity in refusing to accept responsibility for his behavior—coupled with a high degree of egocentricity, in that he justified in his mind whatever he chose to do. Miller was a deceitful person, a social outcast by his work peers. He seemed extremely dejected at his lot in life. It was as though getting married at a young age and having so many children gave him a responsibility that wore him down. He seemed depressed over his family life and wanted a way out. Miller knew by his work assignments that his fellow agents and supervisors did not hold him in high regard. He had little or no job satisfaction. Miller, being a Mormon, was also not held in high regard by his church. He had difficulty with the church and had been chastised on several occasions for his lack of participation. Religion was not the center of his life. Miller had a high degree of depression; he was not a cheerful or optimistic person. His overweight condition added to his depression, and he seemed to have little or no self-esteem. There was little in Miller's life that offered excitement, joy, or happiness. When you took an independent look at all of the factors in Miller's life, you had to wonder how he was ever selected for the FBI. The character traits were not there, and there was little evidence that they had ever existed.

Years later, it was interesting to compare the Miller's life with the lives of the two FBI spies who caused so much hurt and damage to our country, Earl E. Pitts and Robert P. Hanssen.

I had met Earl Pitts years earlier before he was arrested. My contact with him was strictly social, driven by a business relationship with his wife, Mary. Pitts was a very nondescript person, with little or no personality. He seemed to lack social ease. Pitts was more intelligent than Miller and did not have the same negative peer relationship. His married life to Mary seemed normal but somewhat reclusive. Outside of immediate family, there was little evidence of strong ties with neighbors. Mary was a very competent person, fiercely loyal to the FBI when she served in the clerical capacity of secretary. She was extremely good at what she did as a secretary and was very dependable. Earl seemed always to exist in the shadows and never projected himself well in a social setting.

I never had the opportunity to meet Robert Hanssen. The public disclosures on Hanssen leave him as the single most interesting person to analyze regarding his motivations for spying on the United States for the Russians. The amount of damage he did over the many years of cooperating with the Russians was beyond comparison. Pitts, too, was able to inflict extreme damage on the FBI, but Miller was less compromising by far.

What made Hanssen particularly interesting to profile was the set of conflicts within this man's life. His adherence to the Catholic faith, especially to the extreme conservative association with the Opus Dei movement within the Church. His association with a known prostitute for the purpose of saving her. His giving large sums of money to her and being with her on a trip abroad. His large family that he carefully, skillfully enrolled in excellent schools. His spy activities costing the lives of individuals. The fact that he spied for so long.

Hanssen's remaining faithful to his wife of many years. His seeking promotions within the FBI. His back-stopping efforts to enable him to spy further.

Three very different men who hold the same distinction of being FBI agents who betrayed the oath they had pledged to uphold. What these three individuals have in common is the utter distain of every FBI agent who remained faithful to his country and, most importantly, to himself. Other traits these three individuals had in common acted as a basis for them becoming spies: social inadequacy, egocentricity, lack of self-esteem, immaturity, loneliness, willingness to take a risk, deceit, not highly regarded by peers, isolated, and bored with their personal lives. These characteristics are not limited to individuals who spy and are present in many individuals who would never think of betraying their country. In the cases of these three men, no one will ever be able to identify the reason for their betrayal. In Miller's case, it appeared to be money and sex. In Pitts' case, it seemed to be revenge, power, excitement, and money. In the devastating case of Hanssen, the motivation is clouded by conflicting accounts. What makes Hanssen's case more pronounced is the duration over which his treasonous behavior continued, indicating a more established pathology of deceit and cunning behavior. His efforts to seek religious forgiveness through confessing his sins is sheer hypocrisy in that forgiveness is granted only when there is a firm resolve to not commit the act again.

Hanssen's personality is more profoundly disturbed than one can imagine. Any association with a prostitute, based on the premise that he is saving her, is next to ludicrous. If, in fact, he had no sexual relationship with this woman, we get into a far more complex area of sexual fantasy, which can only be revealed after long hours of psychotherapy. Hanssen had a love affair with money, power, and a sense that he was more intelligent than others. He treated life much like a chess game until he ran out of pieces. Hanssen used the tools he was trained in by the FBI as his personal defenses for almost twenty years. He succeeded far more than any other had before, and his activity cost the lives of other human beings. In his compartmented mind-set, this had no bearing on his behavior. His arrogance was complete.

Unlike Hanssen and Pitts, Miller was captured early in his efforts to seek relief from how he perceived life. Miller's surveillance was tight. In an eight-week period, every moment of his odyssey was chronicled. His regular meetings with Svetlana as well as his work routine became a predictable pattern. It was a bright, clear day in late September when Miller parked his VW in a small park south of the FBI office alongside the 405 Freeway. He sat in his car exchanging small talk with Svetlana and spoke of taking a possible trip to Europe. Svetlana had already purchased a raincoat for Miller, and they felt this item would be used as a means of identifying Miller. Miller had no way of knowing that his every word was being monitored. It was interesting to note that Miller's characteristic laziness had a bearing on this meeting with Svetlana. Miller was within two blocks of the FBI office. Without any planning, another FBI car, driven by Paul (PP) DeFlores, pulled into the same park and made eye contact with Miller. Miller was convinced, by this action, that he was under the watchful eye of the FBI and that they knew his actions. It was true that the FBI was watching Miller, but DeFlores was not a part of the surveillance team.

The accidental encounter of Miller and DeFlores, while initially thought to be a disaster, worked in the favor of Miller's investigation. Miller became convinced that the FBI was onto his spying. For the days following the accidental encounter, Miller seemed extremely paranoid. He went as far as going into the office of Brice Christensen, a fellow Mormon, for small talk in an effort to see if Christensen would give any indication that he was onto what Miller was doing. It took two or three days of Miller stewing over whether he had been detected for him to catch Brice Christensen after business hours in his office alone. His timing was perfect; he caught Brice putting his material put away, readying to close his office for the day. Richard Miller came into Brice's office and asked Brice if he could talk with him.

The encounter that was to take place would later create legal consternation. Instead of Brice stopping Miller when he started into his discussion for the purpose of getting another agent to witness what was being said, Brice put on his "father confessor" hat and listened to what turned out to be a confession of Miller's guilt. Brice went as far as having Miller provide a signed sworn statement summarizing the contents of his discussion. In that discussion, he confessed to his turning his FBI credentials over to Svetlana for the purpose of establishing his bona fides with the Russians. Miller was not so specific as to include his sexual encounters with Svetlana, but he did confess that the two of them were planning a trip to an undisclosed location in Europe for the purpose of meeting his future "handler." Because Brice Christensen was Miller's immediate assistant agent in charge, Brice had been made aware of the allegation against Miller and the surveillance that was going on around Miller's activities.

In what turned out to be Miller's confession, there were no surprises. Miller was quick to furnish the identity of the material he had turned over to Svetlana and the Russians. Miller denied turning over any active intelligence investigation. Miller also denied turning over the identity of any sources of information the FBI was operating or had operated against the Russians. Upon reading the confession the next morning, we were somewhat shocked that Christensen had not called us at home to advise us of Miller's actions and that he had waited until the next day. We were confident, however, from what had transpired, that Miller was caught in the earliest step of his spying endeavor. Miller had not met his handler and never was tasked at performing any operation for the Russians. This knowledge was extremely beneficial because in the overall damage assessment, we felt that Miller's activity was nipped in the bud.

The knowledge that Miller had confessed spread like wildfire throughout the office. The level of suspicion had grown so much over the nearly eight weeks of investigation that it was all but a known fact that someone was in serious trouble. There were several sightings of San Francisco agents in the Los Angeles division territory. Questions abounded surrounding their presence, and all sorts of rumors began as to why they were here. When word reached the squad rooms that Miller had confessed to cooperating with the Russians, everyone was full of anger. What made matters worse was that the first defector was regarded by most as a bumbling idiot. In the anger came the finger-pointing. Most were concerned that because Miller was a Mormon, he received preferential treatment from the Mormon management team of Bretzing and Christensen.

The action of Christensen sitting alone through Miller's confession was extremely unwise. However, the allegations that Christensen and Bretzing were soft on Miller could not be farther from the truth. Upon his return from Hawaii—cutting his vacation short once he received word of what Miller was up to—Bretzing vigorously approved the investigation on Miller and was in favor of harsh punishment for him throughout the judicial process. Unfortunately, those in the office who already harbored ill feelings against Mr. Bretzing as a result of the Matt Perez–created "Spanish agent" issue believed the worst and cast much of the blame on Mr. Bretzing. It was not deserved.

With Miller's confession to Christensen taking us off guard, Miller's arrest had to be hastened. After consultation with the USA, Rob Bonner, the arrest of Richard W. Miller was put on the front burner. The most experienced agents in the Los Angeles office were chosen to take part in the arrest. There was much planning performed prior to arresting Miller—not because he created a safety concern but rather to ensure that nothing we did would give Miller a constitutional loophole. Joseph Chefalo was one of the arresting agents. Chefalo had worked banks for years and was currently the bank robbery supervisor. Agents used on the arrest were mostly from the criminal squads, having more current experiences in handling criminal matters. Miller was arrested at home, early in the morning. His arrest shocked his wife and children, and as would be expected, they went into a period of denial. For the arresting agents, there was no sympathy for Miller, but there was immediate concern for Miller's family. The concern was how Miller's wife would be able to provide for such a large family at this difficult time.

After the arrest, which went without incident, Miller was charged and arraigned, and bond was refused. Miller went straight to jail. The media all over the country carried the story with as many details as were available to them. Miller was depicted as a less-than-mediocre agent, with heavy family responsibilities, who chose to betray his country. What the media did not miss was the fact that he was the first FBI agent who spied.

Once the news had spread that Miller had been arrested for spying, Miller's entire career came under a microscope. Much of the talk related to how he was such a disaster as an agent. Lengthy discussion involved how he ever got into the FBI. Former supervisors came forward to defend their efforts to have Miller fired. No matter how much finger-pointing took place and claims that had the agent in charge listened, Miller would long since have been fired, the truth was that for years the FBI accepted his marginal performance and was willing to carry him into retirement, not expecting much from him. It was extremely difficult to fire people from government positions, especially if the individual had veteran's rights. No one was willing to address Miller on either count—performance or fitness for duty. Now there was no choice; Miller committed a crime, and he was arrested for it.

It took some weeks to gather all the information representing the investigation of Miller. Miller, in the meantime, received two court-appointed attorneys to represent him, Stan Greenberg and Joel Levine. Stan Greenberg was no stranger to FBI agents; he had played handball with many of them and had numerous close friends who were FBI agents. Greenberg's friends among the FBI agents were men to admire. Upon getting to know R. W. Miller, Greenberg questioned his handball buddies as to how Miller ever became an agent. Stan Greenberg was about five-feet-nine-inches tall and came across as a feisty prizefighter. He was well known for being tenacious in a courtroom and somewhat brutal under cross-examination—both ethical and tough. He did not share the label of being anti-FBI, but he did carry the reputation of vigorously defending his client.

Joel Levine was regarded as the thinker among the two representing Miller. Joel was slight of build and looked rather scholarly. His approach was very different from that of Greenberg. Levine would wear you down by pointing out inconsistencies in your testimony. Levine was like the chess player who always had a vision of each piece on the playing field. He was methodical and thorough. Each attorney was well chosen for the task of defending the first spy the FBI ever had. While both Greenberg and Levine were highly regarded by the FBI, neither gave the slightest impression that they would be less than aggressive in their defense of Miller.

The R. W. Miller case went through two appeal phases, and as a result there were three separate trials that kept Greenberg and Levine busy representing Miller. The first trial, which took place in 1985, ended in a mistrial. In 1986, at the second trial, Miller was once again convicted, but in 1989, the conviction was overturned because of the use of polygraph material as evidence. Miller was tried a third time, and in October 1990, he was convicted of spying. This time the conviction stuck.

Greenberg and Levine knew a great deal about the FBI but not its inner workings. One of their earliest tactics drew the wrath of both current and retired agents. The defense employed a retired agent by the name of Al Sayers to assist them in their trial preparation and delivery. There was greater anger directed at Al Sayers as he sat at the defense table than there was for Miller. There was instant outrage that a retired FBI agent would stoop so low as to assist a traitor. There was also a sense that Al Sayers believed Miller was being railroaded by the FBI and that he was innocent. Sayers was the victim of severe criticism and harsh telephone calls after accepting the job of sitting at the Miller defense table. Many of his former peers refused to talk to Sayers. What was clear to me was that if Sayers believed in Miller's innocence, then he was never advised by Greenberg or Levine of how Miller was detected.

Miller's three trials could be folded into one. The trials were mirror images of each other. They were marked by long and tedious testimony that attempted to set forth the life of this rather drab agent. During each trial, Miller sat in the same suit with a very stoic face. Although his future depended on the testimony, Miller gave the impression of being disinterested. It was difficult to read any expression on Miller's face. The court artist had no trouble sketching Miller because his look seldom changed. From the government's point of view, Lance Woo supervised the case. Woo was an FBI agent of oriental heritage. Woo's job was to keep the case flowing and organized, and he performed to perfection. Woo was extremely structured and exacting in every minor detail. The responsibility of presenting the evidence at the proper time as well as having the government witness available when called for fell to the responsibility of Lance Woo. Without his discipline and structure, the three trials would have suffered.

Miller's three trials took place in the US District Court of Judge Robert Takasugi. Takasugi was known for being a tough judge, and he ran his courtroom with a sense of seriousness. He was known as fair-minded but a person who would not back away from rigid sentencing. He ran all three trials in pretty much the same manner. He was fair to both sides and showed little or no partiality, giving the government and the defense the necessary time to present their case. Takasugi preferred to run his court on a strict schedule and was not patient with tardy behavior. He gave no indication as to how he personally felt about Miller. After all the appeals, he sentenced Miller to twenty years in federal prison. Takasugi later reduced Miller's sentence to thirteen years, giving him credit for the time spent in prison while he waited for the three trials.

Svetlana Ogorodnikova spent eleven years in prison and was released in April 1995. Her husband, Nikolai, spent five years in prison. Both were convicted on espionage charges. Miller was found guilty of espionage and bribery and was released in May 1994.

The damage that Miller inflicted on the intelligence community was minimal because he was detected early. There is no doubt that if the Russians had more time to operate Miller, he would have had the potential to severely harm the intelligence operations of the US government. Very likely, the planned trip to Europe was for the purpose of meeting Miller on a neutral ground for assessment purposes. Once introduced to his handler, Miller may have been worked for years had he not been detected. The most damaging aspect of the Miller case was that he allowed a penetration by the Russians that had never happened before. This proved to the Russians that it was possible. The sense of being impenetrable was fractured forever. This meant that the Russians would be energized for future penetrations of the FBI. The immediate history, after the Miller case, would prove them successful on at least two occasions.

The case was even more difficult because it went to trial on three separate occasions. The more times such a case would go to trial, the more pressure was placed on the prosecution. What was critical in each trial was consistency. The witnesses testifying against Miller were called to testify in three separate trials, and the defense had the luxury of comparing the testimony from each trial. The greater the length of time from when the events occurred, the greater the chance of memory failing the witness.

Miller's expression during the second and third trials changed from that of his first trial. When he appeared during the second and third trials, he had the look of a person who had been separated from society by incarceration. Miller seemed to enjoy his trips to the courtroom in the later trials. The trials lessened the daily, boring routine of prison. Miller looked as though he actually believed the lies he was trying to spin—that this was his best effort at turning around an otherwise disastrous career as an FBI agent. He also seemed to put on more weight during his time in prison, making him look less disciplined than ever.

Being in charge of the administration of the Los Angeles FBI office, I had the role of introducing into evidence pertinent material from both FBI files and Miller's personnel file. Upon the completion of three trials, I had all but memorized Miller's personnel file. Personnel files in government generally say very little. They hold routine documents, such as annual physicals, transfer letters, letters of censor, or letters of commendation. Seldom does a file document an incident—because if the incident is of significance, a separate investigative file is opened. It was around this time that medical information had to be separated out of personnel files for fear of discriminating against the individual based on medical findings. The most important area of my testimony was entering into evidence the policies practiced, at that time, by the FBI as an institution. Such policies covered medical fitness, transfers, promotions, disciplinary actions, and incentives.

The defense's strategy was unclear in all three trials. The defense placed a great deal of effort in picturing R. W. Miller as someone who suffered because of the FBI's personnel policies. The defense portrayed Miller as a less than marginal agent, full of imperfections. They seemed to play up the negatives concerning Miller and had ample opportunity to do so. Miller sat by, lacking in any degree of pride or self-esteem, allowing himself to be portrayed as a clown. The more the prosecution demonstrated Miller's ineptness, the greater the defense would press the issue. The defense seemed to paint a picture of a man with life-long failures as an FBI agent who was willing to risk it all by taking the ultimate risk of dealing with the Russians on a personal basis. It was the defense's conclusion that once Miller had been directed by the Russians, he would then advise the FBI. Advising the FBI would then place Miller in the role of double-agent.

The concept deployed by the defense would sell spy novels, but it had little or no bearing on the accepted operational workings of the FBI. What Miller did made no sense. What Miller would accomplish in contacting Svetlana and ultimately the Russians would have little or no effect on Miller's already failed career. What made a lot more sense was that the failing operative was Svetlana and that it was her reliability and usefulness that was at issue. Svetlana knew that if she brought an FBI agent into the Russian spy web, she would gain stature and credibility once again. Svetlana, in her younger years, was an attractive person, capable of Russian male influence, and she was a regular to the consulate in San Francisco. Her days had long since passed, and she was well aware of it. Svetlana lived a boring life with her husband, Nikolai, and was looking to relive the days of excitement when she viewed herself as meaningful. In many ways, she duped Nikolai into the plot to trap Miller. Nikolai, throughout all trials, viewed himself as innocent of the charges against him. He was enraged when he was convicted and asked to serve five years in prison. There is little doubt that Nikolai was aware of the comings and goings of Svetlana, but he was not the mastermind behind turning Miller toward the Russians.

What is more reasonable is that loose talk on the part of FBI agents handling Svetlana when she cooperated for the FBI against the Russians led Svetlana to know of R. W. Miller. There were a hundred stories swirling around the life of Miller in the Los Angeles division. Some were funny, some were pathetic, some were dumb—but what all these stories led to was the picture of a man ripe for compromising. Svetlana came into Miller's life offering him what the Hollywood writers would in creating a spy novel. She offered him attention, money, sex, and a false sense of power, which would give him the sense of revenge for his long suffering as a pathetic figure. Miller took the bait in a desperate fashion. He did not require thousands of dollars or the most beautiful Russian woman known to man. Like Judas, he fell for a few paltry pieces of silver and an alcoholic mental case who had long since seen her appeal vanish.

The timing of Miller's defection had a profound effect on the FBI. It was not what Miller did as much as what his actions stood for. The FBI had never been successfully penetrated by any intelligence community, much less the Russians. Miller's defection sent a shock wave through the organization. The timing of the shock wave coincided with other dramatic institutional changes that were not fully assimilated. A decade had not gone by since female agents were first sworn in. There was a high degree of unrest among the agents of Hispanic origins. This unrest quickly spilled over into those agents who were Black and Native American. The predominantly white agent population that existed before these changes occurred observed in disgust what was going on. Like most government organizations, the FBI had difficulty recruiting highly qualified minorities for the FBI agent position. In adjusting to this shortage, they decided to select minorities from a secondary acceptance list, which fell short of the standard that male whites were being selected from. In the late '70s and early '80s, it solved a recruitment shortfall but created problems that would carry forward into the new century.

It was 1972 when J. Edgar Hoover died. The FBI had just been through the assimilation of changes from a very autocratic organization to one now marked by participatory management. There was a body of agents, still active, who had memories of working under Hoover. These memories never included race problems, spies, female agents, and all the examples of shortcomings in personal conduct that were being encountered. Prior to the early '70s, there were incidents of personal misconduct, but they were dealt with quickly and without much noise. These individuals were allowed to resign or were simply fired. This was not the case in the mid-1880s. More and more of what went wrong in the FBI was being aired in the courts with a great deal of publicity attached. The times had radically changed, and in many ways the agents of the FBI had changed dramatically. The agents were no longer predominantly white males from America's law schools and the military but were more and more a cross section of America.

The three agents who chose to betray their country were from the traditional FBI. The climate that was present when they spied was more permissive than during the disciplined years before the '70s FBI. Miller's betrayal in the early '80s set a benchmark of what was to come. Miller proved that the FBI could be compromised, giving the hostile intelligence community a target that no longer had the reputation of being untouchable. In many ways, Miller's defection changed forever the FBI as we once knew it. The change did not necessarily make the public trust the FBI less, but it did make the FBI trust itself less and less.

Miller was released from prison in May 1994 after having served about two-thirds of his prison sentence. During the course of his prison term, his wife divorced him. After leaving prison, he returned to live in Utah. Miller's real sentence in life was the removal of any lasting self-respect he had as a person. He turned his back on his family, his country, and his friends for moments of greed and self-indulgence. Miller will live the rest of his life to the extent that he lived the first part, but now he lives in disgrace.

CHAPTER 10

Terrorism and Corporate America

AUGUST 1986 WAS WHEN I chose to retire from the FBI. The FBI had a way of quickening retirement in that it had a mandatory retirement age of fifty-five. Most agents who could not fully retire at age fifty-five targeted other careers in their early fifties because they were more marketable at that point.

The transition from special agent of the FBI to other jobs was formidable. Retirement meant that you would *holster an empty weapon* for the remainder of your life. What made the transition more difficult was that you were no longer in a position of responsibility that had the same demands as those placed upon an active agent. It was virtually impossible to find another job as exciting and interesting. What made the FBI so interesting was that every day was different. There were many days that were routine and somewhat boring, but those days would be punctuated by days when you came to the edge of excitement and danger. It was in those special days that you made a significant contribution to society that made up the catalogue of memories that would never be forgotten.

Having studied human behavior for over twenty years and becoming actively involved in cases that were so unique to the criminal behavior seen in the United States created a natural reluctance to give up this interest completely. The jobs that FBI members sought after retirement were ones that utilized many of the experiences developed as an agent.

Corporate America had many experiences in dealing with terrorism both domestically and internationally in 1986. Some companies had contingency plans in place to deal with major events. Other companies turned their heads, ignoring that terrorists could target them.

What was of great interest was the manner in which each company responded to dangers from any source, whether people-inspired events or events of nature. Events of nature, such as earthquakes, were a great deal more acceptable to company executives if they were in fact real dangers. Sales of a crisis management plan on earthquakes in the state of California were more readily accepted than such sales of the same plan in New York. Companies spent thousands of dollars purchasing food, water, medical supplies, flashlights, and so on in preparation for earthquakes that rarely came. Business resumption plans were written and exercised in preparation for any business disturbance based on the concept if they were not up and running within three business days, most businesses would be destroyed.

Each company had its own personality. In many ways, it was critical to create a psychological profile on the company personality before proceeding with a plan to deal with disasters or terrorists. The very first company that employed me after my years with the FBI was First Interstate Bank in Los Angeles. The executive management of this company was created out of a potpourri of executives from other banks. They were predominantly men with an extremely aggressive appetite for profit. Created under them were all sorts of schemes to increase business potential. While they preached customer service, they were more concerned with profit margins and the performance of cost centers within the business. This atmosphere made them cautious about any measures put in place for the safety of the employees, especially if the costs ran over. For First Interstate Bank, earthquake preparedness was an easy sell because the corporate headquarters was in the tallest building in downtown Los Angeles. The more rarified aspects of security, such as executive protection and kidnap awareness, went basically ignored, however. Unless they perceived an immediate danger, they were comfortable with not dealing with those kinds of problems.

On the other hand, the company profile of Occidental Petroleum was one of arrogance. Its chairman and president, Armand Hammer, directly affected this profile. Occidental was doing business in one of the most dangerous parts of the world for kidnapping, Colombia. It was not until the company had firsthand experience with a kidnapping in 1985 that it took measures to protect its employees working in such dangerous areas. The kidnapping of Rick Paulsen, a Canadian, taught Occidental that kidnapping not only can interfere with the everyday operations of a company but also can be very expensive. Occidental showed character when it negotiated in good faith for the release of Paulsen even though Paulsen had violated every security precaution prior to his kidnapping. Upon the successful release of Paulsen, some thirteen months after his capture, Occidental Petroleum fired Paulsen for violating company protocol.

The psychological profile of many companies mirrored the makeup of its leaders. One such company was the Coors Brewery outside of Denver, Colorado. In the late 1950s, Adolph Coors was kidnapped and senselessly murdered. This remained as a cloud over the Coors family as it continued its very successful business. Unlike other companies, the corporate atmosphere is very much a family business, and the attitude of its employees is one of pride. The Coors family is a very large one, with many children. They are a close family and a very religious family. The company has a sense of responsibility for the community. Longtime Coors employees are not looking for greener pastures but are content where they are and expect to stay there for the rest of their working years. Management is both sensitive and concerned for their employees, and they lend a listening ear when complaints are aired. Crisis management, with emphasis on kidnap matters, is a reality to the Coors Company. This is a company that is open-minded to crisis events and demonstrates a willingness to prepare for these events whether the crisis is related to people or products.

The cluster of companies that create the Silicon Valley in northern California presents an interesting montage. Apple, Sun Microsystems, Hewlett Packard, Autodesk, and Compaq are all reflective of extremely strong management styles that give uniqueness to each company. Perhaps the best example of a company adopting a company profile from its leader is Microsoft. The dynamics inside of Microsoft, in simplistic terms, is that all of the top managers compete with the leader, Bill Gates, for management style. Like Bill Gates, they have an instilled system of denial that anything bad can happen to them. Formulating a crisis management plan to handle nonbusiness crisis is extremely difficult because of their demand that it be made business related to them and them alone.

When a kidnapping occurs, it matters little what company it happens in or how it should be resolved. Companies with extremely strong leaders have a tendency to create lower management that is paralyzed when it comes to making important decisions.

Hewlett Packard, on the other hand, was extremely aware that adverse events could wreak havoc within the company, especially if the company was not prepared to handle the crisis. Hewlett Packard went to great lengths in not only preparing crisis management plans but also exercising them. It has very responsible leadership with a broad focus on events beyond the scope of the business efforts of the company on a day-to-day basis that could adversely affect the company.

Apple Computer has gone through long years of leadership change, and as a result, its approach to crisis management has been fragmented. The energy and effort have been present to prepare it for the unexpected, but it lacks consistency and continuity. Fortunately for Apple, there has always been an awareness of crisis events that could adversely affect the company, and there is not the atmosphere of denial often seen in other companies.

Sun Microsystems takes on the dynamics of its leader. He is both a resourceful and energetic leader, symbolized by his passion for ice hockey. Sun Microsystems is a company that has a high degree of company loyalty. Like most of the Silicon Valley computer-related companies that have made it big in short periods of time, Sun Microsystems has become home to executives who have left other companies in the valley. Sun Microsystems has responded well to business crises as they have occurred down through the years. This has prepared them to handle nonbusiness-related crises. Their management team is decisive and quick to act. They have made themselves available for planning and responding to events such as kidnappings and violence in the workplace events.

For the most part, Silicon Valley companies are young and new. The wealth curve that has spiraled upward for so many years appears to be somewhat flattening. Smaller and less high-profiled companies, such as Autodesk, are able to function safely in a work environment less concerned about nonbusiness-related events creating major crisis.

Extremely well-established companies such as General Mills are far more difficult to assess with a clear profile. Frequently, larger companies possess not one profile but a series of profiles dictated by the divisions found within the company. The shortcoming in cases such as General Mills is that the corporate head is responsible for crisis planning and responding, and the divisions become spectators until such time as they are directly involved. Preparing a crisis management plan to fit all crisis events that could befall General Mills is virtually impossible. Product tampering and product extortion are two real crisis events that can affect a food-producing company with great frequency. Each division within the General Mills family is required to have its own response plan. This plan reflects the personality of the company segment involved.

Another good example of multiple corporate personality profiles can be seen in Nestle, US. This company is broken into at least five divisions, all handling very different products within the same company. Each division has its own structure, and it is very rare that they interact with each other. Times of crisis are managed within the division. A division will require clearance of major decisions with corporate only when such decisions would involve policy issues or issues that would affect the entire company.

So when we discuss terrorism and corporate America, it cannot be viewed in simple terms. As with human behavior, companies are all very different. The reaction of Exxon to the Valdez incident was a study in itself, filling the spectrum from denial to final acceptance. This spill of oil was an environmental disaster from day one, but the Exxon Corporation went well into overtime before accepting responsibility. Exxon's behavior when one of its executives was kidnapped and brutally murdered in New Jersey was not without exception. Sidney Reso was abducted from the driveway of his home in April 1992 by a husband and wife team who had him under surveillance. In his abduction, Reso was wounded. His kidnappers stored him in a storage facility after they bound and gagged him. Reso had no chance of surviving the intense heat in the storage area when combined with the lack of care for his wound and his not receiving water and food on a timely basis. This kidnapping tested Exxon's personality from the outset. Instead of following existing company plans in handling crisis events, one executive, close to Reso, tried to run the investigation. Fortunately, he recognized the need to bring in the FBI from the earliest moments of the investigation, but he ignored the existing procedures in place within Exxon. Sidney Reso lost his life, however, not because Exxon did anything wrong but because his kidnappers were unprofessional in caring for him and had little concern for human life.

In July 1963, when Steve Wynn's daughter was kidnapped and ransom demanded, he reacted so quickly in obtaining the ransom from the casino floor deposits that ransom was paid and his daughter safely released before law enforcement had the opportunity to get established in its investigation.

Some companies take on an attitude of believing they are so big and powerful that nothing bad can befall them. It is within those companies that you rarely see any formulation of a plan to respond to the unexpected. Companies that have thought out what they should do in the event of a crisis, before the crisis befalls them, manage the crisis best. What many companies fail to realize is that because of their very size, the odds are greatly in favor of them experiencing a real crisis.

In the early years of terrorist attacks experienced by companies representing the United States, for the most part, the companies found themselves dealing with bombing and ransom kidnappings. Many companies resorted to protecting their personnel through additional security and by insuring themselves against such events. Once a company set up an insurance program to cover itself for such events, preventive measures were put in place. Many preventive measures included crisis management training, security awareness, travel security, and even training in kidnap awareness.

What companies soon found out when handling kidnaps in foreign countries was that the US Embassy was not always quick to help. The United States had adopted a very rigid policy in handling terrorists, especially in kidnap matters. An integral part of its policy was non concession, no payment of ransom. Conversely, US companies could not refuse to negotiate for their personnel. Also, part of the US policy was that we would not negotiate with terrorists. This policy was very much promulgated, and it was no secret that the United States had a very hard line when it came to terrorist kidnappings. Henry Kissinger had been the architect of the US policy of non-negotiation, and he was adamant in its support. The forethought that went into making this policy was unclear, but it became a very simple and clear policy to stand for, and we were admired as a country for adopting such a hardline approach. The only difficulty was that when an American would be captured and ransom demanded, the policy left very little room to negotiate. This policy was reviewed on several occasions, once under President Reagan as Presidential Review Matter 31. Many conceded that in the real world we needed more flexibility to allow us negotiating room to save the lives of individuals being illegally held as kidnap victims.

The past two decades of the 20th Century left most American corporations sensing that if they added security to their facilities and better prepared their employees assigned abroad, they would largely solve the crisis problems stemming from terrorism. Corporations were still expecting these terrorist events to happen only abroad. However, between 1980 and 1999, the FBI reported 327 incidents of suspected terrorism in the United States alone. The bombing of the World Trade Center in New York and the bombing of the Murrah Federal Building in Oklahoma City gave them reason for domestic concern.

When the concern and threat increased for US corporations, an amazing event took place across America. Many companies started dramatic cutbacks, looking harshly at their bottom line and seeking ways to cut operating costs. Prior to 1980, many companies had security departments within their framework, looking out for the security concerns of the organization. These departments were not profit centers for most companies; they represented overhead. Security organizations were drastically cut back. Some were so fragmented that only a necessary group of security guards was left behind. What this meant for many organizations was the total absence of security intelligence and security networking. In the absence of security professionals being represented in most American corporations, security awareness, and security training was nonexistent.

With this as a backdrop, American companies were in for their worst nightmare. Despite the violent history of our country, in which we were killing twenty-five thousand people per year coupled with a staggering suicide rate, American companies ignored the climate they were functioning in. Headlines reached across the country, giving horror accounts of how disgruntled employees, fired from their job, returned with blazing guns, killing employees. Companies went into total denial, expressing amazement as to what this society was coming to when such events would happen. It was not necessarily limited to disgruntled employees returning to the work environment; those who were mentally sick were also taking out their paranoid aggression on innocent people. American companies had to be concerned for the "monster" that was within their own environment.

Some of the earlier incidents clustered around the US postal services, and the "going postal" simplification was given birth. While devastating incidents occurred in the post office, perpetrated by current or former postal workers, other organizations soon found out that they were not immune.

Faced with this new crisis, American businesses looked for easy fixes. The immediate cry went up to identify these would-be gunman and neutralize them before the event happened. What companies would not admit was that they were a significant part of the problem.

During the last two decades, there has been a remarkable change in the work environment. Prior to this time, an individual would dedicate his or her working life to one company. There was a connecting bond between the employee and the employer. Many employers would refer to the "corporate family" and actually treat their employees as family members. Many companies had a well-defined corporate culture, and employees responded to this atmosphere with undying loyalty. The loyalty went so deep that an individual would describe himself in terms of employment. Corporations with strong corporate cultures were noted for exceptional leadership, high productivity, strong philosophy, and high morale that resulted in an extraordinary amount of customer satisfaction. Management communicated with its employees and valued its employees' input to the overall success of the company.

Something radically changed in corporate management since the 1980s. Not only did we alter the work environment from a people-sensitive environment to an information-intensive workforce, but technology developed at such a rapid pace that it edged the unskilled worker to the far outer perimeter of the workforce. The work environment became a lot less flexible. The white-collar worker who normally felt safe in the work environment was experiencing the same pressure of dwindling employment options experienced by the blue-collar worker. Foreign competition, military cutbacks, and defense spending cutbacks sent shock waves through corporate America. Corporations were no longer interested in the employee willing to dedicate a lifetime but turned to temporary employees or employees interested in staying one or two years. Seniority in a job equated to increased salary and benefits cost, and soon the goal to hire two employees for the cost of one became a standard.

Many large corporations adopted the attitude that its employees were fortunate to be working for them, and if they left, there would be ten other people standing in line for the job that was vacated. What was unfortunately happening to the individual was a sense of declining options for work and an overall feeling of desperation. This became the feeding ground for workplace violence. It is well known that self-control and an operating sense of inhibitions is what controls behavior and ultimately regulates violence. An inability for self-control and a nonfunctioning system of inhibitions leads to violent behavior. America had already become a society with a demonstrated lack of self-control, and it was clearly performing at a level of little or no inhibitions controlling behavior. What you therefore had was a collision course. On the one hand, corporations were treating people rather shoddily, and on the other hand, poorly treated people had an increased tendency to act out violently.

Corporations came to the psychiatric community for a quick business solution. Identify these people within our ranks, and we will terminate them. It was not quite that easy. Many companies knew well that violence in the workplace does not always begin with a gun but can rather dramatically end with a gun. Many companies were asked to identify the behavior that would be indicative of future problems. There were several areas selected, including work mischief, malicious destruction of property, product tampering, sexual harassment, threats, and acts of prejudice, sabotage, assaultive behavior, and mental sickness. The motivation behind such behavior was clear. It centered on revenge, destructive appetite, boredom, embarrassment of others, attempt to show superiority, and a need to intimidate others.

From a psychological point of view, the motivation behind an individual perpetrating violence in the workplace is the deadliest of all violence because two very different motivators collide. On the one hand, there is a strong motivation to kill. Sometimes it is directed at a particular person; at other times, it is random violence where only the location is the target. More than not, from a study of violent incidents to date, the perpetrator will target a person or group of persons within the company to get even with. On the other hand, coupled with the homicidal behavior is a subconscious desire to commit suicide. Intervention with this type of behavior is difficult, if not impossible. If intervention is to occur, it must come early on before the individual plans his attack on the company. What is interesting in workplace violence that has gone to the extreme is the detailed planning that can take place. Seldom is there a berserk outbreak of violence; rather, there is a well-planned attack at the weakest part of the organization.

On several occasions the courts have been critical of corporations for their failure to properly protect their employees and anticipate violence in the workplace. One such case involved a female employee who repeatedly advised her employer that she was being harassed by a fellow employee. Eventually the employee doing the harassment was terminated and advised by the courts with a restraining order to stay away from this young lady. Within a short period of his being fired and court order to stay away, the individual showed up at the work environment, gained access, and created havoc. He shot the young lady who was the center of his fixation and several others. Multiple lives were lost in that incident. Early on when this potential problem was brought to the attention of the company, they all but accused the target victim of encouraging the pursuant behavior.

Who are these people who kill in the work environment? It goes without saying that they are not the well-rounded individuals of our society. They are people who, if allowed to continue life without being crossed, will live dull lives and never stand out for doing much of anything. They are very inadequate individuals and have a poor self-concept. Many times they will describe themselves in terms of their work. The first response to a question, "Can you tell me something about yourself?" will always be answered in a manner describing what they do for a living (e.g., "I am a teacher…postman…carpenter, etc."). Because they see themselves in terms of what they do for a living, they out of necessity will look upon their employment as having the same level of importance as a family has in their lives. Being fired or laid off from a job is a monumental setback for this type individual. The action of termination is always regarded as a betrayal. Not only is it a betrayal, but it is unjustified. The predictable reaction to these types of events is to get revenge at all costs.

The question of who these people are and whether they can be turned around from destructive behavior is a reasonable one. Many times these individuals talk about impending actions. They will be very upfront in making comments indicating that they plan to carry out destruction. If they go ignored, nothing will stop them from carrying out their worst nightmare. The personality profile of the workplace killer is that he is normally a white male aged thirty-five to fifty-five. He is an individual who has difficulty socializing with others and is often regarded as a loner. He has a demonstrated interest in weapons, whether he is a hunter or shoots at a local range. Symbols of power are very meaningful to him. His psychiatric evaluation would have him sane but with paranoid ideations; with very low self-esteem; hypersensitive to criticism; and basically distrustful of other people. He is a person with a history of depression and thoughts of suicide and homicide. Internally these types of personalities are constantly doing battle with their peers and demonstrate this unrest by being chronically disgruntled. On many occasions they are troublemakers and difficult to get along with. Their assaultive behavior is methodical and selective. They have an inability to control their behavior, and because of this characteristic, they are likely to talk about what is on their mind. It is imperative that any menacing words be taken seriously. It is especially important if this individual starts to "keep book" on a fellow employee or supervisor. Any individual he chooses to keep book on would be at an increased danger level. Outbursts and confrontations with individuals of this nature should never be ignored. Intervention by professionals is highly recommended.

Companies are at a loss in handling individuals of this nature. Most unfortunately, if you were to review the typical profile of the person most likely to commit workplace violence, it could fit fifty or more people in a large company. As with street crime, we are unable to take action with an individual unless he breaks some law. However, within the confines of a work environment, much can and should be done to intervene before a person goes to the final stage of violent behavior.

Handling violent or potentially violent people is somewhat of a science. Ignoring the behavior of violent people and allowing them to intimidate a work environment is totally unacceptable. A company's greatest tool is observation. A company has at least eight hours a day, five days a week to observe the problem. Look for signals, listen for and look for leakage. Leakage refers to the person verbalizing what his intent is, such as, "I'll get you for this!" If the decision is made to terminate the individual based on past performance or because of his instability, it is strongly recommended to deal with the person in a humane manner. Termination for cause is a volatile transaction. Termination for cause performed in a confrontational manner is similar to lighting a fuse and knowing it will go off some day. If an individual has had numerous confrontations with his immediate superior, that superior is the last person who should take charge of the termination process. Many companies summarily terminate individuals through impersonal letters or very indirect messages, leaving the individual uncertain whether he is terminated.

Terminations do not necessarily have to be confrontational. The company must not show distain for the individual but must manifest empathy. The process must focus on the positive aspects of the person's future, even to the point of assigning him to a transitional out-processing agency. Professionals should handle the termination interview with an effort to control emotional outbursts. The most important factor in a termination interview is that the action is final. Leave no doubt that this is an event that cannot be further negotiated. It is imperative that the person being terminated be assisted in overcoming self-doubt and loss of self-esteem. The session should not entail laying out all the person's faults but rather emphasizing positive aspects of the employment period. The person conducting the exit interview must be fully supportive of the company decision for termination and must look and act secure in the role he or she plays. Interest in the welfare of the terminated individual can be manifested through a reasonable severance package, outplacement benefits, and retraining benefits. Retraining benefits are extremely important for the most worrisome terminated employees. Retraining session can give the necessary feedback required on individuals of great concern.

What can be more difficult for an organization is the aftermath of a violent episode that has cost the lives of employees. There have been organizations that return to regular business as usual with holes still in walls, windows needing repair, and blood tracings on carpeting. How a company handles the aftermath of a workplace violence incident tells more about the company than anything else. Demonstrating a total lack of sensitivity to a crisis sends the message to employees that they are not important and that what is important is that no money be lost by a business disruption. It is critical, even if the company stumbled in allowing an incident to occur, that the company place its employees' mental health before all else. Seeing someone killed is a traumatic event. Seeing a close friend—who happens to be a fellow worker—killed is another matter.

Companies operating domestically and internationally have a future in which terrorist events such as bombings, kidnappings, and violent outbursts in the work environment will not disappear. In our society, violence in the workplace is a logical overflow of the violence we have come to live with. The workplace, in many ways, is the most logical place for violence to occur. Marital strife, triangle love affairs, and desperate partners are all potential violent episodes waiting to happen. The husband, banned by the courts from coming near his wife, does not have to go hunting for her if he knows she is working at Home Depot from 8:00 a.m. to 5:00 p.m. The disgruntled employee, angered at a perceived injustice, knows every movement within the work environment to plan his attack. Instead of being shocked that their workplace was chosen for violence, companies should expect it and be prepared for it.

The best preparation an organization can take to offset violence within its premises is to return to the time when organizations treated people with dignity. People need a sense of belonging, a sense of worth, and a sense of value. Individuals strive for a sense of accomplishment and appreciation for the contribution they are making. Work environments need not be institutions where management and staff are characterized by mistrust, hatred, fear, retaliation, and ridicule. American corporations must return to the period when leadership within a company was meaningful. Rewarding the ability to take a group and lead them to accomplish a task is a far better investment than rewarding trickery and deceit.

Corporations must always be on guard for those individuals who have absolutely no connection to the company. These individuals, who frequently commit violent acts in the absence of logical reasons, make up the population of the mentally disturbed. The mentally disturbed will always be with us. They give no warning, but in their minds they have convinced themselves that your organization is to blame for all their plights. The law firm in San Francisco was victim to one such individual. Armed with deadly weapons and ammunition to start a small war, a delusional man traveling from southern California targeted this law firm. That irrational delusion took the lives of many and forever remains as a living nightmare to those who bore witness to it.

Corporations in many ways are similar to individuals. An individual's behavior is very much related to whether or not that individual will become a victim of crime. One of the most-used examples to demonstrate this is the prostitute. By the very nature of a prostitute's occupation, the individual places herself/himself in the high-risk category for violence. Undercover policemen and policewomen, by the very nature of their occupation, are in the high-risk category for violent acts befalling them. A corporation that has built a reputation of creating boring workplace environments where individuals are treated without dignity and terminated for unjust causes is creating an environment where violent acts are not only expected but will occur.

What is interesting about psychological profiling is that it works both ways. Both the perpetrator and victim have distinct profiles. Victim companies on many occasions contribute to the violence that befalls them. Operating with an attitude that says, "We are too big and powerful for anything to happen to us" is a guarantee that something nasty will happen at some point.

Just as corporate America was amazed at the violence occurring on its property, the schools across America were astounded when students showed up not with their homework complete but with a plan for destruction. All across America, the question was heard: why? The answer should have been why not. What is happening in our school system is a microcosm of what is happening in the American society. In many ways, we have created a love affair with violent behavior. We have glamorized it in movies and on television. We have stacked our malls with violent video games. We have carried dramatic accounts of the worst serial killers in our nation's history in the media. Violence is rewarded over good in sports. All of this was present when we had a generation or more of individuals lacking in self-control and operating on an absence of inhibitions. In the words of Sigmund Freud, we were flying on instinct satisfaction alone.

No one will deny that school violence is an extremely complex problem. It can be successfully argued that violence in our society is also an extremely complex problem. The psychological profiles of student killers have many common traits. Contrasting what happened in Columbine with the recent shootings in San Diego, California, teaches us a profound lesson. Student killers can look different and can have different sets of problems motivating them. The students involved in the Columbine killings had for the most part cut themselves off from their peers. They had created a world for themselves in which their differences were pronounced to such a degree that they believed those differences justified their hostile acts. The shooting in San Diego left the picture of a very lonely boy, who was still very much a little boy, transplanted from the east coast and rejected by his new environment. Indications were that he was severely bullied by his newfound classmates and held up for ridicule. He looked incapable of doing what he did, yet the reality told us that he was responsible. More so than in Columbine, you wanted to seek an explanation, relieving this child of the lifelong responsibility for such a serious act.

The common trait that runs through all school shootings is the emergence of the two deadly forces of homicide and suicide. This is the mentality that needs to be explored in greater depth. What is it that brings a person to have total disregard for others based on an absolute disregard for himself?

The study of violent behavior necessitates carefully avoiding forming conclusions that apply to all of society through the lens of violence alone. While it can be proven that we are far more violent in 2015 than we were in 1901, it can also be demonstrated that we are far more responsive to society's needs and to people than we were a century ago. Studying violence in America is very much like the scientist looking through a microscope studying bacteria. The scientist has a clear focus of the bacteria on the exemplar glass, all the while ignoring what is going on in the room he is in. In studying violence, we cannot focus so intently on those who turn to violent behavior that we ignore the legions of individuals leading good and productive lives.

That said, let us focus for a moment on the forces involved in school violence. The dynamics in workplace violence and school violence are interrelated. The major difference is age of occurrence. Workplace violence almost always happens in the adult male. School violence invariably happens in the emerging male adult in his teen years. The most common factor is the simultaneous emergence of both homicidal and suicidal instincts. In simple terms, homicidal tendencies are manifested by a total disregard for others. Suicidal tendencies are an abnormal disregard of self. People who are homicidal turn their violence outward against others. People who are suicidal turn their violence inward against themselves. A willingness to kill and an acceptance of being killed is by far the most pathological state of mind a person can be in. It is a state of total despair accompanied by uncontrollable rage. When we see these dynamics operating in an adult, we look at the dysfunctional aspects of a person's life, such as a broken marriage, terminal sickness, death of a loved one, or loss of one's occupation. If a person acts out in a violent manner, killing his colleagues in the work environment, then we look deeper to understand why this individual could not cope with a stressful life event.

Not everyone who loses a job kills fellow employees. Not all students who are isolated and bullied return to school to destroy their classmates. The infinitesimal numbers of people both adult and teen who turn to destructive, violent behavior are the product of poorly developed and inadequate personalities. These personalities have developed over years lacking in self-discipline and absent a well-formulated system of inhibition control. It is from this population of individuals that mental illness and personality disorders become a pattern of living.

Society is more ready to accept a news headline that says, "Terminally ill man kills boss and self after being fired" than on that says, "Sophomore kills teacher, three students." The reason we accept the first headline is that we can relate to the stress and trauma of the terminated employee. We do not approve of his actions, but we typically say, "He snapped." When a fourteen- or fifteen-year-old boy steals his father's gun and takes human life in a school environment, we are at a loss to explain this behavior.

Several things have to happen to bring about school violence. A significant population of children is being raised today with no boundary of behavior and no inner structure dictating what is right and what is wrong. For too many, God has never been a factor in their lives, much less a moral compass. Many children have grown up lonely, being passed from one parent to another in divorce or totally alone in this world, being born out of wedlock. Some have never been hugged or touched in an affectionate manner. The lesson they have learned well is that people can disappoint you, and it is not wise to get too close to them. They have grown up with criticism, learning to condemn others. Many live with hostility, learning to fight. Others live with ridicule, turning inward with insecurity. Their immediate family has taught them to live with shame, so they feel guilt daily. For many, a family meal is not remembered as a festive table set with candles but as a fast-food drive-through. The steady hand of a father's wisdom is replaced by a fifty-inch TV screen. The warmth of a mother's love is a late evening telephone call questioning whether you ate the right frozen food dinner. Imaginative sports have given way to business-sponsored activities managed by controlling adults. Churches are where you go shortly after you are born and when you die. TV and the movies are the modern-day gospel preaching a message of living for the moment, violence, sex, and disregard for your fellow man. Success is the goal we strive for at any cost, even happiness.

The young person growing up in America in this 21st century is blessed if he/she is given a strong foundation to bring together the relevant tools necessary to succeed. One will admit that with all the necessary tools, it is still a difficult task. Those missing a structure, unable to structure themselves, have a monumental task to survive as a whole person.

Similar to corporations with workplace violence, educational institutions bear a strong responsibility for school violence. There are many excellent educational institutions across the United States. Thousands of teachers have spent a lifetime dedicated to the students who admire them. Schools receive the end product of what society is raising, and they are responsible for their education.

Where schools have failed is that they have rewarded failure and allowed the courts to dictate how discipline should be administered. The fundamental failure is the American approach using the model that all children are entitled to an education. The system of mass public education has failed in that it has not promoted learning as its primary goal but rather the custodial care of a student until the student completes high school. What the system fails to admit and adjust to is that not all students are able to learn. The student with the greatest deterrent to learning is the one without motivation. What mass education needs in America is fresh thinking by looking at a model that provides a work environment for those unwilling to apply themselves in school. In a serious work environment, the realization of the value of being educated is more likely to happen; rather than being promoted without demonstrating proficiency.

Perhaps the most devastating indicator of failed educational systems is the metal detectors and presence of police in the schools. This is an admission that self-discipline is absent and the students are controlled by self-instincts to do whatever they wish to do. A learning atmosphere is missing. Most schools are plagued with regular teachers being absent and classrooms occupied with substitute teachers who found out they were to be there minutes before the class started. In many ways, school unions have busied themselves improving teachers' benefit packages while ignoring teaching as a profession and the fact that the students are the raison d'être of education. Being a teacher is the most important profession in a society. If the teacher is ill equipped and not supported, learning will not take place. We have targeted the mediocre student in our lesson curriculum and feel accomplished when the brilliant student performs at a lower level.

The handling of school violence incidents in America has staged performances that will only ensure violent acts in the future. Desperate people who commit desperate acts of violence crave attention. They will accept that attention in life or death. Columbine was our worst school violence. The emotional outpouring of grief was understandable, but the political use of this incident was unfortunate. No one would argue that school should have been resumed the next day, but the pageant of grief was carried on for weeks. While one might argue that this was what the survivors needed, I would argue that what occurred was not good for those in grief or for the future person bent on suicide by murder of his fellow students.

Discipline has all but been removed from our schools. Teachers were, at one time, respected and autonomous in keeping order in the classroom and school. The threat of legal action against a teacher is real, not imagined, if discipline is carried too far. This environment reinforces the tendency for students to lack self-discipline and respect for others. There is an apparent absence of recourse.

The psychological profile is typically a teenage male who is quiet, shy, not involved in school activities, from a broken or dysfunctional home, intelligent, sensitive, victim of bullying, rejected by his class peers, not popular, with acne, and having few, if any, friends. They are rejected in the school environment and are looking for that one day of acceptance. The rejection has driven them to hatred, the hatred has turned into rage, and the rage has turned into senseless violence. Like the person involved in workplace violence, tomorrow's killers will fantasize and discuss their attack before carrying it out. School authorities and families must do a better job of listening for these cries for help.

The prognosis for violence in the workplace and school violence is not promising because it is about those who have been allowed to develop with severe personality shortcomings and the inability to face life as it presents itself. It is much like any form of violence: we must protect ourselves from it by detection and diffusion. Detection and diffusion are easier said than done. The only other solution that can readily be called a dream is to raise our children more responsibly so that they do not fall out of society by killing others and ultimately killing themselves.

Corporations and educational institutions have a great responsibility. In simple terms, they are both tasked in a very similar manner. They are to treat people as human beings and show respect for them, not deceit. Recognize the worth of every human being under your charge, and give them recognition for a job well done. When you enter into a contract with them, honor that contract and do not betray them. Be interested in the well-being of the person assigned to you. Listen to them because what they have to say is worthwhile. Be interested in the problems of everyday life as they see them, not as you see them.

Corporations and learning institutions cannot be expected to approach their employees or students with a suspecting profile for future violence. Profiles can become future predictors if past behavior indicates a pattern, but profiles are useless in the absence of actual destructive behavior. If problems are occurring with a student or employee and the individual has a history of a troubled life, wisdom would indicate that this individual needs very close attention. If intervention is necessary, it should be swift and conducted by a professional. The intervention should be lawful and, above all, humane.

The face of international terrorism has radically changed over the past thirty years. What is most alarming, at the present time, is the coexistence of the two extreme elements seen in both workplace and school violence: suicidal and homicidal tendencies within acts of terrorism.

The phone rang at 6:10 a.m. on September 11, 2001. My son Ryan's voice sounded serious when he stated, "Dad, something terrible happened in New York; it's on the television." For the next several hours, like most Americans, I was glued to the television, giving witness to the most horrific act of terrorism carried out on American soil.

When I was lecturing years earlier on the psychological profile of people who take hostages, my mind raced back to the type of personality we said was the most difficult, if not impossible, to negotiate with: the religious/political fanatic. The United States had few examples of people in this category until we ran into Koresh in Waco, Texas. Koresh's dedication to his cause is somewhat questionable. Abdul Amass Khalis was another person who was rigidly fixed on his beliefs but fell short of dedication to kill himself to achieve his goals.

On September 11, as I passed minutes and hours watching television, the tragic results of dedicated terrorism became a reality. There was no chance to negotiate. What was set in motion was a well-conceived coordinated plan of destruction. The perpetrators planned not only mass destruction but their own destruction in the process. With the crumbling of the two massive towers of the World Trade Center, it was evident that many lives would be lost and that America would be changed forever. It was clear that the terrorist dealt a massive blow on a powerful nation. It was once again the David and Goliath scenario being played out on World Theater.

In the early hours of September 11, a local TV station asked me, "Could this possibly be a group of American terrorists."

My response was very quick: "No, it is inconceivable." As the hours passed and the tragic events were brought together, including the downed aircraft in Pennsylvania, it was clear that we had suffered an attack on our soil from a terrorist organization that had a dedication far greater than we had ever witnessed. They had an appetite to kill vast numbers of people accompanied by a willingness to kill themselves in the process. This behavior can be witnessed in an individual but it is seldom seen in group activity. Days into the investigation, we would learn there were nineteen individuals responsible for the worst act of terrorism America ever experienced. The aftermath of this event reveals the reality of what has been happening in the Middle East for decades: the ever presence of the suicide bomber.

While Bin Laden was singled out as the mastermind behind this destruction, whether he was ever found appears somewhat irrelevant. What is relevant is the legacy he has left behind as a result of September 11. The legacy is that he has forever raised the level of violence that can occur in our society. For years we studied the mentally driven bomber, assassin, or killer. We took into account the purely psychopathic mind that destroyed for the sheer delicious hell of it. We were shocked by the magnitude of violence that occurred in our workplaces and schools. We came to accept a level of violence in our society that was limited to murder and suicide. We were willing to watch on television the suicide efforts against our interests abroad, including military bases and ships of war. Yet we never imagined that so few could create such devastation in the center of one of our major cities. When the level of violence is raised, it seldom pulls away from shore like a wave in high tide. The violence level has a tendency to remain and seek other targets as acceptable as the World Trade Center on that beautiful, clear morning of September 11, 2001.

The psychological profiler is forced to delve deeper into the psyche of the individual willing to not only kill but also die while killing. The complexity of applying this state of mind to the motivational behavior of a group directed at one target is burdensome. Homicide has all the aspects of hate, rage, anger, destruction, and absence of concern for others. Suicide is the state of mind that sees an end to this existence and willingly embraces the means to that end. The willingness to embrace suicide can have its basis in religious or political beliefs that are inflexible and rigid. When these two ingredients are allowed to develop in a person or race of persons, there is little or no room for appeasement. What is strange from a profiling standpoint is that the nineteen terrorists who killed themselves and so many others on September 11 are the easiest subjects for profiling because their behavior is so extreme. Yet while they may be the easiest to profile, they are the most difficult of individuals for behavior change.

September 11, 2001, has changed the course of many people's lives. In many ways, we were all affected by this act of terrorism. For those who directly lost love ones, the impact was immediate. For those who watched the destruction on television, it took days and weeks to determine the connection to the World Trade Center. A website of a school where I once taught carried the names of thirty people who lost their lives. A retired judge, one-time FBI agent, and college classmate, Jack Duffy, lost his son Michael when the airplanes hit the towers. The ashes were turned over to the Duffy family shortly before Jack passed away of brain cancer, months after the incident. Jack not only went to the grave with the memory of the terrible loss that he and his wife and family suffered, but he went to the grave with the ashes of Michael as they were placed next to him in the coffin.

America is going through a major adjustment as we move beyond our modern-day Pearl Harbor. Yesterday's security measures become outdated with a new battlefield filled with people willing to die for what they believe is true. In many ways, it is like dealing with insanity not of our making. Unfortunately, the insanity will be with us for years to come, and our only response is vigilance based on reason and strength. In the absence of reason and strength, insanity becomes contagious, and we are not immune.

CHAPTER 11

Giving Up the Badge

THERE WAS A MARKED DEGREE of idealism where the journey in understanding criminal behavior first began. Teaching in the New York area and working with students motivated me to take to heart an inspirational passage that I have kept on my desk for almost five decades. The passage reads as follows: *Faith is seeing the brilliant countenance of God shining up at us from every creature.* I have maintained this statement and mounted it on wood, which is now fast decaying. As a teacher exposed to young, well-adjusted students, the statement had more relevance to me at that time than it has today. As the wood has decayed over the years, the application of such a statement was made all the more difficult when studying the types of behavior that this manuscript describes.

The most difficult task for anyone who studies criminal behavior, especially the extreme form of criminal behavior found in murder, is to not have one's focus narrowed to the point that good becomes imperceptible. Studying violent behavior and violent people takes extraordinary personal discipline. It requires not only intellectual curiosity but also an abundance of sensitivity to all human behavior. The art of psychological profiling will never be a science; it will serve only as a guide. Not everyone is equipped to linger in this business for long without it taking a toll. The toll on the profiler will be lessened greatly by the ability to isolate one's feelings from the destructive behavior studied. The sensitivity and insights required to study violent crimes and violent personalities cannot be taken off like an old suit of clothes. They become part of the personality and linger for many years after formal retirement. Undoubtedly, the keenness of observation will be lessened with lack of use, but the intellectual curiosity lives on. What started out as a journey to eradicate violent behavior ends up with the reality that we desperately need to manage the violence in our society if we are to survive.

One year after the death of Jon Benet Ramsey, the opportunity presented itself for me to sit down and talk with the parents, Patsy and John Ramsey, about security matters and how they pertained to their family and business life. The murder of this young child has been a tabloid exploit since the day it happened. Like most murders that happen within a home, the suspicion is placed on someone from within the home. Individuals believing that one or the other parent is responsible have their camp, and individuals feeling them totally innocent champion John and Patsy. While my purpose was not to profile this murder case, the profiler was very active inside of me as we discussed security matters. What I witnessed were two people devastated by the loss of their daughter. This is what murder does; this is the eternal cost of murder. Murder not only blows out the flame of a young life, but it also destroys a significant part of those left behind. For their part, no matter what it is, John and Patsy Ramsey will never be the same. They have been forever changed.

In late October 1977, I was in San Francisco as part of an FBI inspection team. Howard Teten and I, along with others, had long since launched psychological profiling as an investigative tool working homicide cases. The inspection team was staying in the Holiday Inn, not far from the federal building. It was Halloween. At this point, I was very comfortable in my understanding of human behavior...until the famous Halloween parade went past the hotel where we were staying. After all of my formal schooling in psychology and my work at the FBI academy, my best lesson was that day in San Francisco. After watching the parade, and especially the participants, I realized how limited my knowledge of psychology was. That realization became a most valued asset in the years to come. Human behavior does not come in neat boxes; it is different and comes in many variances. Every murder is different, and every planned murder has a different plan. No two murders are totally alike. No individual who murders has a duplicate.

After many years of being directly involved with psychological profiling, we have yet to scratch the surface in studying violent behavior. What intrigues many of us is the cause of violent behavior. In the few cases we illustrated, the cause is complex. Who really understands what led Charlie Manson to kill? Why did Edmund Emil Kemper start his killings and end them with the killing of his mother? What was it that ignited David Meirhofer in his spree of killings? Was Sirhan Sirhan self-motivated? What makes people take hostages and threaten to kill them? Why are we, as a country, hated so much by those who plan to destroy us? The questions are endless. When we talk about the equation of murder, we infer that we are all capable of murder. It is easy to accept the proposition that we are all capable of murder when forced to defend life itself. What is more the object of our study, however, is the individual who has no need for someone or something to throw his equation of murder off balance. This type of individual uses violence as a first option.

One of the most moving experiences I had with violent behavior and its effects came shortly after the bombing of the Murrah Federal Building in Oklahoma City. Within weeks of the bombing, I visited the site and stood holding the fence protecting the site. The fence was covered with mementoes of the victims. There was a silence to the scene that was moving. Joining in with that silence, you had a sense of the magnitude of lives that were lost in this place: 168. Locations can take on special meaning if they represent places where people died. There is a reverence attached to that location. Visits to the battlefield in Gettysburg, Virginia, put you in a place where much suffering and death took place. Harpers Ferry is another place where the rolling mountains and rustling wind remind you of a time gone by in which many people suffered.

A visit to the USS *Arizona*, where many bodies rest in the rusting hull of this once great ship, gives you a sense that you are in a major cathedral. Driving a highway, passing a makeshift cross nailed to a tree, lets you know that someone drew their last breath on that spot. The landscape of Wall Street has been forever changed by the tragedy of September 11. It will be debated for years how to properly memorialize the thousands who lost their lives that day. What will not be debated is that now this site is sacred and special. The World Trade Center site will be visited for decades, if not centuries, beyond where we stand now. It will speak to the same devastation seen at Pearl Harbor and on the shores of Normandy. The World Trade Center site has now accepted the sacredness of a cemetery, and like the grief-stricken mother placing flowers on the roadside where a deadly automobile accident took place, flowers will adorn the site where these two giant buildings reached to the sky. Those who died did not deserve the death they received. Death has a way of lingering, and when it happens with such magnitude as in time of war, it is not forgotten.

Senseless killings can reach out and touch all of us at the most unexpected times. January 24, 1975, a young business executive working in Wall Street made arrangements to meet two of his colleagues for lunch. They decided to have lunch in a historic restaurant in downtown New York. Fraunces Tavern was a very popular meeting place with a quiet atmosphere for conversation. Frank Connor arrived early for lunch and sat waiting for his two associates. Shortly after they arrived, they placed their orders and waited for lunch. Lunch was delivered in a prompt fashion, and they began to eat. Frank Connor and his friends never finished lunch that day. It was the last meal they would order in this life. A terrible explosion ripped through the restaurant, sending tables and chairs flying. Chandeliers were wrenched from their bearings and sent crashing against walls. The front windows gave in to the rush of pressure from the explosion. Shouting and cries mixed with moans of dying people. Frank Connor was killed immediately. He left behind a loving wife, Mary, and two sons, Thomas and Joseph. Frank Conner would never see them grow up. It was the work of a terrorist group fighting for the independence of Puerto Rico, and terror was struck in the heart of all New Yorkers. Willie Morales was the bomb maker, and his instrument worked to perfection. Bomb makers are the most cowardly of killers. They choose a deadly weapon of destruction and secretly go about their business, trying to go undetected. The killer with the knife or gun at least comes face to face with his victim. Not so with the bomber, who intends to get away and live another day to gloat over his actions. Frank Connor never saw the face of his killer. The face of Frank Connor will always be remembered by my brother Tom, however, because he holds a prominent place in his wedding album as his best man.

[photograph with caption: "1 24 75 BOMBING AT FRAUNCES TAVERN, NEW YORK CITY CLAIMED BY"]

For all who tried to make Tim McVeigh into a warrior, he too, fits the profile of the cowardly killer. McVeigh made every effort to run from his destruction and disappear into society after his dirty trick of killing innocent people. Lateral damage being "necessary" is no excuse for the bomber. The bomber usually picks a place as a symbol of destruction. The fact that hundreds of people are present at that place when the bomb goes off only adds emphasis to the destruction. People can be victims of brutal murder while having absolutely no relationship to the perpetrator.

Crime causation has been a subject of study for years. There is no unanimous opinion on the cause of crime. Several areas have been investigated, such as violent behavior having its roots in a biological or chemical imbalance in the brain. Many regard the developmental factors within a person—how the individual was socialized—as the most important factor. Some try to isolate environmental factors as a cause. Others base the foundation of a violent personality on the psychological makeup of the individual. Society would have been satisfied if we could have performed an autopsy on Tim McVeigh that revealed a massive brain tumor located in the area where behavior is controlled. The discovery would have given us reason to wash our hands of the guilt of this man's destruction, but it would do little else to solve the problems of society for the future.

The well-known fact that two individuals can grow up in the same environment, one turning out good and the other turning out evil, bothers us a great deal. What we have come to admit is that no two people react to their environment the same way. The truth probably lies somewhere among all of the potential causes of violent behavior. Some have a root cause of their behavior in biological or chemical imbalances. The environment in which a person is raised also has a direct relationship. It has been proven that children brought up in an abusive home are more likely than other children to become abusive parents when they grow up. When we look at the psychological causation of violent crime, it seems to wrap all the causes together, and we wind up with the end product.

Although Sigmund Freud is no longer held in high regard by many, his breakdown of the personality into three parts gives us something to ponder when we are studying violent crime. The id, ego, and the superego are a personality's components; we can inspect each and determine what is and is not functioning properly in an individual. The id is controlled by animal instincts. Whatever is desired, normally pleasure, to satisfy the appetite for immediate gratification. The ego, on the other hand, is where self-esteem comes into play. The ego acts as the mediator between the person and reality; conversely, the superego acts as the conscience of the personality, determining what is right and wrong in society. Use of the psychoanalytic model in seeking to understand man's behavior assists in determining the level of crime committed.

Understanding this, it is clear that most brutal murders operate at a level far below the superego. In many cases, it appears that the murdering mind, for all practical purposes, either has no superego or has a nonfunctioning superego. Thus, the associated individuals experience no shame or remorse for the crimes they commit and have very little insight into their own behavior. They operate without a conscience. They know right from wrong, but right and wrong do not matter to them.

The level to study intensely in violent behavior is the ego portion of the personality. One might go as far as to say that any individual who turns to senseless acts of violence, such as murder/suicide, is dealing with a severely impaired ego. The individual's self-esteem is nonexistent, and the person views the world in an animalistic manner, relying on id instincts alone—which leads to uncontrollable acts such as murder. This is where we have to stop and study society. We have to honestly ask ourselves how we are raising our young. I have believed for many years that we are raising an ever-increasing number of people who are in this world to satisfy themselves and themselves alone. We have to stop and ask ourselves this: what is it that our culture puts emphasis on? Do we emphasize satisfying basic needs, or are we more concerned about the controlling factors within society that dictate what is right and wrong? Do our movies and TV shows establish role models emphasizing the self-esteem and dignity of the individual, or are they reinforcing destructive behavior?

We all know the answers to these questions, yet the American society demonstrates a willingness to accept a certain percentage of our population turning to violence. We are willing to pay to institutionalize them after their violent episodes, and then we entertain ourselves with their behavior by producing the *Dog Day Afternoon* of tomorrow.

When we discuss crime in America, we tend to concentrate on the scores of individuals growing up who achieve positive lives, contributing to society. This is like trying to find the cure for cancer while concentrating on all the perfectly healthy people on earth. Society has a choice: surrender to the violence we have come to live with or take drastic measures to turn the trend in violence around. The drastic measures are quite natural. They begin at home from the time of birth and end in the classroom when the person is eighteen. That is the window we have to work with, and it is front-end loaded. By the age of fourteen or fifteen, the person has already developed into either a well-adjusted individual or one with major problems.

The most tragic comment made about the American society is that we are the most violent of all civilized societies. Earlier we discussed the volume of murders and suicides we experience annually. A visual picture of a person who kills either someone else or himself would be the equivalent of a crowd attending an NFL Sunday football game.

All too often, when we study violent crime, we are drawn to the things we believe will deter it. We look at the punishment model, which consists of incarceration and the death penalty. This model has a tendency to make the rest of society comfortable with what it has done about crime. Remove the individual from society, and if the individual is bad enough, remove him from life, too. It is important to note, though, that incarceration works in only one manner. It removes the most dangerous from society and protects us from them. However, incarceration seldom, if ever, works to rehabilitate a person. There are rare instances when an individual makes a complete turnaround in prison and upon release reenters the world with self-esteem and respect for others. Yet 95 percent of the individuals within our prison system today are classified as sociopathic or psychopathic. These individuals, for all practical purposes, have neither an ego nor a superego level of personality and are beyond rehabilitation. They are classical repeat offenders and seldom learn from their crimes. They are individuals who experience no guilt for their actions, lack respect for life, and treat the world as a chess game they must win.

The normal person who struggles with the correctness of the death penalty is convinced that this ultimate punishment would stop all from committing murder. Our judgment is colored by our sense of values and by our own capability to adhere to the superego, which demands that we have high standards. For us, the death penalty alone would act as a checkmate for violence. We would never conceive of murdering someone, even if only for fear of facing the death penalty because of this one act. However, the psychopath does not have the time or capability for such evaluation. Punishment for his actions never enters the mind of the psychopath—much less the ultimate punishment of the death penalty. The normal person witnessing an execution is emotionally moved, if not scarred for life. The psychopath witnessing an execution looks on with ridicule, viewing the person as stupid because he got caught. The psychopath is incapable of drawing the connection between his future behavior and the correlating potential punishment. He operates based on what is good for the moment and satisfies immediate needs. If anyone gets in the way of that immediate gratification, the person's life could be in danger.

The death penalty does nothing more than get rid of those we fear the most. It is not a true deterrent for violent crime and is in fact a punishment that many find inconceivable. The killers among us do not concern themselves with whether they might be executed because they believe they are too smart to ever be caught.

We have examined many types of behavior. Much of the behavior we have studied relates to homicide. Psychological profiling is not limited in its function to homicides alone, however. There are many practical applications of profiling human behavior as it relates to crimes of a very different nature. The compulsive arsonist lends himself quite readily to profiling for detection purposes as well as for predicting the when and where of the next fire. Child molesters, who are basically driven by obsessive-compulsive behavior patterns, are excellent candidates for psychological profiling. Behavior that is controlled by obsessive-compulsive traits is generally adaptive to psychological profiling. Such behavior would include the obscene phone callers, obsessive gamblers, voyeurs, exhibitionists, pedophiles, and deviant sex offenders. On many occasions, the police treat these offenses as individual cases and seldom need to establish a relationship between offences. If the incidents increase and public attention is paid to the conduct, then psychological profiling can make a major contribution to the apprehension of the individual involved.

We have looked at many varied types of behavior, from the puzzling makeup of the political assassin in Sirhan Sirhan to the individual who carries out his feeling of hate in the schoolyard. What is interesting is that in most cases, there was a time in the perpetrator's life when he or she appeared perfectly normal. Charlie Manson as a youth appeared as normal as the next person. David Meirhofer, although he grew up quiet, was well liked in his community. Edmund Emil Kemper, while harshly treated by his mother, seemed interested in other people and fairly well adjusted. The lives of the most notorious killers in our country's history reflected normalcy at an earlier age and then regressed into behavior that was shocking in its brutality. Cannibalism, unimaginable to the normal person, has become a selective behavior in many of these more bizarre killers. This strange and perverse behavior makes killing out of anger, with a gun, a far more normal crime than it ever should be. What has been manifested in the study of criminal behavior is that man can reach down to the darkest abyss in his behavior, defying the dignity of human kind. I am convinced that there are no limits to the indignity that can be inflicted on another by the murdering mind.

Psychological profiling of homicide cases has grown increasingly popular by the treatment the media has given it. Long before the movie *Silence of the Lambs*, the entertainment business was interested in filming suspense-packed drama that delves into the inner dynamics of the human mind. There has always been an interest in what influences people to commit crimes of this nature. The news media has long since been on board with a mysterious "who done it" type of mystery. The missing Washington intern with the close relationship with a congressman is made for TV. The coverage of it becomes endless and sometimes mindless. We cannot get enough of it. Respectable news stations turn into couch-potato detectives, looking for e-mail input to aid in solving the case. When the most vicious killer is apprehended, we are fascinated, waiting to hear his life story. All too often, we unfortunately turn his life story into a thrilling, R-rated movie. Hannibal Lector was the composite of three vicious killers. The normal person viewing these movies will come away somewhat moved but not so moved that he/she cannot get past the movie. However, the violent personalities among us who have yet to act out may never fully get beyond the violence portrayed.

Has the profiler himself/herself become victim to the darkest killers we produce? Is the intrigue in understanding murderers' behaviors so captivating that it is impossible to let go? Has the profiler, like the media, become a spectator in the violence that surrounds us? Have the sharpened mental insights into behavior become a personality trait? Every profiler must ask these questions of himself/herself. One can never run the risk of believing he or she possesses supernatural powers or some special gift. It is important to never lose sight of the fact that psychological profiling is a technique for apprehending the most vicious killers in our society. Good psychological profiling enhances the hard work of law enforcement. The goal of both is to apprehend before the killer acts again. The achievement of that goal is like preventive medicine—we will never know how very sick the patient would have gotten had the medicine not been administered. Stopping a killer before he kills again is the greatest memory a law enforcement officer will ever have.

Society needs to stop and consider the contribution law enforcement makes. We ask the young police officer, whether he is working the jail or the street, to deal with the worst segment of society. Such officers have often been regarded as the blue line separating the good people in society from those who would inflict harm. By its very nature, the role of law enforcement officers places at risk the finer aspects of the officers' personalities. Very early on, they learn to isolate their feelings, and cynicism takes over; they become distrusting of others and critical, and they often isolate themselves. Due to the nature of the job, they tend to socialize with other police officers and take on a bunker mentality toward those not involved in law enforcement. They begin to feel comfortable only with their peers at work because no one else understands what they are doing.

Being married to a police officer is not easy for the spouse. The quietness, moodiness, and depression can be difficult to live with. Divorce among police officers is common. The everyday elements of what the police officer is exposed to on the street are not easy to witness. The car accident with two fatalities, one a two-year-old girl and the other a seven-year-old boy, are memories that rarely leave when the ambulance door closes. The suicide investigation involving an elderly man who took a shotgun and blew his head off is a gruesome sight. Yet the young police officer has to journey into these scenes, study them, take pictures of them, and make chalk markings around the bodies—and perhaps prepare herself to testify in court what she witnessed in the investigation. We frequently force the role of mediator on the officer dealing with the physically and sexually abused children of our society. We ask them to walk into the middle of a bar fight and return order. We ask them to respond to armed robberies and chase felons. We ask them to walk on the perimeter of the drug culture and not be lured by the smell of big money. Society really asks them to do the superhuman, and when they fall, they are held accountable and face severe judgment.

Importantly, though, most police officers choose their occupation not because of the money but because of their belief that they are making society a better place for you and me. I was reminded of this recently when I was asked to review a terrible double homicide. I sat and talked to three wonderful, dedicated people who were doing an excellent job. One was a seasoned veteran female officer who had the looks of a movie starlet. She loved her job and gave it her all. She was not only beautiful in looks but also bright and street smart. The other two were dedicated detectives who had worked long and hard on the case. Both of these individuals were excellent investigators. The three of them had put together a remarkable case file.

When the call came for me to participate in this review, my heart picked up a beat, and my ego went into overdrive. I realized that it had been a while since I had done one of these, and I wondered how much would come back. Ten minutes of review erased almost fifteen years. The feeling of having not lost a step came over me. The profiler inside was ready for action.

It was a particularly brutal double murder—that of a mother and her daughter. They had been dismembered, the torsos neatly laid out near a landfill. The first officer to the scene was the female officer in charge of the investigation. Her description reflected the keen insights of an investigator but also the human qualities of a mother. The torsos remained Jane Does for almost two weeks. It was a mystery; nobody knew what neighborhood or area they were from. After two weeks, a missing person's report was filed in an adjoining police department, and then the Jane Does were quickly identified as the wife and daughter of the person who had filed the missing person's report. His story, however, had more holes than Swiss cheese. He now sits in prison with the memory of these brutal killings, having confessed almost one year later.

In my mind, the motivation for these killings was clear. The cover-up was extraordinary when it came to disposing of the bodies. The ability to establish a tight alibi, however, was severely lacking. When I arrived at the main crime scene, vivid memories of the crime scene pictures were in my mind, but those images were less vivid than for the first responding officer. We both had similar reactions: the person responsible must face justice.

This hardworking police detective put in focus what profiling and police work is all about when she said to me, "We have to make this case for these two victims; they can no longer help themselves, so we must make someone answer for their senseless killing." Good police work entails giving innocent victims a voice from their graves. In this case, justice will be well served.

Once again, this case demonstrated the dark depravity that mankind can inflict on others. The killer of these two innocent people will never be called a serial killer, because he will not kill again. The behavior displayed in this homicide is every bit as sick as the killings of Ted Bundy, John Dacy, David Berkowitz, Edmund Kemper, Richard Speck, and Jeffrey Dahmer. The treatment of the bodies after death was barbaric and indicates severe pathology. What is clear is that the killings were performed by a person who knew what he was doing and did it in the face of insanity.

What motivates profilers? Empathy for the victims of violence; a feeling of rage for the senseless, animalistic killers who prey on their victims; a need to represent the victims; and a passion to stop them from killing again—these are the attributes that clearly represent the makeup of a profiler. The psychological profiler knows that his or her efforts must not fail in stopping a killer, because the killer cannot stop him or herself.

Acknowledgements

To Annie McKeon and Peter Mullany for immigrating to this country
from Ireland, marrying and having four children
you gave the opportunity to succeed
by giving us a great education.

To all those that gave me the privilege to
carry the title
Special Agent of the Federal Bureau
of Investigation

To Robin Roberts ABC for suggesting to write a
book while filming *Vanished*
with 20/20

To Howard Teten for his brilliance,
Insight, knowledge, and resourcefulness.
He was truly a great partner in this journey
to attempt understanding
Criminal Behavior

To all the men and women in
Law enforcement
That put their lives at risk every day.

Printed in Great Britain
by Amazon